Gatesℏead CRAWCROOK LIBRARY
Council

TEL No: 413 8164

Due for Return	Due for Return	Due for Return
8\20		
1 4 SEP 2020		
− 4 AUG 2022		

Visit us at:

www.gateshead.gov.uk/books

Tel: 0191 433 8410

MORGAN'S MEN

NICK HOULT AND STEVE JAMES

MORGAN'S MEN

THE INSIDE STORY OF ENGLAND'S RISE FROM CRICKET WORLD CUP HUMILIATION TO GLORY

ALLEN&UNWIN

First published in Great Britain in 2020 by Allen & Unwin

Allen & Unwin
c/o Atlantic Books
Ormond House
26–27 Boswell Street
London WC1N 3JZ

Phone: 020 7269 1610
Fax: 020 7430 0916
Email: UK@allenandunwin.com
Web: www.allenandunwin.com/uk

A CIP catalogue record for this book is available from the British Library.

Hardback ISBN 978 1 91163 093 7
E-Book ISBN 978 1 76087 483 4

Printed and bound by CPI Group (UK) Ltd, Croydon, CR0 4YY

10 9 8 7 6 5 4 3 2 1

CONTENTS

To Bethan Amy James, daughter of Steve and Jane and sister of Rhys, who died aged just 21 in February 2020. Such a beautiful, kind and caring girl taken so early. She wanted to be a journalist like her dad.

ONE
FINE MARGINS

THE WORLD CUP FINAL –
ENGLAND V. NEW ZEALAND

LORD'S, LONDON

14 July 2019

Sunday, 14 July 2019 dawned grey and overcast in north-west London. Umbrellas were required for those arriving early at Lord's for this the 12th Cricket World Cup final, the fifth at the grand old ground and the first there since 1999. But the forecast promised ever better weather throughout the day, and there was going to be a new name on the trophy by its end, with England in their fourth final and their first since 1992. New Zealand were beaten by Australia in their one final appearance in the previous tournament in 2015.

So, the frisson was understandable, but nobody could ever have envisaged what levels of excitement would be seen before that trophy finally was presented just after 8pm.

Because of the dampness, with the rain having only just stopped, the start was delayed by 15 minutes from its scheduled 10.30am slot. Once the covers had been removed, a green-looking pitch was revealed, although England captain Eoin Morgan, a Lord's veteran, having only played his county cricket for Middlesex, had said the day before that its looks could be deceiving. 'From afar, it looks greener than it is,' he said. 'There isn't a lot of grass on it.' He knew that would be bad news for his big hitters and good for New Zealand. It levelled the playing field between the two sides. Home advantage was significantly reduced now.

Speaking on the popular BBC *Tailenders* podcast, broadcast live from the ground that morning, England Test bowler James Anderson was adamant that it was a morning on which to bowl first.

The old adage at Lord's when assessing what to do at the toss has always been to look up rather than down – in other words, take more notice of the skies above (it was still cloudy when Sky Sports' Nasser Hussain gathered Morgan and Kane Williamson, the New Zealand captain, together with Sri Lankan match referee Ranjan Madugalle for the toss) than the pitch down below.

The further complication was that England had built a reputation in the previous four years for being supreme chasers. But this tournament had challenged that thinking considerably. A combination of the slow pitches and the pressures of the tournament meant that batting first had become ever more fashionable.

What to do? There was much to consider. The decision at the toss here at Lord's was always going to be tricky.

Morgan tossed the coin, and Williamson called tails. It

fell as tails. Williamson elected to bat, but he admitted some 'confusion'.

'It was a tough decision,' he said. 'If you look at the surface, I think it is a bat-first surface, but then you look up above and that brings in a bit of confusion.'

England were going to bowl. Just. Asked if he was disappointed to lose the toss, Morgan said: 'No, not at all. It was a bit of a 50–50 call. It is always difficult here at Lord's with the overheads.'

In the England dressing room, team performance analyst Nathan Leamon was happy. 'Oh, thank God,' he said. England had got what they wanted without the pressures of inserting the opposition.

'We thought the wicket would get stodgier as the game went on, and we also knew that the first ten overs were going to be very difficult, so we were trying to make a decision that took New Zealand's easiest routes to victory off the table,' said Leamon to *The Times* after the final. 'But we were on a knife edge. If the sun was shining, we were going to bat, and if it was cloudy, we were going to bowl. So, it was almost the perfect outcome. We didn't have to decide, and we got to do what we wanted to do anyway. The idea of having got the decision wrong in a World Cup final and that affecting how the game went was not something I wanted to have to go through.'

And Morgan admitted afterwards to Sky Sports that it was a decision that took up too much of his time on that morning. 'It took up so much of my head space,' he said. 'And it normally doesn't.'

The first ten overs were going to be crucial. New Zealand's openers had had a poor tournament up until that point. Martin Guptill was the leading run scorer at the 2015 tournament but was having a shocker here, while the left-handed

Henry Nicholls had only been brought into the side after Colin Munro had failed to deliver and was dropped.

When in the third over Nicholls was adjudged lbw to Chris Woakes without scoring, it could have been a rather predictable tale. But Nicholls reviewed the decision by the Sri Lankan Kumar Dharmasena, who was not exactly the most reliable of the umpires in the tournament, and the ball was shown to be going over the top of the stumps.

Guptill, having survived a vociferous caught behind appeal off Jofra Archer in the second over – a brilliant piece of umpiring from South African Marais Erasmus, who saw that the ball had brushed the batsman's back trouser pocket rather than bat – began to show signs of his aggressive best with an uppercut six over third man off Archer and then a drive down the ground for four in the fourth over after advancing down the pitch to the same bowler. It felt as though the first wheel was coming off.

At this moment Andrew Strauss, the director of England cricket at the start of this England team's four-year plan in 2015 but now at the game working for Sky Sports, arrived in the writers' section of the Lord's press box. 'Just hope that this is not the day Guptill comes off,' remarked a member of the media to him in a moment when making conversation prompted a departure from impartiality to patriotism.

Calm as anything Strauss replied: 'Just relax, there is nothing we can do about it up here.' It was a fair point. It was also why he was such a fine captain of England, although even the excitement must have got to him by the day's end.

Guptill soon went for 19, leg-before to Woakes, who bowled yet another probing opening spell, in a tournament full of them from him, of seven overs for just 19 runs. Guptill then wasted his side's only review by referring his decision upstairs. It was plumb.

As Guptill walked off up the stairs into the Lord's pavilion, Hussain remarked on the television commentary: 'His tournament with the bat comes to an end.' Nobody in his or her right mind could ever have thought that that statement would then be proved wrong later in the day. But then this was not going to be any normal day.

For New Zealand to end the opening powerplay of ten overs at 33 for one represented something of a triumph for them, though. Nicholls and Williamson, who took 12 balls to get off the mark, slowly and carefully built an important partnership.

In pulling Liam Plunkett for four, Nicholls moved to 31 and to his highest score of the tournament. His tenacity and grit epitomised the Kiwi spirit in these most high-pressured of circumstances. Plunkett, such an important bowler for Morgan, struggled in his opening spell as nerves looked to be taking hold.

The outfield might have been lightning fast, but this was not a belter of a pitch. Like so many in this tournament, it was a little too slow and a little too easy for the ball to linger in the surface rather longer than any batsman wishing to drive through the line of the ball would ever want.

The New Zealand score passed 100 in the 22nd over, and England desperately needed a wicket. Step forward Plunkett, who had swapped ends after his first three overs from the Pavilion End had gone for 19.

'As soon as I came up the hill [from the Nursery End] I felt comfortable attacking the crease, it felt a lot better,' Plunkett said afterwards.

Plunkett's fourth ball was to Williamson and, as is so often his style, was held across the seam. It was pitched on a good length, but Williamson viewed it as being fuller than that and drove at it. It went through to wicketkeeper Jos Buttler, and, as he took it, Plunkett and the rest of the England team appealed demandingly. Umpire Dharmasena was unmoved.

Not out, he decided.

England reviewed immediately.

The edge seemed obvious and was soon proven as much. Williamson, a rock amongst Kiwi batting sandcastles for so much of the tournament (he was the fourth-highest run scorer overall with 578 runs at an average of 82.57 and had scored a staggering 30 per cent of New Zealand's runs before the final), was gone for 30 from 53 balls. It was a huge wicket for England, and a huge moment.

'Kane is a massive player, and to get a crucial wicket is what I do pride myself on. So, it was nice to get that,' said Plunkett. 'I tried to get as much out of the pitch with my variations as I could. That's my role. I use the cross-seam ball more than the seam-up.'

Nicholls passed his half-century off 71 balls in the 26th over, with a single off the leg spin of Adil Rashid, who was bowling a decent spell from the Pavilion End. Indeed, in eight overs Rashid conceded just one boundary, a heave over wide mid-on for four by Williamson.

But Plunkett soon snared Nicholls as well with another cross-seamed delivery, with Nicholls bowled off the inside edge for 55 from 77 balls, so that the bowler had taken two for five in 14 balls, and the New Zealand innings suddenly took on a very different look.

This was gripping stuff. Lord's was rapt. Trafalgar Square was too, with a big screen being watched by many thousands of fans. It was a wonderful advertisement for cricket, with the final also being shown on UK free-to-air television, after Sky, whose considerable investment in the game had contributed in no small way to England reaching this final, had allowed Channel 4 to screen it, the first time a live

England international had been on that platform since the 2005 Ashes. And it attracted a peak viewership of 8.3 million. What a match this was for this expansion of the game's audience to see.

It was a remarkable sporting day in general, with the men's tennis final also taking place at Wimbledon, where Novak Djokovic eventually beat Roger Federer in what would turn out to be the longest final in the tournament's history. Meanwhile, Lewis Hamilton was also winning a record sixth British Grand Prix at Silverstone.

Back at the cricket, by the time 30 overs had been bowled, New Zealand had reached 126 for three. It did not look an especially threatening platform from which to launch their push for a big score, but this was classic New Zealand: workmanlike and unfussy, crafting and grafting their way to a workable total. It was what they had done to India when shocking them in the semi-final at Old Trafford. There they had made just 239 for eight after electing to bat first, and then India had failed by 18 runs.

New Zealand were not going to break any run-scoring records again here, but they were damned determined to make a score that would test England. That has always been New Zealand cricket's way: to make the very most of what they have, however unflashy it might appear.

Chasing in a World Cup final on a sticky pitch is the ultimate test of a one-day-international side. More so for a team at home that had entered the tournament as favourites, courtesy of their no. 1 world ranking. New Zealand were really going to investigate the true extent of England's mettle here.

'We sort of wanted 250, 260. We knew that it wasn't easy,' said Williamson afterwards. Given that totals of over 250 had only been successfully chased down twice in the tournament before this final (Bangladesh in making 322 for three to beat West Indies and India in surpassing Sri Lanka's 264 for seven), it was not a bad aim.

Ross Taylor, in at no. 4, did not last long, however. The 35-year-old veteran, in his fourth World Cup, had made a vital 74 in the semi-final but scored just 15 here, adjudged leg-before to Mark Wood, who, though expensive in conceding 23 runs from his four overs, had bowled like the wind in his first spell from the Nursery End. He had hit 95mph at one stage and equalled (at 95.69mph to be exact) the fastest ball of the tournament, alongside Jofra Archer and Australia's Mitchell Starc, and had swung the ball sharply.

Now Wood returned from the Pavilion End. As with Plunkett swapping ends earlier, this was more shrewd captaincy from Morgan. Wood's first ball was again fast – 90mph – and nipped back into the right-handed Taylor down the slope.

Wood often falls over after delivering the ball, but not this time. Instead he was soon squatting with arms in the air pleading for the leg-before decision. Umpire Erasmus granted him his wish, but for once – he was the umpire of the tournament in many observers' eyes – he was wrong. It looked high upon first viewing, and this was proven to be the case by subsequent replays, but because Guptill had already burned New Zealand's only review, Taylor did not have the opportunity to use them. He walked off ruefully, but without any histrionics or any words of anger. He took it remarkably well.

To rub salt into the wound, Wood then changed to around the wicket to the new batsman, the left-handed Jimmy Neesham, and proceeded to bowl five dot balls. He had bowled a wicket maiden in the 34th over! It ended up as the only maiden of the innings.

Along with another southpaw, the wicketkeeper Tom Latham, Neesham set about guiding New Zealand towards that competitive total that they so desired. Neesham is strong on the leg side and was soon launching Ben Stokes for two fours in the 35th over to that side of the field.

Latham, a good enough batsman to have made 264 not out in a Test match, was another to have had a poor tournament up to this point, with his only score above 13 being the 57 he had made against England at Durham in the group stage. But he was another to rise to this grandest of occasions. He was especially quick onto the short ball, pulling Plunkett for a four that was so nearly a six and then later going the whole hog with a six off Wood over straightish deep mid-wicket, which, following Guptill's earlier effort, was the second maximum of the innings.

Latham also played one glorious extra-cover drive for four off Wood, and Neesham had just cut Plunkett for four when, from the very next ball, he tried to loft the same bowler over mid-on but was caught by the fielder, Joe Root, positioned there. New Zealand were 173 for five at the end of the 38th over. It really was a struggle, but a wonderfully gripping struggle.

Wood continued to push his body to the limit – so much so that with three balls to go of his last over he suffered a side strain that, along with a knee condition that required an operation, kept him out for the rest of the season – as the speedometer kept going above 90mph. The fielding continued to dazzle, with Jonny Bairstow, despite a groin injury sustained while batting in the semi-final victory over Australia, throwing himself around the boundary edge as only a supreme athlete of his standing could. It was not bad work for the Test wicketkeeper.

Plunkett finished his allocation of ten overs with two dot balls to the new batsman, Colin de Grandhomme. He had taken three wickets for just 42. He brought his hands together as if to say that his prayers had been answered and then gave a thumbs up to his colleagues, who began to shout their congratulations. He took his cap from umpire Dharmasena and walked down to third man at the Nursery End, where he received a standing ovation. What a moment it was for the 34-year-old. He had certainly done his job.

Jofra Archer now returned at the Pavilion End. His third ball, timed at 87mph, was top-edged onto his helmet by de Grandhomme, a sharp reminder, in every sense, of the threat Archer had posed throughout the tournament with his pace and hostility. It hit the batsman hard. But de Grandhomme, a Zimbabwean by birth and upbringing, whose late father Laurie was a no-nonsense off-spinning all-rounder for the country before Test status came their way, is a tough man and was soon wearing a wry smile after undergoing the now mandatory concussion test.

Not that New Zealanders ever lack toughness, of course. The sight of former All Black hooker Sean Fitzpatrick, the utter epitome of that quality on a rugby field, sitting in the Lord's crowd was a reminder of that.

England did not relent in their use of the short ball, with de Grandhomme being struck on the back as he tried to avoid another bouncer from Wood (timed at 91mph), with the ball flying off over wicketkeeper Buttler for four leg byes.

De Grandhomme is known as a decent player of the short ball but it simply did not look like it here against the brilliant Archer. Missing Archer's slower-ball bouncer (timed at 74mph) – again hitting de Grandhomme on the back – did not present quite as much danger, but the fast bowler's mixture of pace (two consecutive bouncers later in the over were bowled at 80 and 88mph respectively) was just so difficult for the batsmen to set up to hit.

Slower-ball bouncers are a very modern invention. Some of the old-timers chuckle and maintain that they were merely called long-hops back in the day, but they are only long-hops in today's game if there is very little difference between their pace and those short balls delivered at full speed. Then a batsman can set himself for the slower one and know there is no danger of being hit by the quicker one. That is simply not possible with Archer. The physical threat is very real. Prime yourself for the slower one and you could be setting yourself up for a horrible ending if it happens to be the quick bouncer that is sent down.

Archer would bowl five overs on the trot at the death here, a significant ask for any bowler, let alone a 24-year-old who had only made his international debut just a few months previously. He would concede just 22 runs in those five overs – having gone for only 20 in his opening spell of five – and in the final over of the innings he would also take the wicket of Matt Henry.

Wood finished his ten overs with one for 49, but was in obvious pain because of the side injury. He should really have left the field there and then – and Jason Roy gestured for him to do so – but this was a World Cup final. It was not a stage that could be left easily. Wood understandably did not want to go. He remained on for two more overs, but then had to admit to the reality of the situation. It was no place for the injured – throwing is not easy with a side strain – even if we had not seen the last of this whole-hearted player for the day.

With four overs of the innings remaining, and New Zealand's score standing at 214 for five, James Vince arrived as Wood's fielding replacement. Vince was soon into the action. Chris Woakes returned to the attack, and his fifth ball was a slower off-cutter that de Grandhomme attempted to whip to the leg side. The leading edge looped gently to Vince at mid-off. De Grandhomme was gone for 16 from 28 balls. It had been hard work for him.

Latham began the 49th over by going a long way across his stumps to Woakes and attempting to swing to leg. England's appeal for leg-before was turned down by Dharmasena, and the subsequent review confirmed that the ball had indeed pitched outside leg stump.

Latham had advanced to 47 from 56 balls when the substitute Vince was again in the action as he took a second catch at mid-off, from another slower Woakes off-cutter, which this time was a low full toss. The next ball, to Mitchell Santner, was of the much higher – and much more dangerous – variety, a beamer in fact, that was suitably punished by a call of no ball and therefore a free hit to come.

Woakes's last ball was smashed over mid-wicket for four by Henry, but the bowler still finished with the hugely impressive figures of three for 37 from his nine overs and, remarkably, Archer's over, the last of the innings, went for just three, including that wicket of Henry, bowled trying to heave away on the leg side.

The final ball of the innings was a bouncer, a slower-ball bouncer no less, and, unfathomably, Santner, the bespectacled left-hander, ducked underneath it. He might have been hoping for a wide to be called. He might have just had a brain fade. But would that be critical later on?

It is easy to look back on these small moments and extrapolate their significance to later in the match. In the 49th over there were five wides when a Woakes slower-ball bouncer to Latham went way down the leg side, and on its second bounce, which turned sharply, it defeated keeper Jos Buttler, who was trying to stop it with his pads. Four fewer runs to chase might have been quite handy for England later on.

New Zealand finished on 241 for eight. In a bilateral

series you suspect that England would have quite fancied chasing that. But in a World Cup final was it enough for the New Zealanders? Opinions, unsurprisingly, were divided.

'If you had offered that to Eoin Morgan at the start of the day, he would have bitten your hand off, I really believe that,' said Andrew Strauss on Sky Sports. 'If England are not bowled out, they will win this.'

'It's enough,' argued the former New Zealand captain Brendon McCullum. 'The wicket is wearing. If Trent Boult takes some wickets up front, then I think the captaincy of [Kane] Williamson will squeeze this middle order of England's.'

Even in the England dressing room there was some mixed reaction. Coaches Trevor Bayliss and Chris Silverwood said the side had done well to restrict New Zealand to 241 and told them they would knock them off the runs if they batted well. The bowlers weren't so sure.

As for Eoin Morgan, he said afterwards: 'I thought it was a very chaseable total.'

Well, Trent Boult very nearly did take a wicket up front, as McCullum had hoped. He almost took the wicket of Jason Roy from the very first ball of England's innings. Bowling from the Pavilion End, Boult swung the ball sharply down the slope, the ball crashing into the knee roll of Roy's front pad. It looked out. But umpire Marais Erasmus rejected the appeal, and Kane Williamson reviewed almost immediately.

It was so close. The ball pitched in line. The ball hit Roy in line, but, agonisingly for the New Zealanders, it was only deemed as an 'umpire's call' on where the ball was hitting the stumps.

'I am almost speechless,' said the quite brilliant Kiwi commentator Ian Smith on television. 'I can't believe that. I cannot believe it.'

It was another huge moment on this huge day. There were

jitters in evidence everywhere. At the second ball of the second over of the innings, a good-length delivery bowled by Matt Henry, Roy drove hard and so nearly had his stumps tickled by a ball that nipped back up the slope. The next ball moved in the other direction down the slope and kicked off a length. Roy was nowhere near it. The ball was talking as much as the New Zealanders. 'This is going to be fun,' chuckled Smith.

Roy's response? He decided to skip down the pitch next ball, if only to defend. Two balls later he played the most gorgeous on-drive for four. What cricket. What tension.

Jonny Bairstow was off the mark with a fortuitous inside-edged single off Boult, who then 'nutmegged' Roy with a beautiful inswinging yorker that somehow missed the stumps too. Roy replied with a cover-driven four. Punch and counter-punch. With the sun now shining, this was fascinating and utterly engrossing cricket. There was fortune, but there was also tremendous skill being shown by both sides.

By the end of the fifth over, England were 24 without loss, the identical score that New Zealand had at the same stage. It was to be that sort of afternoon and evening.

New Zealand deserved a wicket, and in the sixth over they got it, as Henry dismissed Roy for 17 with a beauty of a ball. It was pitched on a good length and moved away from the batsman down the slope, with Roy unable to do anything more than edge behind for wicketkeeper Tom Latham to take a good low catch.

Joe Root arrived. He stayed some considerable time but did not score too many runs. In fact, he made just seven from 30 balls. The ball before he was out, he ran down the pitch and had a horrible slog at Colin de Grandhomme. He missed. He then drove wildly at a wide length ball to edge behind.

Root later described it as 'the worst innings of my

professional career'. It was certainly uncharacteristic, and it underlined both the difficulties of the pitch and the pressures under which England were batting. For a gifted batsman, who had played his entire career behind a paywall on Sky, this was a missed opportunity to showcase his talents to a wider audience.

De Grandhomme had been introduced as first change from the Pavilion End, bowling a maiden immediately in between two maidens from Henry, whose initial seven overs cost just 22. Three consecutive maidens! What was happening to England?

De Grandhomme's nibbling medium pacers, unusually for ones so modest in pace, with the wicketkeeper standing back from the stumps (at least until Ben Stokes and Jos Buttler started advancing down the pitch later in his spell), were fabulously frugal on this surface. He might have snared Bairstow too on 18 had he taken the relatively simple return catch, but he ended up bowling his full allocation straight through, bowling another maiden (to Stokes) and finishing with the astounding figures of 10-2-25-1. Of those who bowled more than 50 overs in the tournament, he finished as the most miserly with an economy rate of 4.15.

'He basically replicated what Tim Murtagh does here on a regular basis in County Championship cricket [and then did for Ireland in the Test against England just ten days later, with five for 13 in the first innings],' said Eoin Morgan on Sky Sports. 'He was extremely difficult to get away.'

It was time for a captain's innings. But Morgan's appearance at the crease, unsurprisingly given some previous travails with the short ball in the tournament, coincided with the introduction of New Zealand's fastest bowler, Lockie Ferguson, who had bowled only one over before Morgan arrived. Ferguson regularly touched 90mph and often, predictably, tested Morgan with the short ball, once clipping his helmet as the left-handed Irishman turned his head away, and on another occasion even defeating keeper Latham such was the pace and bounce of his bumper.

But it was the wicket of Bairstow that Ferguson took first, persuading the opener to inside-edge onto his stumps for 36 from 55 balls. It was a familiar mode of dismissal for Bairstow, although his bottom-handed jabs away from the body can be mightily effective too, and indeed one of them had brought a majestic four through the covers just the ball before.

Morgan could easily have been caught at deepish mid-off from de Grandhomme in the 24th over, and, like Root, he never really got going. He made nine from 22 balls. And it was indeed Ferguson who got rid of him, but not as the bowler. Instead, Ferguson, so recognisable in his black boots, took a catch for the ages on the deep-cover boundary, running in and diving forwards at full stretch after Morgan had slapped Jimmy Neesham's very first ball, which was wide and short, in his direction.

As Morgan hit the ball he screamed 'No!' He knew it was going to Ferguson and not the boundary as intended. He knew the importance of this period of the game. He knew he had made a mistake to a poor ball. His side were 86 for four in the 24th over.

Jos Buttler joined Ben Stokes at the wicket. This was the game, surely.

'We knew we just had to bat some time,' Buttler said afterwards. 'In one-day cricket recently, that hasn't been the mode of operation. But we knew if we batted for 50 overs, we should be there or thereabouts.'

Sky's win percentage predictor had it at 51–49 in England's favour at this moment, and that was about how it felt. It was going to be tight, so tight.

'I was distraught about getting out,' said Morgan. 'But I took my pads off, and I was sitting there trying to devise a plan and think how it would look in ten overs' time. And the best possible scenario was that Buttler and Stokes were still there in ten overs' time.'

The pair began conservatively, as you would expect. This was no time for frippery, or indeed undue aggression. By the middle of the 26th over, the required run rate had, for the first time, crept up to a run a ball: 147 runs required from 147 balls.

Today's players playfully mock the old guard who recount tales of six-an-over being the top of the mountain in run chases. Anything above that was indeed often insurmountable. But this, with the pitch always asking awkward questions and the burden of history chipping in with some even weightier queries, was an old-school run chase. It required nous and character more than power and abandon. Risks had to be calculated carefully, and Stokes took one such successfully in running down the pitch to Neesham and smashing the ball back past him. When Buttler then decided to go aerial, to the very last ball of de Grandhomme's spell, he needed some luck as the ball flew off the outside edge down to, but just short of, third man.

With 20 overs remaining, England still required 127. Stokes had been circumspect, making 18 from 38 balls. Buttler, who despite that edge off de Grandhomme had timed the ball probably better than any other batsman in the match, had made 13 from 15 balls.

Mitchell Santner's jerky left-arm spin was afforded three overs, and they only cost 11 runs. Both he and his captain Williamson would have been extremely happy with that, especially with such an inventive player of spin as Buttler at the crease. It was almost as if Santner had bowled those overs without anyone noticing.

Buttler had a little more fortune when, in the 32nd over, his carve off Trent Boult just evaded Martin Guptill's grasp at backward point and sped away for four. After 35 overs, England were 141 for four, requiring 101 runs at a rate of 6.73. The win predictor was swaying in their favour at 62 per cent.

Moments later, on 25, Buttler was rapped on the pads by Matt Henry as he looked to play to the leg side. Umpire Dharmasena ruled it not out, but Williamson reviewed. This was crucial. Williamson knew the value of Buttler's wicket. The immediate impression was that the ball was slipping down the leg side, and that was confirmed by the technology. Buttler was not out.

The run rate required was on the rise, however, now going over seven for the first time. Though Stokes was beginning to find run scoring easier, it was Buttler who was still playing the more eye-catching strokes, hitting Jimmy Neesham down the ground in the air for four and then, more outrageously, ramping Henry for four down to fine leg, even if there was a man stationed there. The fielder was simply too wide.

Lord's was starting to find its voice now, with the noise to greet that Buttler straight four being quite extraordinary. Just by dint of its tradition and the character and age range of the members it attracts – which is not a criticism, just a statement of fact – it is never going to possess an atmosphere like the raw raucousness the summer would later experience when Stokes played his miracle Ashes innings at Headingley, for example, but this was an occasion when it was very different from its norm. The ground was loud and buzzing now. The tension and the magnitude of the prize on offer saw to that.

England needed 72 off the last ten overs. Stokes had 43 from 68 balls, Buttler 42 from 45 balls. But only 13 runs came from the next three overs. The required run rate was now up to 8.42.

However, while England were desperate for a few more runs, so New Zealand were also desperate for a wicket. A summit meeting ensued between Williamson, Ross Taylor and wicketkeeper Tom Latham. The upshot was that Trent Boult's left-armers were recalled. A wicket please, Trent, they pleaded.

On the flip side, Buttler sensed that it was time to up the tempo. Boult had his mid-off fielder up, and Buttler, always so strong just wide of mid-off because of both the natural shape of his stroke and also a head position that tilts slightly to the off side, decided that was his area to target, even if the resultant four eventually went more over extra cover. It took Buttler past his fifty, off just 53 balls, a truly incredible rate of scoring on this pitch and on this occasion. The celebration was muted, as it was later in the same over when Stokes passed his half-century too, this time off 81 balls. The milestones did not matter. There was a World Cup to be won.

Buttler hit a Lockie Ferguson full toss over extra cover for four, but three balls later he was gone, having made 59 from 60 balls, caught superbly by substitute Tim Southee diving forwards out on the cover boundary. The partnership had been 110.

The dismissal changed everything. 'I thought we were in trouble,' said Eoin Morgan. 'We needed something.'

With the greatest respect to the incoming batsman, Chris Woakes, it was down to Stokes. No pressure, Ben. Just the burden of England never having won a global 50-over trophy.

England's plan, as articulated by Buttler, had clearly been, in the modern parlance, to take the game as deep as they could, but that will always be rendered useless unless one or two of the batsmen who have taken it deep are still there.

'I was disappointed we weren't both there at the end to finish it off,' admitted Buttler. In fact, he was a little more than disappointed. Apparently, he spent some time punching the physio's couch in frustration at not having seen the chase through.

'I was berating myself for getting out,' Buttler told the *Mail on Sunday*. 'I wanted to be there at the end. I'd had a quiet few games with the bat, and I felt this was my time and that maybe it was meant to be.

'Every dot ball I would kick something. And then I thought: "This isn't really helpful for the guys who are waiting to bat."

'You go through all the emotions: "Oh my God, we are going to lose, and I am going to have the rest of my life thinking about that." Then Stokesy would hit a four or a six, and you are thinking: "We could actually do this, and how good would that be."'

England needed 46 from the last five overs. The pitch was so slow now as to be funereal. This was why Williamson had opted to bat first. This was the situation on which he had been banking.

Stokes's flicked four to the leg side from the last ball of Jimmy Neesham's over meant it was then 39 required from four overs. Woakes needed to play some shots too, but he was out to the first ball of the 47th over, looking to hit Ferguson's cross-seam ball away on the leg side and only skying to the keeper Latham.

Liam Plunkett walked out to bat. The run rate was rising and in the England dressing room there were people hiding behind chairs. Mark Wood apparently felt sick.

Plunkett almost immediately clubbed Ferguson over mid-wicket for four. Plunkett can strike a cricket ball, but this was an extraordinary shot in the circumstances.

Now it was 34 off three required. What a finale. And what a

cricketer England had at the crease in Stokes. He was already absolutely shattered, as well as shouldering the responsibility of a cricketing nation, but the first ball of the 48th over, from Boult, was smashed into the leg side for four.

Plunkett hit two twos in that over, with Stokes having to summon every last drop of his incredible stamina to run each of them. At the end of the over, Stokes was down on his haunches in the middle of the wicket attempting to gather some more air. He could barely speak to his partner. He had made 62 off 89 balls at this stage. It was truly heroic stuff.

With two overs to go, and Plunkett on strike, England needed 24 to win the World Cup. After one ball of that 49th over, and a single off Neesham for Plunkett, commentator Ian Smith first mentioned the prospect of a Super Over should there be a tie. 'A Super Over is still possible,' he said. Yeah right, never going to happen, said everyone else. England had only tied six one-day internationals in their entire history, for goodness' sake, even if two of them – against Australia in 2005 and India in 2011 – had occurred at Lord's. There had only previously been four ties in World Cup matches too, even if England were involved in one of them, against India in 2011. The chances of a tie happening in a World Cup final at Lord's? Come on.

From the third ball of the over, Plunkett was caught at long-off by Boult. But the batsmen had crossed. Jofra Archer came out, but Stokes was on strike. England needed 22 off nine balls. They needed a six really. They had needed one or two of them for a while. So, what did Stokes do? He only went and hit a six, sweep–slogging Neesham's slower ball out towards wide long-on.

It required some good fortune. Coming around from long-on, Boult caught the ball, but, having done so, he trod on the boundary rope. Only then did he throw it to Martin

Guptill, who was waiting nearby. If Boult had got rid of the ball immediately, Stokes would surely have been gone, and with it England's World Cup chances too. It was another huge moment in a game studded with them.

It will be of no consolation whatsoever to Kiwi fans to point out that, previously in this tournament, Boult had taken a similar catch to dismiss West Indies' Carlos Brathwaite and seal victory in an agonisingly tight group match. Guptill sportingly signalled with his arms that it was six as soon as he had received the ball. Stokes signalled it too, having initially, upon hitting the ball, given the impression that he was a goner, and then umpire Marais Erasmus raised his arms as well.

As Jonny Bairstow said: 'I did think the game had gone. But it ebbs and flows, doesn't it? I said to Nathan [Leamon], our analyst, with seven overs to go: "We need three sixes here."'

That was the first of them.

Stokes took a single, leaving Archer to face the last ball of the over. It was another slower ball from the back of the hand from Neesham, and Archer slogged at it, missed it and was bowled.

England were eight wickets down with 15 needed from the final over. Stokes was on 70 from 92 balls. He could barely move he was so tired. The bowler was the left-armer Boult. The non-striker was Adil Rashid.

'I would have had the Kiwis as big favourites,' admitted Eoin Morgan afterwards. 'Simply because Ben needed to face a lot of the balls, and it was against one of the best bowlers in the world. The angle a left-armer creates when he is accurate makes it difficult to get away.'

The first ball was a yorker that Stokes could only squeeze out to extra cover. No run. Fifteen needed from five balls now. The second ball was similar, full and wide outside off stump. Again, Stokes could only hit it to extra cover. No run again. Fifteen off four balls. This was only going one way. New Zealand's way. England could not win from here, could they?

So, what did Stokes do now? Only hit another six, the second of those demanded by Bairstow all those overs ago. This time Boult could not quite find the yorker, and Stokes used the length to go down on one knee and sweep–slog the ball high over deep mid-wicket and onto the fence at the bottom of the Mound Stand. It was the sort of shot you play to a spinner, not a bowler of Boult's pace. Not in a World Cup final. It was extraordinary. Stokes admitted it was the first time he had played a slog–sweep to a quick bowler. What a time to do it.

The crowd went bananas. Yes, even the Lord's crowd went bananas. The scenes were incredible. It is fair to say that even the press box, supposed to be that haven of impartiality, objectivity, cynicism and reserved reaction, was becoming a little animated and noisy too.

On the cricket writers' WhatsApp group, it is usual around this time of an international day for suggestions to be made to Danny Reuben, England's hugely popular and highly effective head of team communications, as to whom the press corps might like to speak to at the post-match press conference. It was at this moment that one of the more mischievous of the group sent a message, reading: 'Farby tonight?'

There were some chuckles at that. It was a reference to Paul Farbrace, the personable and likeable coach who had been an assistant to this England team until just before the World Cup, when he joined Warwickshire as their director of sport. During his time with the squad, he was often brought out to talk to the press on the really quiet days. This was not a quiet day. It was a day the like of which none of us had ever seen before and may never see again.

It was difficult not to feel some sympathy for Farbrace. He had been there right at the start, taking over as interim coach for England's first ODI series against New Zealand in 2015 before Trevor Bayliss arrived. He had played a huge part. But he was not here now. Farbrace was actually listening to the last hour of the match on his car radio. He had been at Chelmsford watching Warwickshire's County Championship match against Essex, and he was driving back to his rural home outside Birmingham. He arrived there just as both sides were about to complete their 50 overs. Little did he, or any of us, know what would happen next.

This was ridiculous, truly ridiculous now. Nine runs were needed from just three balls.

Cricket suddenly entered the realms of fantasy, because what happened next is still so difficult to believe. The ball bowled was a full toss. Stokes hit it out to deep mid-wicket, where Guptill was the fielder. Stokes and Rashid simply had to run two. Stokes came haring back for that second, and Guptill, sensibly given Stokes's state of fatigue, threw to his end, the wicketkeeper's end, even if it meant a much longer throw. It was going to be close to a run-out, close enough for Stokes to have to dive to make his ground.

As Stokes dived, so the ball arrived too, hitting his outstretched bat – right in its middle ('It's the only one I middled all day,' Stokes may or may not have whispered in jest later on) – and sped away to the boundary under the pavilion, with Colin de Grandhomme chasing vainly after it.

'I do not believe what I have just seen,' screamed Ian Smith on the television commentary.

Stokes, still on his knees with his shirt dirtied from the dive, immediately raised his hands in apology. What had happened had been completely unintentional. He did not even look at the throw. He certainly did not change the direction of his run or the position of his bat. It was simply a freakish accident.

'I said to Kane Williamson I'll be apologising for that for the rest of my life,' said Stokes afterwards. 'I have apologised countless times for that fluke. It's not how you want to get them.'

The irony was not lost on anyone. Here was Stokes, born in New Zealand, apologising to a group of New Zealanders for something that could easily now cost them the World Cup. 'Playing against New Zealand is always a great event. They are a seriously good team and really good lads,' said Stokes.

Stokes was even nominated for the New Zealander of the Year award after the final. He turned it down. He said he was 'flattered' and 'proud' of his New Zealand and Maori heritage, but that 'it would not sit right'. Just like these runs, but he had to accept them. Cricket's laws demanded so.

It was with typical magnanimity and calm that Kane Williamson said the overthrows were 'unfortunate' for his team. 'I don't wish to nitpick. I just hope it never happens in such moments ever again,' said Williamson. You suspect many other captains, nay, most other captains, would have reacted rather differently. Williamson truly is a gentleman of our game, a wonderful guardian of its values and principles.

There was talk in some quarters that Stokes had asked for the four overthrows to be taken off England's score, but that was simply not true. Had the ball not reached the boundary, of course, the batsmen would not have taken any extra runs. That is cricket's etiquette. But it is also one of cricket's laws that the runs must stand if the ball does cross the boundary. The only way England could benefit from the bat deflection was the ball reaching the boundary.

So it was that umpire Kumar Dharmasena signalled with the four fingers and thumb of his right hand, along with the thumb of his left hand, that it was six runs.

The England dressing room exploded in a flurry of excitement and noise. It had been exceptionally quiet up until that point. Players just could not watch. Most thought they were dead and buried. Jos Buttler was on his haunches. Jason Roy was on a table. Suddenly players were shouting things like: 'Come on, you ginger ninja!' The atmosphere had changed.

And Bairstow had his wish. 'When Stokesy dived and it deflected for four, that was the third six,' he said. 'Then we [Bairstow and Leamon] looked at each other and went: "OK, we've got our three sixes!"'

After the match, it became clear that only five rather than six runs should have been given, that a horrible mistake had been made by the umpires. The claim came first from Simon Taufel, the Australian former umpire. Taufel said that, according to Law 19.8, which relates to overthrows, the second run should not have counted because Stokes and Rashid had not crossed when Guptill released his throw from the boundary.

'They should have been awarded five runs, not six,' said Taufel. 'It's a clear mistake. It's an error of judgement. In the heat of what was going on, [the umpires] thought there was a good chance the batsmen had crossed at the instant of the throw. Obviously, TV replays showed otherwise.

'The difficulty you [umpires] have here is you've got to watch batsmen completing runs, then change focus and watch for the ball being picked up, and watch for the release [of the throw]. You also have to watch where the batsmen are at that exact moment.'

Nobody even mentioned this at the time. Nobody, not even gnarled old veterans of the game, even thought about it. Most did not know that the laws were written like that.

Eoin Morgan had an inkling, though. 'I probably thought it was five, not six, naturally,' he said. 'But I didn't celebrate. I was still trying to work out what was going on. When the replay came up, I could not believe what I was seeing. I could not believe what had just happened.'

Dharmasena, who confirmed that Stokes did not ask for the four runs to be deducted, later admitted his error. 'I made a judgemental call after consulting my colleague Marais Erasmus,' he said in an interview with the Sri Lankan newspaper *The Island*. 'It was like calling a no ball or a wide, and I couldn't consult the third umpire. I was 100 per cent sure that the batsmen had crossed. I admit that I was wrong. I will never regret the decision I made.'

It was outrageously fortunate for England, outrageously unfortunate for New Zealand. But it is not something that will ever be altered now. And it does have to be said that England would, of course, have played very differently if they had had one run fewer going into the final two balls, even if Rashid had then been facing.

But with the decision made as it was, England now needed three runs from two balls. There was a lengthy delay. The umpires were conferring while Stokes was trying to regain his breath and composure. Then Williamson went to speak to Boult about his field.

It was pandemonium around the ground. People were seen praying. Some just could not watch. And all the while, on the England players' balcony, captain Morgan was sitting with his cap on, arms folded and visage impassive.

'If he is cool now, he is not a human. He can't be,' remarked Ian Smith on commentary.

The next ball was full again, and Stokes drove it out towards long-off. As he hit it, he slipped over. He and Rashid simply had to try to run two though. Stokes had to be on strike for the final ball.

The fielder was Mitchell Santner. He threw to the non-striker's end. It was a mistake. He should have thrown to the other end, where Stokes would have been struggling to make his ground.

Yes, Rashid was run out by miles anyway, but imagine if Stokes had been run out instead? As Boult took the bails off (he actually did extremely well to take Santner's throw on the half-volley), he gestured both hands towards the other end before mimicking a throw there. He knew. They had run out the wrong man.

England needed two runs from one ball. It was completely incidental that Stokes was now 83 not out from 97 balls. What an innings. What a cricketer.

Coaches and cricketers often talk about batsmen taking full responsibility upon themselves, never leaving it to others and being there at the end of a run chase, being out there to shake the opposition's hands at the end of the game. Well, Stokes was there all right.

Mark Wood was the last man, required only to run. He had been fully padded up since no. 8 Liam Plunkett had gone in. And he was indeed fully padded up, with a chest-guard, thigh-pad and arm-guard on. He didn't need all that just to run, and he might have been better off without it all. No wonder he admitted later that he felt sick and very nearly threw up at one stage.

Wood was so fast out to the middle that Ian Smith compared him to Usain Bolt. Side strains clearly do not affect one's running, and his knee seemed fine here too.

James Vince, the twelfth man, also appeared in the middle. What if England only scored one run off that final ball? Would they win? Would New Zealand win? Would there be a Super Over? Stokes did not know, and Vince apparently offered some erroneous advice.

'There was a little bit of confusion,' Stokes revealed afterwards on the *Broad and Fry* podcast. 'I don't think anyone knows this. Vincey came up and said I think if we get one, we'd win, because Colin Munro [New Zealand's twelfth man] had also said that to him, and he then relayed that message to me.

'But I was like, "I am not taking that risk," so I had to go up [to umpire Marais Erasmus at square leg] and ask. I think he knew exactly what I was going to ask and cut me off halfway through my question and said: "Yeah, it's a Super Over." So that's as far as my cricket knowledge went as regards that.'

England had already lost one more wicket than New Zealand, and in days gone by the side losing fewer wickets would have won in the event of a tie, but not now. Not under these tournament rules. If England scored one run, there would be a Super Over.

Stokes's mind turned to a match between Bangladesh and India in the T20 World Cup in 2016. There Bangladesh required two runs from three balls, and first Mushfiqur Rahim was out caught, then to the penultimate ball Mahmudullah had a slog and was caught too. Off the last ball, Mustafizur Rahman was run out, and India won by one run.

'All I could think about was Bangladesh in the World T20 when they needed the same and they just hit it in the air,' said Stokes. 'All I was thinking was: "Don't get caught. Try and get one and get it to a Super Over at least."

'Then, if I hit it into a gap, maybe we could get two. That was my process: just don't hit it in the air and get caught. I was thinking: "Don't try and be a hero and do it with a six."'

Stokes remained true to his word. The ball from Boult was a full toss. Rather than trying to smash it for four or six, Stokes just placed it. But he would have preferred to place it wide of long-on. Instead, he hit it almost straight to that position and the fielder, Jimmy Neesham.

'I've told him this, so I can say it,' Eoin Morgan later said with a laugh. 'He got a ball that he had been waiting the whole of the last five overs for, and he chipped it down the ground for one. It just shows how detached he was from the emotion of the game and how focused he was. He said: "If I had timed it and got it in the gap, we would have won the game there and then. If not, it was a Super Over, and we had a strong chance."

'I was thinking: "That is really good." I wasn't thinking like that. I was thinking that it was our game to win, and we had brought New Zealand back into the game.'

Wood sprinted back for a two, but the throw from Neesham was superb under pressure. Boult also did magnificently well to take the ball in front of the stumps without disturbing the bails first. Wood was way out. England had one run, and the scores were tied. The final was to have its first ever Super Over.

Stokes was distraught. He kicked his bat some distance in frustration and then slammed his gloves together.

'I wish it had gone for two and it hadn't come to that [a Super Over], because my emotions were high,' he said. 'I wasn't best pleased with myself walking back to the changing rooms for that ten-minute turnaround.'

Indeed, Stokes spent much of that walk back to the Lord's pavilion with a glove over his face, still disbelieving.

Wood walked behind Stokes clapping his gloves in appreciation at one of the greatest one-day knocks the game has ever seen. The ground rose to Stokes, but in a strange, bemused sort of way, because everyone was still trying to comprehend and come to terms with what was happening.

Stokes had ended 84 not out from 98 balls. Rarely can a player have had to dig so deep into the combined wells of character and stamina to complete an innings. It truly was remarkable.

And his day's work was still not done. This, already the greatest ODI ever, was not done either . . .

TWO
FROM ROCK BOTTOM
TO REVOLUTION

England did not tie with New Zealand when they met at the previous World Cup in 2015. They did not even compete with them. They were completely embarrassed and humbled by them.

When Eoin Morgan, who was of course England captain in that tournament too, says of that match in Wellington, 'It was as close to rock bottom as I've been,' it provides a very clear indication of the turn of events that day of 20 February 2015.

It was scheduled to be a day–night match, but the floodlights were never required. England won the toss and batted, a decision Morgan soon regretted as Tim Southee swung the ball lavishly. Even the captain was not at his sharpest that day. 'With hindsight, I wouldn't have batted first if I had known it would swing for that long', he said. 'There was not a cloud in the sky, and it had not rained for a while. If it looked like it was going to swing, obviously I would have had no hesitation in bowling first. Everything said bat, and I just got it wrong.'

England managed just 123, with Southee taking seven for 33. Worse still, it took New Zealand just 12.3 overs to smash off the required runs for the loss of only two wickets, with captain Brendon McCullum hitting 77 off just 25 balls. His fifty came off only 18 balls, and it remains the fastest ever half-century in a World Cup match. Steven Finn conceded 49 runs from only two overs!

'Being beaten off the park like that is humiliating,' says Morgan. 'I didn't know what to feel, because things were so bad, but we still had games to play. It was weird.

'It was a terrible day, one of those moments in my career that will stand out for ever in my life as a day where I was devastated not only with the way we performed, but also the way we carried ourselves.'

England had already lost their opening match of the tournament to Australia in Melbourne, a heavy defeat too, by 111 runs, after Australia had made 342 for nine. James Taylor was left 98 not out and should have been able to go on to a maiden international century but for a glaring umpiring error – which the International Cricket Council later admitted was a mistake – when James Anderson was given run out. Taylor had been given out leg-before but reviewed the decision, and it was overturned. In the confusion, though, Taylor and Anderson had attempted a single, and Anderson had been run out. The ball, quite clearly, should have been declared dead once Taylor had been adjudged leg-before.

It was cruel on Taylor, who did at least go on to make a one-day international century – against Australia – later that year before his career was even more cruelly ended by a heart problem, but it was the fact that Taylor was batting at no. 6 rather than the no. 3 position he had occupied in the tournament's build-up (that spot going to Gary Ballance), as well as Chris Woakes suddenly being demoted to first-change bowler, that gave the impression that yet again England were making significant tactical changes just before a major tournament.

Sometimes impressions can be misleading, and Paul Farbrace, who was then assistant to Peter Moores (who had been appointed in 2014 for his second stint as England head coach), certainly thinks so. 'Unfortunately Gary Ballance got injured in the warm-up games, so when the changes were made before the World Cup after the Tri-series [England played five matches against Australia and India in Australia, losing the final to Australia], it looked like they were last-minute panic decisions,' Farbrace said. 'But actually had Ballance been fit and not broken his finger he would always have batted at three.'

But England had, of course, already made a big change in replacing captain Alastair Cook with Morgan after a poor ODI tour of Sri Lanka in November and December of the previous year (2014). They had lost 5–2. It was too late to be making such an important decision, with only that Tri-series to come before the World Cup. It should have been made long before. England were simply playing a brand of cricket that was not in line with the rest of the world.

England had been fooled by the fact that, for the first time since such rankings began, they had risen to no. 1 in the ODI rankings in August 2012 after a 4–0 home series victory over Australia.

Off-spinner Graeme Swann, who was a member of that side, has long said that this was an anomaly, that it was because that team played so many games at home and that the seamers revelled in damp conditions.

It had been Swann, by now retired and working for BBC *Test Match Special* as a summariser, who had tried to alert everyone to this fact in the summer of 2014 before the World Cup. It was on a rainy day at Bristol, where the first ODI of a series in which England would be beaten 3–1 by India was eventually abandoned, that Swann let rip. It irked his friend Cook no end, but these were not spiteful and unnecessary comments. There was truth dripping from them.

Swann said that England did not have 'a cat's in hell's chance of winning the World Cup' and that the one-day teams were picked on Test form.

He urged his friend Cook to give up one-day cricket and argued that players like him, Ian Bell and Gary Ballance were not going to win a World Cup for England, while players like Alex Hales, Jason Roy, Jos Buttler, and Eoin Morgan would.

Swann cited the statistic given to the players at the 2011 World Cup, that if they scored 230, they would win 72 per cent of their matches. He thought England's conservatism was 'crazy' and pointed to a match against Sri Lanka in Colombo where England made 229, with Jonathan Trott making 86, and everyone thought they had done well. Sri Lanka knocked off the runs without loss in 39.3 overs.

There is irony in some of this. Alex Hales never made it to the 2019 World Cup, and, mainly because of the slow pitches prepared, some of the cricket in the 2019 edition, including the final, was almost played in a time machine that was taking us back to the type of play Swann was criticising. But overall he was right.

On England went, though.

'Cooky and Mooresy were a good pairing,' says Farbrace. 'We were starting to make strides in Test cricket. I was one who was adamant that we shouldn't sack Cooky before the World Cup. I thought we should stick with him, not necessarily because he was the best captain for one-day cricket, but because his relationship with Mooresy was very good. I didn't want the sacking of Cooky in one-day cricket to affect their relationship in Test cricket. I was strong on that. Paul Downton was the boss at the time [managing director of England cricket] and could see the merits in that.

'In hindsight, maybe we should have changed the captain 12 months before, but I will hold my hand up and say I was adamant that he stayed on. It just didn't seem right to make the change just before the World Cup.

'We lost that Sri Lanka series 5–2, and at the end of that everyone felt it was time to make a change. What it meant, though, was that Morgs in effect captained Cooky's team to the World Cup.

'It was always going to be a difficult situation. We tried very hard to have a new approach to the World Cup, and we talked a lot about being more positive and aggressive. But whatever we did at that World Cup, I don't think we would have done any better. We just had no chance going into it.'

Morgan was also appointed at a time when his batting form was awful. 'It was a horrible tour of Sri Lanka where we had got hammered,' he said. 'My personal form was terrible. I'm not quite sure why. Just on that specific tour it was really, really poor.' Morgan averaged just 12.85 in the seven matches. 'I was given the captaincy over the Christmas–New Year period [2014–15], and it is obviously important to lead from the front. You can't have the captain being a bit of a liability.'

Morgan did make 121 against Australia at the start of the Tri-series in January, but when he made a duck in Melbourne in the opening World Cup match it was his third nought in four ODI innings, with the other score being only two.

'It was the toughest time of my career,' he said. 'It was a bit too late, but we were trying to change the way we played to catch up with the rest of the world, trying to get 300 every game, if not 320.

'We were going through a transition that we needed more time to get used to. We needed players who naturally played an aggressive game, because the tough thing about playing high-risk cricket is, when you get knocked back, traditionally a lot of our players resort to just batting time and spending time at the crease, playing orthodox shots. When you get knocked back, you need a guy who is going to come harder and harder.'

So, England did not exactly go to that 2015 World Cup brimming with confidence then. 'To be fair to Mooresy, we knew before we went to that World Cup that we were behind the eight ball and going to find it a difficult tournament,' Farbrace said. 'Even leading into the World Cup, we knew that we had players who were not necessarily playing the modern one-day game. We weren't scoring the big runs. We had a lot of people who had played a lot of one-day cricket in the older method.

'We thought that if we got Australia and New Zealand out of the way, we could crack on and try to qualify for the quarter-finals. We thought that wouldn't be terrible. To win and get to the semi-final would have probably been as much as we could have hoped for. We were limping towards that World Cup from quite a while out.'

But England did not get those games against Australia and New Zealand out of the way. They got beaten so badly that there was simply no way back.

'As it was, we were absolutely blown away in Melbourne by the Aussies and got hammered, and then we went to New Zealand and got bowled out cheaply in Wellington, and McCullum absolutely gunned us down,' said Farbrace. 'We literally never recovered. We were gone after that second game. We knew we were struggling. We had nothing. We literally had nothing after that.

'Not much went right for us, but when you are not playing well the luck doesn't go for you. We got everything we deserved. We played poorly. We didn't really have the team to cope against other sides.'

Morgan agreed. 'Those first two games, against Australia and New Zealand, we knew they would be difficult,' he said. 'We were playing against two of the favourites in their home conditions. We envisaged a possibility of losing our first two games. But not by those amounts.'

But it was the defeat by New Zealand that had the greatest impact upon Morgan, and upon England's ODI cricket as a whole going forwards. Morgan resolved that if he retained the captaincy after the tournament, his side would play in a similar style to McCullum's. That defeat in Wellington truly was English ODI cricket's watershed moment.

'The way his New Zealand team played, the way they did it their own way, was important. It's important for any team to get their own identity and stick with it,' said Morgan. 'New Zealand proved a point that you can actually be really good humans and grow the game, and play cricket in your own way and win at the same time.'

Having first played together for the Kolkata Knight Riders in the Indian Premier League, Morgan and McCullum have become very close friends. McCullum was master of ceremonies at Morgan's wedding in Somerset in 2018.

'Baz and I, we are close mates,' said Morgan. 'We talk cricket a lot. I watched how he implemented the changes in New Zealand cricket. Behind what looked like a free-spirited, wild, exciting game there was a bit of structure. I learnt a lot from that.

'He is a fantastic leader. He will consult others, but it has to sit right with him. During that 2015 World Cup, I certainly fell victim to taking in too much information and going with a safer option instead of going with what I would have gone with four months later.'

The pair would be seen embracing warmly the day before the 2019 final at Lord's. The link from that day of defeat in Wellington was complete, and it even gave McCullum a tricky dilemma of allegiance on the day of the final as a pundit. 'You can't lose, can you?' asked Sky Sports' presenter Ian Ward.

'That's right,' replied McCullum. 'I normally have quite a strong feel for who might win, but not today. I'm just so pleased. I love what Eoin Morgan has been able to do with the England side, and the flip side of that is what Kane Williamson has done with the New Zealand side. To me, they are two great custodians of our game, and two great men.'

McCullum fits those two descriptions pretty well himself and was the ideal exemplar for Morgan to follow, but before he could do so, there was still the rest of the 2015 World Cup campaign, however ill-fated and dispiriting, to be completed.

England beat Scotland in Christchurch but then returned to Wellington for another hammering, this time by Sri Lanka, by nine wickets, when 309 for six proved utterly inadequate because of a poor bowling performance. The next game, against Bangladesh in Adelaide, was lost too – by 15 runs – and England were out of the World Cup.

When England met Bangladesh in the 2019 version at Cardiff, it was suggested that that match in Adelaide had been a turning point for Morgan and his team, but Morgan was having none of it, returning again to the New Zealand match in Wellington.

'Not that [Bangladesh] game in particular,' he said. 'We

weren't humiliated. We were beaten by a better team who deserved to win on the night. The humiliating games were the ones that happened previously, ones where we might have been competitive but were blown away. The New Zealand game in Wellington was the big contribution to us making steps forward and good decisions.'

It was after the Bangladesh defeat in 2015, though, that in an interview with the BBC head coach Peter Moores was thought to have said: 'We'll have to look at the data.'

It caused a mighty furore, but he didn't actually use the word 'data', not in that BBC interview anyway, even if he did then use it in another interview with Sky Sports.

And apparently England were not as obsessed by data as everyone thought. Other teams were using it much more. 'When we won the T20 World Cup with Sri Lanka in 2014 [Farbrace was Sri Lanka head coach then], we had six analysts working overnight on every game and giving me information to help us against the next opposition,' said Farbrace. 'Their data helped us beat the Indians in the final. This Indian company that the Sri Lanka Board employed came up with this stat that the Indians attacked the opposition's third and fifth overs in the powerplay [of six overs]. So, we bowled our two best bowlers then.

'They also came up with a stat that bowling wide yorkers at the end was the thing that M.S. Dhoni found hardest to score against. We won the final based on statistical data and analysis. We used more data than England did in that 2015 World Cup, yet Pete was constantly harangued for saying about the data.'

What Moores had said to the BBC was: 'We will have to look at it later.' But with emotions high and scapegoats being sought, once the whole data bandwagon – which chimed neatly with Swann's earlier criticisms – had been set in motion, it was almost impossible to stop, even after a BBC apology to Moores.

Worse still, even though they were already out of the tournament, England still had one game to play, against Afghanistan in Sydney. England duly won that match, by nine wickets, but it did not matter.

The day afterwards, 14 March 2015, Moores called a meeting at the team's hotel, the Intercontinental Hotel in Macquarie Street in Sydney. This was the day and the meeting at which England's one-day revolution began, even if nobody had the faintest idea that was going to be the case. Of course, it began badly – what else would you expect? – but at least it was a beginning.

'If we are all honest, it was an absolute disaster,' said Farbrace. 'Mooresy called the meeting, and rightly so, because he wanted to get some things off his chest, and he wanted the team to say what they felt.

'We all had our say, but it became a finger-pointing meeting and people blaming others. There weren't too many saying: "I messed up. I made a mistake." It was a negative meeting. In some ways, it summed up our World Cup. It was a disastrous meeting at the end of a disastrous World Cup.'

Apparently, Essex's Ravi Bopara was especially vocal and did not spare too many of his fellow squad members, even accusing some of them of dragging his own cricket down by the way they were playing.

'Ravi made some quite memorable comments,' Farbrace said.

But Bopara, having featured in the side before the World Cup, had been omitted at the start of the tournament to allow James Taylor to bat at no. 6, and his only appearance in the tournament came against Afghanistan when it was all over.

A flavour of what was on his mind came in an interview with the *Guardian* soon after the tournament. 'We should develop braver players and stop fearing. There is a sense of fear in the team which we need to get rid of,' he said. 'We need to be a bit more free as players, to stop worrying about the consequences. If you look at other countries, they are more open about things and more honest about things.

'For too long we have been worried about what people think of us. We should be honest with everyone. Say it straight up. We weren't good enough in the World Cup. Other teams have developed their skills a lot faster than we have because they were honest enough to say it earlier.'

Eoin Morgan assiduously keeps a diary, and he still has his notes from that meeting. 'The thing I have written down in them, which I still have, is that not very many people looked to themselves,' he said. 'The blame was elsewhere. It was not a productive meeting.

'There was an emotional frustration from everybody. It went around in circles for quite a while. There were a couple of home truths, but they were painted over by guys blaming other people or things around them.

'The best of the best show complete honesty in their own performance. They are always the first to say: "Right, I'll do something about it. I should have been the one to win the game." It is not really built on excuses.'

Farbrace did not think it was a seminal meeting. 'It wasn't a turning point,' he said. 'We all knew we were battling going into that tournament.'

But Morgan looked at it slightly differently. 'I don't think it necessarily ruled out any players for the future, but I think it emphasised the need for change,' he said.

Of course, there is always some change after a World Cup. 'The way we work in cycles, the change was probably going to happen anyway, because after Ashes and World Cups you normally draw a line under things and start building towards the next one,' Morgan said.

But this time there was considerable change. From that 2015 World Cup squad, Bopara, Ian Bell, Gary Ballance, James Tredwell and James Anderson never played ODI cricket for England again. Stuart Broad has only played two more ODIs and Chris Jordan just nine more. Just five players – Morgan, Jos Buttler, Joe Root, Moeen Ali and Chris Woakes – from that 2015 squad were at the 2019 tournament.

Within a month of the tournament having ended, Paul Downton, after only 14 months in his job, was sacked as England's managing director of cricket by the ECB's new chief executive, Tom Harrison. Downton had taken up the post at a difficult time, when the furore over the sacking of Kevin Pietersen from the England team was raging, but there was always a lingering suspicion that he was not up to speed with the modern game, a point reinforced when he made his infamous comment after England had been knocked out of the World Cup. 'What has struck me has been how much influence T20 is having on one-day cricket,' he said.

It had struck the rest of the cricketing world a long time before then. Downton went, but for now Moores remained. 'This doesn't impact Peter Moores' position at all. This is with respect to delivering an environment for the future,' Harrison said, with England about to begin a three-match Test series away against West Indies (that was eventually drawn) with Moores still as head coach. It was the dreaded sporting vote of confidence.

On 8 May, England were playing their next ODI after the World Cup, a one-off match against Ireland in Malahide, Dublin, that was eventually washed out. The team selected for that match was very different from the one that ended the World Cup and included some interesting new names. Adil Rashid (inexplicably omitted from the 2015 World Cup squad after averaging just 18.64 with the ball in List A cricket in 2014) was in that side, as was Jonny Bairstow, and there were five debutants in Jason Roy, Mark Wood, James Vince, David Willey and Zafar Ansari. With Morgan away at the IPL, James Taylor was captain.

'Mooresy's last game was actually the first game with the new group of players,' said Farbrace. 'Pete knew we had to change a lot at the end of that World Cup. He was trying hard to effect that change.

'Morgs stayed at the IPL, which caused a stir. We made some significant changes to the shape of the team, but Mooresy never got to see that through.'

That was because, while the rain fell during that match, rumours began surfacing that Moores was going to be sacked too. The journalists in the press box knew before he did.

Andrew Strauss had been due to commentate on the match for Sky Sports, and when he pulled out, it became clear that he was about to replace Downton and that his first move would be to move Moores on. This was all confirmed officially the following day. Moores had been sacked by England for a second time.

'That World Cup wasn't Pete Moores's fault,' said Farbrace. 'Ultimately the ECB could have got rid of all of us at the end of that World Cup. I could have gone too. I was involved in the decision-making. We all had our chances to input. It is easy for people to point the finger at him.'

'It is never nice when things like that happen,' said Morgan. 'I still think Peter has a lot to offer. He has proved that in county cricket.'

But Strauss knew that England's one-day game needed a drastic overhaul. 'I was watching the [2015] World Cup, working for Sky, and I was genuinely angry [about] what I'd seen,' he said during the 2019 World Cup. 'Not because of anything those guys were doing, but the same mistakes made in the two previous World Cups that I'd been involved in, and prior to my time as well, were being made again: playing the wrong brand of cricket, picking Test players and hoping they'd put some of the best one-day players in the world under pressure.

'I still remember my quotes from the 2007 World Cup that two threes are as good as a six. That was trying to justify something that you just couldn't justify. To me, and this was before I was appointed director of cricket, we just could not do this again.'

Now aware of his fate, Moores flew home on his own on the night of that Ireland match. The next day, when the team returned, Strauss met Farbrace at Birmingham airport.

'I spent three and a half hours with Straussy, discussing everything – Test and one-day cricket,' said Farbrace. 'And one of the questions he asked was: "Is Morgs the right chap to be captain of the one-day team?" I was unequivocal.

'"Yes, he is," I said. "He is a positive bloke, he captained Cooky's team, he captained the team at a tough time, and it probably wouldn't have been the team he wanted to take to a World Cup." So Straussy continued with him.'

It sounds as if Strauss needed little persuading anyway. 'Once I was appointed director of cricket, it was a case of, well, if we're going to prioritise one-day cricket, what do we need?' he said. 'If we want to play that type of style, who is the right captain to embody that?

'That led me very quickly to Eoin Morgan. He was exactly the sort of person I was looking for. I knew Eoin well. I knew what he brought to the party. I knew the way he played his cricket and knew him as a person, because I had played a lot with him for England and Middlesex.

'He has always been a guy who hasn't been afraid to do things his own way and to stick out from the crowd. He always had a very strong friendship with Brendon McCullum and an instinctive desire to want to play that high-tempo cricket. You can't force anyone to do that. It's got to be very comfortable for them.

'Eoin had only just started in the job, and it would have been very harsh to blame him for what went on in the World Cup. He did not have the team he wanted, and I just felt he could do something special. So, it was natural that he would carry on.'

Strauss immediately called his one-day captain in India. Morgan was in Hyderabad, having breakfast at the Sunrisers' team hotel, before practice for a game two days later against Royal Challengers Bangalore. When Strauss's name appeared on the screen of his mobile phone, Morgan feared that he might be about to lose the captaincy.

'I hadn't heard from anybody since the World Cup,' Morgan said. 'The only communication I had was that I wouldn't be needed for the Ireland game, and I was quite nervous about that phone call, because I wasn't quite sure which way he would go.

'Normally when someone comes into a big role with a lot of responsibility, the first thing they do is have an inquiry, and that takes six months, and then they spend the next three or four years trying to implement it. It takes quite a lot of balls to make the decision to keep the captain who got you knocked out of the previous World Cup and to make the big decision that we are going to change the way we play immediately and say: "These are the right guys I am going to entrust to do that."

'I am very appreciative for that, for someone like Straussy to come in for the right reasons and make the right calls. I have never come across anyone in a senior position who has done that before. There is normally a corporate process they go through.'

Morgan now realises that it needed England to reach 'rock bottom', as he put it, because if they had not plumbed such depths, then the necessary changes might never have been made. 'I have to be extremely thankful for that time, because if we hadn't been as bad as we were, if we had limped into the quarter-finals, if we'd beaten Bangladesh in that game in Adelaide where we were knocked out, I'm not sure there would have been as drastic a change with the team and with the employees at the ECB,' he said. 'Paul Downton might have still been in the job, which would have meant that Andrew Strauss might not have come in. He was a huge contributing factor to us, especially with the freedom with selection and the way we wanted to play.'

It was only a short phone call between Strauss and Morgan, emphasising the need for a complete change in England's attitude to one-day cricket, but it considerably enthused Morgan, who had looked so glum and downbeat at the end of the World Cup campaign.

'We were talking about the changes we might make, and Straussy stopped me in mid-sentence and said: "No, you are going to be in on the selection meetings. You are all going to be on the same page, with the coaches as well,"' said Morgan. 'It was brilliant. It was such a change in attitude. We were talking about batting lower and lower, and going harder and harder. It was just like, "This is the way we are going to go. Happy days!"'

Strauss's next task was to find a coach to replace Moores, preferably someone with significant white-ball experience and success behind him. In the Australian Trevor Bayliss, he found exactly the right man.

Bayliss had coached Sri Lanka to a World Cup final in 2011, New South Wales to Australia's domestic 50-over title, Kolkata Knight Riders to the IPL twice, the Sydney Sixers to Big Bash titles and the Champions League, and he had taken brief charge of Australia's T20 side the year before. He certainly had the CV.

Bayliss, who was a solid batsman for New South Wales without ever playing for his country, was then coach of New South Wales and had been interviewed by the ECB the year before when they had reappointed Moores. They had decided they wanted an Englishman.

'It definitely wasn't an easy decision, because I was very happy with New South Wales Cricket, having already left them once to spend four years with Sri Lanka,' said Bayliss. 'And I could have signed to stay for three more years with Kolkata Knight Riders in the IPL. Talking to Andrew Strauss, it got to a point where it was something I couldn't refuse.'

Bayliss was also someone with whom both Morgan (at Kolkata Knight Riders) and Farbrace (Sri Lanka – he was Bayliss's assistant at that 2011 tournament) had worked before.

'Not a lot of people knew him,' said Morgan. 'He has this incredible ability to take pressure off when he knows you are under pressure. It is very down to earth. It is very realistic. He is also not afraid to coach. A lot of head coaches are worried about managing people all the time, but they need to coach as well.'

Bayliss's appointment was not confirmed officially until the day after the first Test of that summer, against New Zealand at Lord's, for which Farbrace was in temporary charge. And it did not appear that Bayliss did a huge amount of swotting up on his new players during this time. Sitting on the balcony at Cardiff during his first Test in charge, an Ashes Test no less, he apparently leant across and asked Jos Buttler which team he played for. Buttler was rather taken aback and replied: 'England.'

'No, no, which county?' asked Bayliss.

Buttler told him it was Lancashire (he had moved from Somerset at the end of the 2013 season), and there were some bemused glances amongst the England players about their new coach.

This actually became a bone of contention throughout his tenure. There was much criticism about Bayliss not watching any county cricket, but the truth is that there is so little time to do that when you are head coach of England. The schedule is too busy.

Before Bayliss arrived, Farbrace made a hugely important decision for the future of English cricket in that first Test against New Zealand in 2015. He promoted Ben Stokes, who, like Rashid, had been a shocking omission from the World Cup squad, to bat at no. 6, back to the position from which he had made his maiden Test century against Australia in Perth in 2013–14. Stokes responded with scores of 92 and 101, as well as taking three second-innings wickets as England won a memorable Test by 124 runs.

'I think that was the turning point for me in international cricket,' Stokes told Sky Sports. 'It's a place where I made my debut, batting at no. 6 and being that fourth bowler. I was then in and out of the team, and if I was in, I was batting at 8.

'So, when Farby gave me the opportunity to come back into the side at no. 6, again there was that self-belief, knowing that I'd done this role successfully, whether for England or back at Durham.

'Farby was great at getting the best out of the individual

– even for myself, who has played quite a lot, he was constantly saying go out, do what you do best and commit to it.'

Bayliss was obviously the first Australian to be head coach of England, and that quite naturally created a lot of interest back in his home country. On the day that the new coach was appointed, Farbrace was standing outside the Grace Gates at Lord's, and right next to him were an Australian television crew waiting for some reaction to Bayliss's appointment. What they didn't know was that Farbrace was actually on the phone to the man himself, discussing the composition of England's ODI squad for the New Zealand series, which would follow the two-Test series. Bayliss would not start his job until the Ashes later in the summer, after which there would be one T20 international and five ODIs against Australia.

'We had our one-day selection that day,' explained Farbrace. 'Mick Newell, Gus Fraser, Jimmy Whitaker [the three selectors], Morgs, me and Straussy. I had spoken to Morgs about the types of players I thought we needed, and I stood outside the Grace Gates that morning for about three quarters of an hour talking to Trev [Bayliss], next to an Aussie media crew who had no idea who I was.

'I was talking to him back in Sydney about the one-day selection. I said: "What are the key things you want me to get over in this meeting to get the ball rolling before you get over here?"

'He wanted a spinner who could spin the ball both ways and to play two spinners. He was also very strong on Jason Roy because of his character, his attitude, his "up-and-at-'em" type of approach. So, Roy got picked, and Adil Rashid came in as that spinner alongside Moeen Ali.

'He also wanted people with athleticism in the field, as he has always built his sides around the fielding because that is the one area when you are together as a team. I relayed all that in the selection meeting.'

This was the exciting 14-man squad selected to face New Zealand in that first ODI series of five matches after the 2015 World Cup: Eoin Morgan (c), Sam Billings, Jos Buttler, Steven Finn, Alex Hales, Chris Jordan, Liam Plunkett, Adil Rashid, Joe Root, Jason Roy, Ben Stokes, James Taylor, David Willey, Mark Wood.

It was a big decision to leave out both Stuart Broad and James Anderson. 'Taking Broad and Anderson out was a significant thing,' said Farbrace. 'In that first World Cup match against Australia, along with James Taylor [who made 98 not out], they were our two stand-out players, both with the ball and in the field. They were the two that coped with the 80,000 at the MCG better than anyone else.

'Broady caught a skyer at long-on with about 20,000 people behind him saying: "Broady is a wanker!" Now, there were a lot of people on the field who would have dropped that catch. It was a massive call not to continue with Broad and Anderson, as it had been not to continue with Cook.'

Eight of those players selected would play in the World Cup final of 2019. Jonny Bairstow actually got one game in this series as well but would have to force his way into the side on a regular basis through sheer weight of runs. Jofra Archer obviously came late to the party, as did Tom Curran, who also made the 2019 tournament squad but didn't play. James Vince and Liam Dawson were the other members of the 15-man squad.

Chris Woakes was injured for the New Zealand series. And Moeen Ali was left out in order to concentrate on long-form cricket ahead of the Ashes. That created a vacancy at no. 7 in the batting order, and England chose Sam Billings, a fire-cracker of a batsman who would surely have made the 2019

World Cup squad had he not dislocated a shoulder in early season while fielding for Kent in Cardiff. It was an important signal of their attacking intent.

'Someone said at the end of the meeting we could be 70 all out with that batting line-up,' said a team source. 'It was said as a joke but was also serious too. But we stuck with it, and that selection was a big statement. It was a crucial start.'

'We wanted Mo to go back to Worcestershire and bowl some red-ball overs ready for the Ashes,' said Farbrace. 'That was the only reason he didn't play. He was always going to play in our best one-day side, and we were always going to play two spinners.'

Until the actual World Cup in 2019 that is (Rashid and Moeen were a formidable duo in the intervening years), when spinners had a rough time of it, and Moeen was left out of England's XI for the final.

So, the revolution began on the field on 9 June 2015. That was the date of England's first ODI against New Zealand at Edgbaston. It was England's first series, but looking back, it was still probably the most important series in the four-year period leading up to the World Cup. There needed to be definite signs of change and of improvement. That the opposition were New Zealand helped, given they were the model Eoin Morgan wanted to follow, and Brendon McCullum was still captaining them.

Two days before that match at Edgbaston, England held a meeting, a very different one from that in Sydney three months before. Farbrace was in charge as interim coach, but Andrew Strauss also wanted to speak to the squad in his new role.

'Straussy wanted to address the players in the dressing room and speak to them about how things were going to change moving forward, just quickly, because I wanted to give my views too,' Morgan said. 'I sort of started after Straussy, and nobody was saying anything because they were quite intimidated. For a split second I forgot that half the people in the room had barely played a game for England, and Straussy would have been one of their heroes, as he is mine. So, I politely asked Straussy to leave. I said: "Mate, nobody is saying anything while you are here." He was like: "OK, I'd better go."'

This was an early signal that this was very much going to be Morgan's team, and that was how Bayliss wanted things to be too when he arrived. 'Trev is very much about the captain being the leader, and the coaches are there to support the leader,' said Farbrace. 'Morgs is a leader, a front man. He doesn't say a lot, but when he does, it counts. He's got Buttler, Stokes, Moeen and Root around him who have all been fundamental in England's success.'

There was a T20 international against Pakistan in Sharjah later in 2015, which ended up, coincidentally now, going to a Super Over. Pakistan had equalled England's score of 154, but Chris Jordan had been England's most expensive bowler, going for 39 from his four overs. Apparently, Bayliss and Farbrace asked one another at the end of the innings who might bowl the Super Over. At the same time, both said: 'It can't be CJ.'

At that moment, Morgan appeared. 'CJ is bowling the Super Over,' he said.

'Great idea,' said Bayliss, with Farbrace agreeing.

Morgan was in charge. And England duly won. Jordan bowled his yorkers superbly, so that Shahid Afridi and Umar Akmal, who was bowled off the final ball, could only take one single and two leg byes from the over.

Morgan's chat at Edgbaston with his players was short, but the message was clear. 'He told them to go out and play the way they played for their counties, be aggressive, play on the front foot, no backward step, and make sure to take the positive option every single time,' said Farbrace.

Morgan can recall the enthusiasm in the room. 'Everyone was very excited,' he said. 'We were going to try to play a game that came naturally to everyone in the room. Part of the selection was that everybody in the room played an aggressive brand of cricket. All they needed to do was apply it against international teams. It was no different, except the wickets are better.

'We needed to strive to be better than we already were. It was a four-year plan for us to get to the stage where we were contenders for the World Cup, so the initial period of about a year and a half was about testing our limits.'

Those limits were certainly tested to their upper reaches on that very first day. England scored 408 for nine at Edgbaston, which was then their highest score in ODI cricket. After Jason Roy was out to the first ball of the innings, Jos Buttler made 129 off 77 balls and Joe Root hit 104 off 78 balls.

'Nobody thought we would have got off to a start like that, not even ourselves,' said Morgan. 'If we had played that series and just got 380 in one of the games that would have been enough for me to show we were going in the right direction.

'You have to remember that we were playing against New Zealand too. These guys had just made it to the World Cup final.'

At the time, their centuries (Buttler's came off 66 balls and Root's off 71 balls) were the second and fourth fastest by England players in ODI cricket. At the time of writing, they are the 11th and 14th fastest on the list. That illustrates very neatly the dramatic change this game began to set in motion. England were also to pass 400 on three other occasions before the 2019 World Cup (and made 399 once too, as well as 397 in the tournament itself).

The excitement beforehand had been carried into the game itself. 'We don't want to get carried away at one performance and think like English ODI cricket is fixed and we're going to win the World Cup,' said Buttler. 'But I think just looking round – the two training days were really exciting, watching what some of these guys can do in the nets, the energy they have brought to the group. There's definitely been an extra buzz.

'Everyone has seen in county cricket how guys like Jason Roy and Sam Billings have played innings that make people stand up and take notice. When they do that in international cricket, there will be a wider audience taking note. When we realise the potential of everyone as a group and can all do that at the same time, it will be a really exciting place to be.'

And Morgan said again after the game: 'The guys were outstanding. I'm surprised it's happened so quickly, but given that we have two or three new faces, I thought we were brilliant. You can look back and wonder about the World Cup, but today I'm looking forward and I'm really excited.'

Farbrace thought they had some fortune too, though. 'Where we had no luck in the World Cup, we had an unbelievable slice of luck at Edgbaston,' he said. 'We were 202–6 after 30 overs. Jos Buttler and Adil Rashid were there. Jos played unbelievably well, but Rash made 69 [off 50 balls], and that is still his highest score in ODI cricket.

'He could easily have been caught at slip off Mitchell Santner early on but then hit him down the ground for six and he was away. When he was out, Liam Plunkett hit two of the last four balls for six and we had 408.

'We had a plan that we were going to be very positive and aggressive, and if we got bowled out in 40 overs in getting

280, then so be it. We could have got bowled out for 260 or 270 in 35 overs and everyone would have said, 'Nothing's changed. They might have changed the personnel, but they are still shit at one-day cricket.

'We won the game by 210 runs, and all of a sudden the new England revolution was up and running. But we had had a lot of luck, which we hadn't had in the World Cup. Yeah, you can say you make your own luck, but we certainly got a bit in that game.'

Ironically, whereas nothing could go wrong for Morgan (he made 50 from 46 balls), little went right for his opposite number, Brendon McCullum, the man he was looking to copy. Although Roy was out first ball, McCullum's decision to bowl first was hardly vindicated, as the ball did not swing, and he then used up Trent Boult's overs too early, allowing England to make that recovery from 202 for six. McCullum then made just ten with the bat.

But New Zealand were never just going to lie down in this series. They duly won the second match at the Oval, even though England again showed their new aggressive intent in valiantly chasing the Kiwis' huge total of 398 for five, despite the rain not helping their cause at all.

Morgan had again played superbly well in making 88 from 47 balls, but when England slipped to 275 for seven, still requiring 124 for victory, it looked too tall an order. But Rashid came to the rescue again, this time in concert with Liam Plunkett, so that when the rain did arrive, 54 were needed from 37 balls. It showed England's batting strength, with Plunkett eventually making 44 from 30 balls. Not bad for a no. 9, with Chris Jordan, who had three first-class centuries under his belt, still to come in at no. 10.

'Most of the time we played with ten batsmen so that people could keep going hard and being positive,' said Farbrace.

Upon the resumption, though, England needed 34 from 2.1 overs, a stiff ask, but still Morgan's message to his team was: 'It's our game to win.'

They didn't quite win it, falling 15 short, but they had hit 14 sixes in the innings, equalling the record they had set in the first game at Edgbaston. This really was something different.

'We're enjoying this brand of cricket and having the guys in the changing room to play that way naturally – not making it such a big deal,' said Morgan.

England lost the third game of the series too, by three wickets at Southampton, but again there was an important message contained within the defeat. England lost five wickets for 14 to be bowled out for 302 in 45.2 overs. Not using up your overs had long been considered a cardinal sin in one-day cricket. Not now, not with this team.

'It's not a huge thing for me that we have to bat 50 overs. It doesn't disappoint me,' said Morgan afterwards. 'We're trying to change our process and mindset with the bat, which may take time. We've come a long way in the last three games, scoring 300-plus in each of them – which is a huge achievement, and a big turnaround.

'I want the guys to continue with that mindset and not worry about batting 50 overs. I think that makes guys hesitate and question their natural way of playing. I don't want that to happen.

'For a long time in this game we looked like getting 350 to 360. That's a huge plus for us, because for a long time we've never even thought about getting that sort of score. As long as we set the standards really high, we'll win more games than we lose playing in this manner.'

The time for a little more conservatism and smartness (maybe in a World Cup final) would come later. 'Yes, there will be a time for that, absolutely, but we're trying to get as much natural ability out of the new guys, and those around them, as we can,' said Morgan. 'I think, as early as we are into changing things, at the moment there's no need for it – unless things go drastically wrong. But they haven't, and guys are really enjoying playing the way we are.'

Before the next match at Trent Bridge, Morgan called a meeting to discuss the team's progress. It did not last long. 'We had a meeting before training the following day to discuss what we were going to do, because we had been set back,' he said. 'The meeting lasted about 30 seconds. I spoke about how we wanted to play and that it wasn't after one game that we were going to change things. I said: "I'm delighted that we played well for 46 overs. We just need to be better for four more overs."'

Interestingly, there was another occasion against New Zealand, three years later in Dunedin, which required a similar meeting to reinforce that message that England's positive attitude was still very much worth pursuing. 'We lost eight wickets for 46 in just over ten overs at the end of our innings in Dunedin,' said Paul Farbrace. 'And we lost the game. We had a clear-the-air meeting afterwards, discussing whether we had been too gung-ho, and it was agreed that: "No, we haven't. We stuck to what we have always said we would do and been true to ourselves." We went to Christchurch at 2–2, and we hammered them [by seven wickets] to win the series. We cleaned them up and smashed them.'

And England smashed the Kiwis at Trent Bridge in 2015 too, winning with a whopping six overs to spare, with Morgan at the forefront again in making 113 from just 82 balls. Joe Root also made an unbeaten century.

'The single biggest factor behind the resurgence was that Eoin Morgan played the way that he asked the team to play,' said Farbrace. 'He has never wavered from that, even when he hasn't been scoring runs. He is such a tough, thick-skinned bloke.'

England needed 350 to win. The first over of their innings was, remarkably, a maiden, but by the end of the ten overs of the first powerplay, England, through Alex Hales and Jason Roy, were 97 without loss.

Hales made 67 and Roy 38. It is easily forgotten that Roy struggled a little in this, his first ODI series. He had not batted on debut in Ireland and then had suffered that first-ball dismissal at Edgbaston. His highest score in the series was 39 at the Oval. He averaged just 19.60, but his selfless and fearless approach was already becoming evident.

'Jason didn't get many in that series, but he played for the team,' said Farbrace. 'The next series we lost to Australia 3–2, but Jason got his rewards [averaging 40.20, with two fifties and a strike rate of 112.92]. I was adamant he stayed in for that whole New Zealand series because he kept playing for the team and at no stage just tried to get himself a fifty just to get picked for the next game.'

To illustrate Morgan's attitude, Farbrace has told a story of that game at Trent Bridge. Farbrace was sitting with Hales and Jos Buttler watching the captain bat. 'He was batting with Root, and Matt Henry was bowling,' Farbrace told the *Guardian*. 'So, Jos says: "Look, we've scored five off this over already. Rooty has hit a four off the first ball and a single off the third, so all we've got to do here is bat sensibly."

'And as he says it, Morgs runs down the wicket and flat-bats Henry over wide mid-off for this huge six, one of the biggest I've ever seen him hit. And all three of us just fell about laughing.

'It summed him up, really. There are so many times I've seen him do things that other people wouldn't have dreamed of doing, but for him it's a natural thing. Always has been.'

Morgan was enjoying himself. 'The carefree attitude is helping my batting, concentrating on the process rather than the result, and I've really enjoyed going up to no. 4,' he said. 'I still think the style is more important than the result now up at Durham.'

Yes, there was a decider now to be played at Durham. Farbrace had a slightly different opinion about the significance of the result: 'Everyone was saying it didn't matter whether we won the decider because of the way we had played, but I said: "It does matter. It really matters, because if we lose this, nothing has changed. This is our chance to really make a difference."'

And they did make a difference, complete with an unanticipated nod to their eventual World Cup final side in the inclusion of Jonny Bairstow, winning the game by three wickets after rain had affected England's pursuit of New Zealand's 283 for nine in their 50 overs. England were asked to score 192 in 26 overs. They won thanks to 83 not out from Bairstow, batting at no. 6 and making his first-ever ODI fifty after being called up to replace Buttler, who had injured a hand in practice.

Setting aside the abandoned match in Dublin just before this series, it was Bairstow's first ODI since September 2012. He had understandably not been happy about his exclusion. 'I'm without doubt capable of doing a very, very, very good job for England,' he had said just before his unexpected summons. It was an attitude we would see a great deal of in the following years, as Bairstow desperately attempted to prove his worth to the England ODI side.

Morgan was out first ball, caught at deep mid-wicket off the left-arm spinner Mitchell Santner, with only two fielders permitted outside the fielding circle in the reduced five-over powerplay, leaving his side at 20 for three, which soon became 45 for five, but it did not diminish his efforts in the series one bit. It might even have reinforced that aggressive mindset he wanted to encourage. It was after all the very thing Farbrace, Buttler and Hales had been laughing about at Trent Bridge.

'Everyone said: "New England, new approach, new selection,"' said Farbrace. 'But I still say the single biggest factor was the way Eoin Morgan played.'

Some of the statistics to emerge from the series were quite astonishing. The overall run rate was 7.15 runs per over. No ODI series of two or more matches had ever seen a rate that high before. And there were 3,151 runs scored in total, at that time more than in any ODI series featuring five or fewer matches. It truly was a defining moment for England's ODI cricket.

Morgan's friend, Brendon McCullum, was certainly impressed. 'There is some exciting talent there amongst their group, and they're going to be a tough team over the next few years,' he said.

As already mentioned, the ODI series that followed the Ashes (which England won 3–2) was lost 3–2, making it 5–5 in the ten ODIs played that summer, but they were all against New Zealand and Australia, the two finalists from the World Cup a few months earlier, the two sides that had absolutely thrashed England in their first two matches of that tournament.

'It showed how far we had come in such a short space of time,' said Farbrace.

Indeed it did.

THREE
COURAGE, UNITY, RESPECT

In the early morning of 25 September 2017, Andrew Strauss travelled to Bristol, where he met up with a distraught Clare Ratcliffe, Ben Stokes's partner and mother of his children. It was a month before their wedding.

Stokes, one of the world's most-prized cricketers, the most expensive overseas player in the IPL, and the beating heart of England's red- and white-ball cricket teams, had been arrested overnight on suspicion of causing actual bodily harm after becoming involved in a fight outside a nightclub that left another man with a fractured eye socket.

Stokes and many of his England colleagues had been out celebrating after completing a one-day international series win over West Indies. The end of a long summer was drawing near, and even though there were still two games left to play in the series, players needed to let off steam. Drinking began as soon as the game finished, carried on in the bars of Temple Meads, where they posed for selfies with fans, and ended with most drifting back to the team hotel after midnight, but Stokes and Alex Hales decided they wanted one more beer.

It would be a fateful decision that would drag English cricket's name through the gutter, destroy the carefully laid plans for that winter's Ashes series and call into question the culture at the heart of England's one-day team, a side that was heading for no. 1 in the rankings and was rightly considered hot favourites to win the World Cup.

For the two men involved, Stokes and Hales, it would change their careers. For Stokes, it would lead to the stress of a Crown court case, a damaged reputation only partially recovered by a not guilty verdict, and the inevitable loss of form that followed.

For Hales, the cricketing cost was far greater. He had not been arrested that night, but his England career would go into free fall. He lost the trust of his team-mates, and when Strauss banned both players for the rest of the West Indies series, Hales let go of his place at the top of the order.

The suspension of Hales allowed Jason Roy to come back in with a point to prove, having been dropped a few months earlier during the Champions Trophy, and he would go on to form England's greatest-ever opening partnership with Jonny Bairstow. Hales was heading for international oblivion.

Under the management of Trevor Bayliss and Eoin Morgan, there had been a relaxed attitude to team discipline. Bayliss hated to get involved in disciplinary matters. He believed it put the coach in an awkward situation. Resentment could build between a coach and a player who felt hard done by for what he saw as a minor transgression. Bayliss far preferred an old-fashioned team manager to be in charge of discipline, leaving the coach to be a father figure who could be firm but also offer a kindly shoulder when needed.

Morgan believed in trusting his players and allowing them to be responsible for their own actions. If you play an aggressive, free-spirited style on the pitch, then it is hard to inhibit individuals off it with a strict rulebook.

But over the course of 2017 something shifted. It was not just within the one-day side, but the Test team too. Perhaps it was the changing of the guard with Alastair Cook's time as captain coming to an end, a series of long, exhausting overseas tours and the frustration of coming close in two big tournaments. There is a lot of crossover between England's Test and one-day sides. The talent pool is not big enough for both to be totally separate. Many of England's one-day side had endured a tough tour to India that winter, losing the Test series 4–0, and the popular Cook resigning.

England also disappointed badly in June 2017 at the Champions Trophy, going out in the semi-final in Cardiff to Pakistan when they misread the pitch and could not recalibrate their attacking style. The same group had also lost narrowly in agonising circumstances in the World Twenty20 final a year earlier to the West Indies when Carlos Brathwaite stunned Stokes by slamming him for four sixes in the last over at Eden Gardens.

So perhaps Bristol 2017 had been building for some time. The laid-back, avuncular Bayliss and Morgan, the steely, focused captain but someone who hated straitjackets being put on players by overbearing coaching staff, had let discipline slide.

The night they smashed Australia in the 2017 Champions Trophy to set up a semi-final against Pakistan they drank late into the night at Edgbaston and carried on until the early hours of the morning in the Malmaison Hotel. It was a sign that players had entered a comfort zone. Professionalism had slipped. Four days later, they were knocked out of the Champions Trophy. They learned not to get ahead of themselves in the most painful way.

It would have to change. Radically. There was no team curfew in place that night in Bristol. Players were free to come and go as they pleased. After Stokes's arrest, Strauss started a review of team culture and discipline. He fined three players who were also out that night – Liam Plunkett, Jonny Bairstow and Jake Ball – for 'professional misconduct'. The review was still in its early stages when the 2017–18 Ashes tour started that November without Stokes, who was at home being interviewed by police and waiting to hear what charges he would face.

The players arrived in Perth for a four-month tour to Australia, dumped their bags in their rooms at the Hyatt Regency Hotel on Adelaide Terrace and headed to the bars of Claremont. There, in a nightclub popular with students named the Avenue Bar, Bairstow greeted the Western Australia opener Cameron Bancroft with a gentle headbutt, the kind of hello used by rugby players, and something he thought of as just banter.

A bemused Bancroft thought it strange but laughed it off. However, during his Test debut a few weeks later in Brisbane, he mentioned it to more seasoned members of the Australia side, who spotted an opportunity. Bairstow was sledged mercilessly, and the Australian team obligingly let the broadcast media know what was behind it all. The story was broken by Fox News sports reporter Neroli Meadows. She tweeted: 'I understand there was an incident in a bar in Perth, The Avenue, where Jonny Bairstow's head connected with the side of Cam Bancroft's.' It sounded serious. It wasn't, but after the Stokes affair the last thing England needed was more headlines about boozing and violent behaviour (even in jest), and the Aussies knew it.

After winning the first Test at the Gabba, Australia went to town. Steve Smith and Bancroft appeared together at the post-match press conference and basically took the mickey out of England. 'There was certainly nothing malicious about his action. I just took it as . . . I don't know Jonny Bairstow, but he says hello to people very differently to most others,' said Bancroft. England were a laughing stock.

Strauss was in Brisbane to oversee the start of the Ashes. Witnesses say he gave the squad a blistering telling off. 'It was ferocious. It was a headmaster getting stuck into school-boys,' said one who was present.

Publicly he backed them. 'These guys are not thugs,' he said at a press conference in Brisbane's Sofitel Hotel, where, just to add to the sense of rising panic, four years previously the then England head coach Andy Flower had revealed Jonathan Trott had left an Ashes tour suffering from stress. England were whitewashed. 'These are good, honest, hard-working cricketers who sacrifice a lot to play for England, and I will back them to the hilt,' Strauss continued.

But Strauss had reached the limit of his patience. A midnight curfew was enforced. Players had to be back at the hotel by that time, and the team's security staff would check them off a list when they returned. Anyone who stayed out later would be reported to the management. The curfew was still in place in 2019, now an integral part of the England team code.

Strauss also accelerated his review into team culture and put Morgan at the forefront of devising a new moral code that every player in the future would live by. It would take another 12 months to complete. But when Morgan and Joe Root, the Test captain, delivered it to the players in another five-star hotel, this time in Sri Lanka, there would be no going back.

The Shangri-La Hotel in Colombo is now synonymous with tragedy. It was one of the targets hit by bombers during the Colombo terrorist attacks on 29 April 2019, when staff and tourists were killed in its popular Table One restaurant by a terrorist wearing a suicide vest. England spent almost 40 nights at the hotel during their tour to Sri Lanka in October and November 2018. They loved the Table One restaurant so much that they engineered an extra night's stay at the hotel, using the excuse of breaking up the journey from Galle and Kandy between the first and second Tests.

Morgan was stunned by the terrorist attack. He remembered the staff who were injured and killed. He knew how long he and the other players had spent in the Table One restaurant. It could have been them. Morgan is a man who has life in perspective anyway, but it was another reminder of the world outside the cricket bubble.

It was in the Connect Cafe, one floor below the Table One restaurant, in early November 2018 where one of the most important team meetings of his England captaincy took place.

Morgan hates team meetings. Bayliss too. They both feel they are hot air ventures, usually achieving nothing. But this one was different. It would be the moment when Morgan and Root would reveal months of hard work that had been conducted away from training, nets and matches. It was the culmination of Strauss's review into team discipline that had grown into something else, something substantial and real that could be passed down the generations.

As his captaincy grew, Morgan became fascinated by leadership, reading up on the subject and listening to podcasts featuring interviews with chief executives and senior business figures. He met with author James Kerr who wrote *Legacy: What the All Blacks Can Teach Us About the Business of Life*, a book about the All Blacks rugby team and leadership. Kerr told Morgan how the world's greatest sports team teaches its players humility, why it is important young players learn the history of the All Blacks and how it relates to them, and finally why values on the pitch provide a code by which players should behave off it.

Kerr writes about the All Blacks' mantra of 'sweeping the sheds', which basically means no individual is bigger than the team and its history. It is about the small details too, and why no one individual is too important to clean the dressing rooms after a game. 'Sweeping the sheds' is the responsibility of every player.

Kerr also told Morgan how the All Blacks put the new generation of players in charge of updating the Haka, a process that took 12 months. It gave Morgan an idea.

David Young, the ECB's national lead for performance psychology, helped Morgan and Root identify what they wanted to change. It was decided they needed their own mantra, a code that was simple for all to understand. Young, who also works for Wolverhampton Wanderers, used his football contacts. The England management met with Manchester City's team psychologist, Pete Lindsay, at a hotel in Leeds during a one-day match against India in 2018. Lindsay read the poem 'This is the Place', written by Tony Walsh, that celebrates Manchester's cultural and industrial past.

A quote from the poem – 'Some are born here, some are drawn here' – is written on the wall of Manchester City's circular dressing room at the Etihad Stadium. Pep Guardiola, the Manchester City manager, has it translated for new recruits, introducing them to the city's culture. It shows nationality does not matter in a multi-cultural team. It would be the same for Morgan's squad. He is Irish. His team are representative of modern, multi-cultural Britain. The England management were moved by the poem and its meaning. The team's code could not be just about England and being English. It had to be more wide-ranging.

Cricketers live out of suitcases, following a transient life-style. They spend their lives in hotel rooms, but Morgan identified the thing that stays with them wherever they go: their England cap. It is presented to a player on debut, and they wear it until retirement.

After several meetings it was decided to settle on a three-step mantra. The first is the cap as a metaphor for a player's career. Guard it and treasure it. Second, the crown emblem on the cap stands for taking the team forwards, on and off the field. It represents always doing your best for the team. Third, the three lions below the crown were each given a meaning: one for courage; one for unity; one for respect.

Courage is about playing the team's way even in tough times when matches are on the line. Unity is about playing as one and bringing the country together behind a diverse team. Finally, it is about having respect for your team-mates, opponents and the England shirt.

As an Irishman, Morgan is keen to embrace outsiders, those from different countries and cultures. In his presentation to the players at the Shangri-La he used the example of Andrew Strauss, Kevin Pietersen and Jonathan Trott – players who had come to Britain from overseas, South Africa in their cases, and become successful England cricketers.

It was important to Morgan to make Jofra Archer feel part of a collective, with a common goal in mind, when he later came into the team. He was also aware of the different cultural backgrounds of Moeen Ali and Adil Rashid. 'It shows a good place culturally where we are,' he said about his team's new code. It is about a 'sense of belonging' where 'nationality is not relevant'.

But it was also about something else. Courage, unity and respect were also rules to live by on and off the field. Play hard and play fair. But also live your life in a way that respects your team-mates and what you are trying to achieve together. Alex Hales was about to discover the consequences for ignoring this new ethos.

At the age of 29, Alex Hales's career was faltering. He had lost his England place as a result of his involvement in the late-night street fight in Bristol, his gamble to play only white-ball cricket had not resulted in big offers from the main Twenty20 leagues, such as the IPL and the Big Bash, and he had become estranged from Morgan, who had been such a pillar of support earlier in his career.

Perhaps Morgan spotted the danger in Hales. He perhaps sensed this was a cricketer who would struggle to uphold the ethics that he and Root outlined in Sri Lanka. Hales was not unpopular with his team-mates, but they knew he could be reckless off the field. Some kept their distance.

He incensed the England management the morning after Stokes's arrest by going off to play golf and failing to inform them that his team-mate was in a police cell. Hales thought he was protecting his friend. England felt it showed selfishness and that he did not care. Shortly after Stokes was arrested, and with a hungry media picking over the story, lewd photographs of Hales emerged on social media.

Hales would later be fined for the embarrassment caused. He then made headlines in the tabloids when his girlfriend dumped him two months before the World Cup after she found out he was cheating on her during the tour to the Caribbean in March 2019. Hales could be trouble, and England knew it.

But Hales is also talented. At 6ft 5in he is an imposing figure at the crease, with enormous power to clear the boundary. He broke Robin Smith's 23-year record for England's highest ODI innings when he hit 171 against Pakistan in 2016 and is the scorer of England's only Twenty20 century to date. He can devastate attacks, and even if Roy and Bairstow were the no. 1 choice, Hales offered brilliant back-up. His presence no doubt pushed Roy and Bairstow to maintain their high standards.

Hales had been named in England's preliminary 15-man World Cup squad on 17 April and was thought a certainty to make the final cut, so when his county, Nottinghamshire, announced on 20 April he was taking a break for two weeks for 'personal reasons' it caused few ripples. The breakdown of his relationship with his girlfriend had been made public, so perhaps he needed time to clear his head before the pressures of a home World Cup took hold of his life.

But there was a darker secret, and only a very small handful of people knew the real reason for his absence: Hales had failed a second test for recreational drug use.

Hales had played for the England Lions alongside Surrey's Tom Maynard, son of former Glamorgan and England batsman Matthew, on a tour to Bangladesh in early 2012. It was a strong Lions side that also included the backbone of England's World Cup team in Joe Root, Jos Buttler and Jonny Bairstow.

Maynard played his last game for the Lions on 18 January of that year. Exactly five months later, in the early hours of 18 June, he died on train tracks in Wimbledon. At his inquest it was revealed his body contained traces of cocaine and Ecstasy consistent with the level of a 'daily or habitual user'.

After his death the England & Wales Cricket Board introduced random hair sampling tests to target recreational drug use. Players would be tested twice a season, at the start and end of the summer. A first failed test was kept confidential and treated with counselling. Recreational drug use was treated as a lifestyle issue consistent with gambling or alcohol addiction. A second failed test would result in a two-week suspension and the player's employer being informed. A third would equal a 12-month ban.

When Hales failed a second test, Nottinghamshire were informed; so was Tom Harrison, the chief executive of the ECB; and because he was employed on an incremental white-ball contract, Ashley Giles, who had taken over from Strauss as the England team director, was also told. Harrison and Giles were furious. They knew how hard the England team had been working on its culture. But the legal advice was they had to keep the news confidential. It was a protocol that did them few favours.

It seemed to many that the ECB had swept it under the carpet because they did not want to lose a key player in a World Cup summer. But the tight protocols in place even prevented Giles from telling Trevor Bayliss or Morgan about the failed test. Colin Graves, chairman of the ECB, and the board were kept in the dark too.

On 26 April, just 24 hours before Hales was due to join up with England on a pre-summer training camp in Cardiff, the *Guardian* cricket reporter Ali Martin broke the news that Hales was serving a two-week ban for failing a second drug test. It would be the scoop of the World Cup.

Hales's England team-mates had been texting him during his break to check if he was OK. They had no reason to suspect anything was wrong. He told them he would see them in Cardiff. All was fine. He had even told Martin in an interview in the *Guardian* in early April that 'sometimes I make mediocre decisions – I always have – but I don't want to make them any more'. Prophetic words.

Bayliss, Morgan and the England team only learned the truth when the *Guardian* story about his drug ban broke on the Friday afternoon. When Hales showed no contrition over the weekend in Cardiff, and acted as if nothing had happened, Morgan called together his senior core of players – Stokes, Buttler, Root, Moeen and Woakes – and they decided Hales had to go.

A statement was issued by the ECB: 'Consideration was given to creating the right environment within the team and ensuring that there are no unnecessary distractions and that the team is in the best position to succeed going into this crucial period.'

England flew to Dublin three days later to prepare for an ODI against Ireland. Giles spoke to the press but gave little away, still bound by the confidentiality agreement. It was Morgan who took the firm line. He was adamant Hales had broken too many rules. Courage, unity, respect. It had fallen on deaf ears. Hales had not been listening that night in the Connect Cafe in Colombo.

In a press conference in a marquee at Malahide Cricket Club, where Morgan had played as a youngster, he revealed his anger. 'We believe the right call has been made considering everyone in the squad,' he said. 'We have worked extremely hard over the last 18 months to establish our culture and work towards values that everyone across all three formats could adhere to, respect and relate to.

'We have been at that stage for six or seven months. They are in place. There has been a complete disregard for those values. There has been a complete breakdown in trust between Alex and the team. Everybody in the senior players' meeting agreed that the best decision for the team and the culture moving forward was for Alex to be deselected. We don't make that final call. I communicated this to Ashley Giles, and the decision was made.'

Morgan had spoken and Hales was out. 'It's not just a message to the players in this team. It's a message to the rest of the players in England, throughout county cricket,' added Bayliss. 'Those sort of decisions [about taking recreational drugs] will not be tolerated. It's got to start somewhere. It's got to start at the top. Hopefully county cricketers learn from it as well, that there's not going to be any future for you if you go down that track.'

Courage, unity, respect. If you are an England player, remember those words when playing cricket, and in life.

Morgan had made his decision and had gathered around him a trusted group of fellow players to endorse his call. The strength of that group had grown over four years, and Morgan himself had reasons to be thankful for their backing. They had saved his job just two and a half years earlier.

On 1 July 2016 England were in Cardiff, training at Sophia Gardens in preparation for the final ODI of an unremarkable series against Sri Lanka. That evening in Dhaka, Bangladesh, terrorists attacked a bakery popular with foreign tourists. It took a raid by Bangladeshi Armed Forces to end a ten-hour stand-off at the Holey Artisan Bakery in the upmarket Gulshan district of the city. By the time they regained control, 29 people were dead.

Events thousands of miles away from the England team in Cardiff would soon plunge Morgan into the greatest crisis of his captaincy. It would be the only time since the last World Cup when his leadership would be called into question and his mettle for the job doubted. He even worried he would be sacked.

England were due to tour Bangladesh in October to play three ODIs and two Tests. As the news of the terrorist attack sank in, security teams from the ECB accompanied by the Professional Cricketers' Association visited Bangladesh demanding guarantees for the safety of the team otherwise the tour would not go ahead.

A sign of the importance of the England tour was the fact that Bangladesh's Prime Minister, Sheikh Hasina, met personally with Reg Dickason, the ECB's head of security. She assured him the players would be given presidential-style security. They would be safe.

The ECB knew this would still not be enough for some players and gave them the option of making a personal choice. Strauss assured them if they decided not to go to Bangladesh, it would not be held against them in future selection meetings. After a long team meeting in London during the final Test of the summer against Pakistan at the Oval in which Strauss and Dickason addressed the team, two players pulled out of the tour.

One was Hales. The other was Morgan, who became the first England captain to skip a tour on security grounds. Strauss was furious. Morgan was the captain, and England expected him to show leadership, but, having told the players their personal choice would be respected, they could do nothing but grumble in private.

'Whilst we understand and respect Eoin and Alex's decision,' said Strauss in a statement, 'we are disappointed they have made themselves unavailable for selection for the tour.' For the understated Strauss, 'disappointed' was a strong word. Strauss believed captains should not expect players to do something they were not willing to take on themselves. They had to lead from the front.

But Morgan had always been stubborn. He is his own man. That was evident early in his career when he left Ireland to pursue his dream of international cricket and then as an established England player opted to play in the IPL rather than bat in county cricket for Middlesex, even though he knew it would harm his chances of being picked for the Test side. He felt the IPL made him a better player and improved his form, not playing on dicey early-season county pitches. Once he had made his mind up not to go to Bangladesh, that was it. Morgan would not be leading his side. Instead Jos Buttler would be captain, Ben Stokes his deputy.

Nasser Hussain, writing in the *Daily Mail*, said Morgan 'should be with his team in Bangladesh'. Michael Vaughan, in his *Daily Telegraph* column, said: 'You sign up [as England captain] knowing that, at times, you will have to do things you do not want to do. One main trait of a strong leader is they never ask a team-mate to do something they would not do themselves. This is why Morgan has made a huge mistake. The players will support him in the press, but there will be a little thought at the back of their minds that he went missing at a difficult time for the side.'

But times had changed. Hussain and Vaughan grew up in a tougher era, when a decision such as Morgan's would be seen as weakness in the dressing room; respect would be lost and never regained.

However, Morgan's team-mates lined up to support him. They were behind him 100 per cent, and it was not just for show. There was no resentment. In fact, they respected him for making a brave decision. It would have been easier to go and not cop flak.

It also allowed Buttler, Stokes and Root to grow into their own leadership roles within the team. Bangladesh would be a tough tour due to the stifling security, but also because their hosts were a spiky, talented side that rarely lost white-ball series at home. The turning pitches, heat and vociferous home support made Bangladesh a testing place for non-Asian teams to tour, especially without an inspirational captain to lead them through the tricky moments.

England knew the moment they left the Hazrat Shahjalal International Airport in Dhaka on 30 September 2016 that this tour was going to be different. The short drive to the newly built Radisson hotel in Dhaka was conducted on deserted streets, which anyone who has experienced the city's choking traffic jams will know must have been incredibly hard for the authorities to organise. Roads had been closed for the VIPs. The team bus was flanked by members of the Bangladesh government's khaki-clad Rapid Action Brigade, a specialist anti-terrorism unit, toting automatic weapons, and wearing sunglasses and flak jackets while sitting on the back of armoured vehicles.

Dickason had chosen the Radisson hotel not for its pool or tennis courts but because it was set back from the main road, making it far harder for attackers to ram with a lorry packed with explosives. The media were also housed with the team. All were told by Dickason not to leave the hotel without an armed guard. Roads would be closed whenever the team convoy had to travel to the stadium, a journey of around five miles but which in the Dhaka traffic could take two hours.

When journalists went jogging on the streets around the hotel unaccompanied by guards, they were told off by Dickason. When one again ignored the instruction and then fell down an open sewer on his daily jog, it gave everyone a laugh but did not please Dickason. There was no more running outside after that.

Harrison, the ECB chief executive, and Strauss accompanied the team to Dhaka. They had to show support. 'We're really happy to be here,' said Strauss at a hastily convened press conference in the basement of the hotel. 'It's been a long journey both physically and metaphorically.

'Quite rightly the players had concerns over security, and Reg Dickason has done a tremendous job allaying those fears. We feel very comfortable and satisfied with the security we've been given. It was great to see the guys in such a positive frame of mind when they met up at the airport. Once you've made that decision it becomes a lot easier mentally, and the guys are now thinking about some tough cricket they've got ahead of them.'

Even when only a handful of players decided to net at the stadium in Dhaka, they were given full protection, and the locals trying to make their way to work had to wait hours as diversions were put in place so the roads could be closed for the team. Only once was the security convoy breached. On the way to a warm-up match in Fatullah, the garment dyeing district of Dhaka, an auto rickshaw containing three elderly ladies briefly pulled out in front of the team bus before the Rapid Action Brigade shoved them off the road.

Strauss was right. The cricket would be tough and harder without Morgan in the middle order and staying calm under pressure.

Buttler had barely captained a side before. This was the biggest test of his career, but by his side was Stokes. His maiden ODI century in the first game and five wickets for Jake Ball eased England to a 21-run win after some early jitters. It took a rallying call from Stokes to calm the team when Bangladesh looked likely to reach their target and Buttler dropped a crucial catch. 'As much as you can, you try and stay calm,' said Buttler. 'Ben Stokes really brought us back and said: "Let's not give it to them easy." I think that belief and hunger to win really came through.'

Morgan's side were growing stronger in his absence. When Bangladesh levelled the series two days later, it was a different Buttler speaking after the game. This time he was incensed by Bangladesh's tactics in a feisty match played on a hot, humid evening in front of 25,000 partisan fans. There was sledging, send-offs when batsmen were out and a nasty incident at the end of the match when Jason Roy and Tamim Iqbal exchanged angry words.

Buttler was goaded by fielders when he was dismissed. 'I was just a little bit disappointed in the fashion they celebrated,' Buttler said. 'Rightly they are happy to get a wicket, but there is no need to run in someone's face and celebrate. I'm disappointed to get out, the emotions were high but that happens.'

Buttler is quietly spoken and modest. This was the first time he had lost his cool on the field for England. 'Maybe you don't know me as well as you think you do,' he replied when asked if it was out of character.

England took the series in Chittagong a week later, winning the third ODI by four wickets, thanks to a solid opening partnership from Sam Billings and James Vince, a cobbled-together first-wicket pairing caused by injury to Roy and Hales's absence, and 63 from Ben Duckett. England chased down 278 on a tricky, turning pitch.

Stokes and Buttler had formed the leadership core. One incident stood out. In Dhaka, Stokes berated Adil Rashid for some poor fielding after he fumbled a routine pick-up and throw at fine leg. An angry Stokes made his feelings plain. Minutes later he had his arm around Rashid, praising him for a diving stop. Rashid was one of the weakest fielders in the team, but he worked hard on that aspect of his game and held his own in the World Cup nearly three years later. Stokes can be the enforcer, but he has a softer side too.

Buttler had grown as well. Morgan now had a deputy with experience of captaincy in the hardest of circumstances. 'It is hugely satisfying,' Buttler said. 'It should not be under-estimated what we have achieved here. Physically it's been a tough tour for us, and mentally as well, with everything that's gone on before, and then to come here – a pretty young and inexperienced team – to win in Bangladesh, who have had success in their recent series, I thought we played really well, but with room for improvement as well. It's great to learn when you're winning, and good teams win games when they are not at their best. Moving forward, this tour will stand us in great stead.'

Throughout the tour the players stood by Morgan and said he would be back as captain. Morgan had no regrets. 'We're a tightly knit group who back each other's decisions no matter what, and in particular in this case where every decision for the individual was right for him,' he said as he prepared to take over the captaincy again for the tour to India the following January. 'I think creating the platform for everybody to feel comfortable, and not begrudging anybody for going or not going, shows the strength within the side.'

In private Morgan feared he would be sacked. He could not judge the reaction of the ECB if he soon lost form and results took a nosedive. He thought Buttler would cope in his absence, but if the tour to Bangladesh had gone badly and the players turned against him in his absence, it would have eroded his authority. Would the ECB still take their chance to punish Morgan for letting them down? Not many play-ers trusted the ECB after the sacking of Kevin Pietersen, so Morgan was aware of the risk he had taken. He was deter-mined not to give the board a chance to make him pay, but he was also reassured that if he was ever injured, or absent for any reason, the team had a strong core. They could cope without him. Morgan said his family had been 'offended by some of the criticism' over his decision, but he knew it was part of the job. What came next would be a different challenge, one that questioned the culture of the side and English cricket.

The first thing Ben Stokes did when he saw Andrew Strauss waiting for him at a city-centre police station in Bristol was apologise.

'I just remember going down to the police station. I spent a long time with Clare, his partner, waiting for him to come out of the jail, and what struck me as soon as he came out was actually his character,' said Strauss, speaking nearly two years later and just hours after England's World Cup win. 'Because he stood up and said: "I've got this horribly wrong. I apologise sincerely for what I've done here."

'From that moment on, I thought this was going to be a good thing for him. I also thought this was going to be very noisy and very hard for us to navigate.

'Anyone who knows Ben, who has played with him, knows what an incredible person he is to have on your team. I think what we've seen is some of those rough edges just smoothed a little bit over the last 12 or 18 months, without him losing that incredible desire and hunger to win and that competitive streak.

'It's an easy story to say what happened in the World Cup final is redemption for him, but I just think it was one of English cricket's talents showing what he can do on the greatest stage. It was amazing to see, and not just him doing it, but to see his family there who had been through so much alongside him.'

The bare facts were that Stokes and two other men had been arrested for a fight outside the Mbargo nightclub in Bristol, an everyday occurrence in British cities but a huge story because it involved England's biggest cricketing star. It also exposed holes in the team's security. Why were they out that late during a series? Only bad things can happen at 2am in a city centre after drinking for hours. The first Clare knew of the arrest was when he called her from the police station. She contacted Strauss, who jumped straight into his car to go to Bristol.

When a student in the city sold footage of the incident that he'd filmed on his mobile phone to the *Sun* newspaper, Stokes's reputation was in tatters. He could be seen punching a man, who looked to be backing away, to the ground. Stokes broke his finger in the fight, an injury that would have put him out of the start of the Ashes tour a month later – a gross neglect of professionalism let alone an act that led to his arrest. He was wearing a bandage on his hand as he married Clare a month later. Stokes would not be going to Australia. The fight ended his hopes of a second Ashes tour and crushed England's chances of competing.

Branded a thug, Stokes had to wait until January 2018 while the wheels of British justice and the overloaded court system creaked into life and he was eventually charged with affray. When the charge was announced publicly, Stokes was immediately called up for the one-day series and Tests in New Zealand. The first thing he did in New Zealand was apologise to his team-mates during a dressing-room meeting. They forgave him immediately, such is the popularity and respect he commands. ECB figures had taken a hard stance towards Stokes and one wanted him banned for a long time. But all disciplinary action was postponed until after his court case.

Stokes stood trial at Bristol Crown Court in August 2018, 11 months after his arrest. The court case lasted eight days, during which the prosecution accused him of 'a sustained episode of significant violence' and alleged he had 'lost control'.

Stokes told the jury he had acted partly in self-defence and had 'stepped in' to protect two gay men who were being verbally abused by his co-accused, Ryan Ali and Ryan Hale. Ali was seen on the video wielding a beer bottle, while Stokes was defending himself and team-mate Hales, who could also be seen getting involved in the scuffle, at one stage aiming a kick at a man lying on the ground.

During the trial a prosecution witness claimed Stokes had himself mocked the two gay men outside the Mbargo nightclub, at one point flicking a cigarette at them. Just weeks earlier the ECB had become the first governing body of a major sport to take a float in the annual Pride march through London. Allegations of homophobia against one of its leading players were disastrous for the governing body. But Stokes maintained his innocence. He denied the allegation he was goading the two gay men. They would support his version of events, thanking him in public after the trial for protecting them from a beating.

The jury believed Stokes. All three men were acquitted. Stokes was cleared of affray. Ali, who was knocked unconscious during the brawl, was also found not guilty of the same charge. Hale had earlier been released from the dock halfway through the trial by the judge for lack of evidence.

Clare, by now his wife, cried in the public gallery when the verdict was read out by the foreman of the jury. Neil Fairbrother, his agent, was also in tears. The stress of the whole affair had taken its toll on those close to Stokes. But he issued no apology in a statement read out by his lawyer on the steps of the court. He still had an ECB hearing to answer to later in the year.

When the ECB's Cricket Discipline Committee finally met in December, Stokes was banned for four matches, with another four suspended, but he was cleared to play cricket because it was decided he had already served his suspension by missing the Ashes tour.

It was only then that a grovelling apology was made public. Stokes had already said sorry to his team-mates. He did that in New Zealand on his first day back with the side after missing the Ashes tour. But this time he made a vow to all England fans, and by association his team-mates, to make amends. 'I regret the incident ever happened, and I apologise to England supporters and to the public for bringing the game in to disrepute,' he said. 'Cricket and family are my life. This incident has been a huge burden for the last 15 months. I am relieved to get back to playing the game that I love without this hanging over me. Although the disciplinary process is now over, I have learned lessons that will stay with me for much longer.'

Stokes would repay his debt in the World Cup final, playing the hero for his team and rehabilitating himself in the grandest style. After his court experience, no other player embraced the team's values more than Stokes. He had learned his lesson. Courage, unity and respect were stitched into his character.

FOUR
PUSHING THE
BOUNDARIES

Press conferences at the Oval are held in the Ken Barrington Indoor School. It can sometimes be hard to hear what is being said, particularly when players in the gym on the mezzanine floor overlooking the net lanes start playing loud, thumping music while they lift weights.

It was in the Barrington Centre that Eoin Morgan was asked about his team's chances of winning the World Cup on the eve of their opening game against South Africa. The gym had been cleared. This was an important moment, and the ICC did not want booming beats wrecking their press conference. Morgan had to be heard. His team were favourites after four years of buccaneering cricket that Barrington, that old master blocker, would barely have recognised as the same sport he'd played for England. 'It [winning the World Cup] would mean a huge amount,' said Morgan. 'The World Cup alone raises the profile of the game and [provides] a platform for every young kid in this country to have a hero or inspiration to pick up a ball or a bat. To go on and win it, I couldn't imagine what it would do.'

The last time Morgan had appeared at a press conference during a World Cup was in Sydney four years previously as his team exited the tournament in tatters. Nobody that day asked what winning a World Cup could do for English cricket. They would have been laughed out of the SCG for such a preposterous question. But nobody was laughing at England any more. Morgan's team were ranked the best in the world for a reason. He sat in the Barrington Centre in charge of a team that was respected rather than ridiculed.

For four years Morgan and Trevor Bayliss had performed major surgery on England's white-ball cricket. After being teamed together in the summer of 2015 by Andrew Strauss, the pair immediately struck up an understanding. An Irishman from Dublin, and a country boy from Penrith, New South Wales, spoke the same cricketing language. England moved on quickly from the Peter Moores era. The 2015 World Cup had to fade in the rear-view mirror fast or they would not be contenders at their own tournament four years later.

The players bought into the methods. The management and players spent 18 months working on a tactical document that would be the blueprint for their World Cup win. The document covers two sides of A4 and was written by the players. The management wanted them to feel in control of how the team played. This was not going to be a dictatorship, but it was clear Morgan and Bayliss would only select players who bought into their methods.

The secret tactical document remains under lock and key at the ECB office, but it is understood to be a simple digest of the methods that brought them so much success. The openers going hard at the new ball, the middle order scoring at a run a ball against spin and closing out an innings with boundaries.

For the bowlers it was about dismissing batsmen and not saving runs. David Willey with the new ball would not worry about being driven for four. His job was to take wickets. Mark Wood and Liam Plunkett attacked with pace. The old-fashioned method of trying to go at lower than four an over was thrown out the window. England picked two spinners to bowl in the middle overs with one to contain (Moeen Ali), the other to attack (Adil Rashid). Rashid was told that if he bowled ten overs and took four for 80 England would not be worried about the 80. It meant his four wickets in the middle overs left the opposition with only two or three in hand for the end.

Fielding would be done with real intent, players encouraged to pick up and throw in one motion rather than take time to steady themselves. The players were told if they attacked the ball one-handed and missed it, it was no problem as long as they had worked on it in practice sessions. Gone were the days of safe fielding, being balanced and throwing in. Throw at the stumps. Take risks.

The management team of Morgan, Bayliss and Farbrace presented the written gameplan to the squad during a series against Pakistan in the UAE in October 2016. 'The players started telling us what they wanted in the gameplan. When we presented the document, they felt they had delivered it,' said Farbrace.

One of Bayliss's first acts was to ban whole team meetings. Statistics would be made available, but they would be tailored specifically for individuals to use in actual situations they would encounter. And they were now to be interpreted in a different way. Instead of limiting players' ambitions, statistics would be used to liberate them – 'here is a target, go and beat it'. Selection would be more considered and consistent.

Nathan Leamon, the England team's performance analyst, was commissioned by Strauss to write a one-day strategy. He studied previous World Cup winners, runners-up and semi-finalists and uncovered patterns. He discovered batting strike rates were more important than bowling. Also, for the two years going into a World Cup the quarter-finalists and semi-finalists came in the top two or three in batting strike rates, team strike rates, had the best win-loss percentages against major nations, and the highest total number of team caps and average caps per player. The only exception to successful World Cup teams not being in the top three in those categories had a pattern too. They were always the host nation. Playing a home World Cup gives teams a huge advantage.

'It was really clear that no team wins a World Cup that is not ranked in the top three in the world going into the tournament,' said Strauss. 'The only exception was India in 2011. They were ranked fourth, but they were the hosts.'

Leamon, a Cambridge maths graduate, was appointed the ECB's first analyst in 2009. His data was credited with helping the team win the World Twenty20 in 2010 and reach no. 1 in the Test rankings a year later. But there was an inevitable kickback when the Test team fell apart and the 2015 World Cup was a disaster. Data had become a dirty word – just ask Moores – but Strauss knew that it was a case of interpreting the numbers in a way that supported your natural instincts.

'In the New Zealand series [straight after the 2015 World Cup] we just whacked it,' Leamon said. 'Then the research started to back up the way they were playing and got us to double down on the shape of our cricket that we had in our heads.'

The average of 70 to 80 caps per player was important, and the insight informed selection. England recognised they only had 88 games between World Cups, so they had to identify players and stick with them.

'The batsmen realised that if you got picked for the first game of a series you were pretty much going to play the whole series,' said Paul Farbrace. 'Jason Roy was a great example during the Champions Trophy [in 2017]. He was battling [for form], but it was important to send a message to the rest of the players that if you play in the right way you stay in the team. That has been really important. It breeds confidence.'

Roy was eventually dropped, but only by the time the tournament had reached the semi-final stage. The 85-cap mantra was also conveniently ignored when the ECB changed its registration rules and suddenly made Jofra Archer available for selection. And the two spinners tactic was dropped during the World Cup due to the pitches. Plans also have to be flexible.

Bayliss had coached Sri Lanka to the World Cup final in 2011, and Farbrace took the same team to the World Twenty20 final in 2014. Both sides were run by a senior core of players. England had to surround Morgan with cricketers he could trust and that meant giving them games.

'We needed to completely reset our relationship with white-ball cricket,' said Strauss. 'These opportunities come along very infrequently. Once you have got an established team it is quite difficult to make wholesale changes. You almost become committed to a bunch of players after a year or two of developing a side. But we had this opportunity at the end of the World Cup that if we wanted to play this way, we could make it happen.

'We wanted a top seven that were all match-winners and not too many of those kind of playmaker guys who set the game up. We wanted a spinner who turned it both ways. We wanted those sort of players who scare the opposition.'

Leamon is very good at judging his audience. He knows Bayliss does not like to be overburdened with numbers. He wants life to be kept simple, and when another eager analyst within the England set-up once overdid his brief and gave Bayliss statistics on opponents he had not asked for, the coach lost his temper – a rare sight.

Leamon tailors his packages for each player. His analysis breaks down pitches into 20 blocks of 100 centimetres by 15 centimetres, called the grid, to provide the ideal area for a bowler to aim for. A comprehensive dossier is given to Morgan before every match that includes an opposition batsman's record against right-arm seam, left-arm seam, off spin, leg spin and left-arm spin with an average performance against each type. If a player's average, for example, against leg spin is higher than his career average, then he is given a plus score (for example, plus 5). His score will be minus if his average against the type of bowling is worse than his overall career record and nought if it is the same. A brief 30-word summary of strengths and weaknesses is included in the dossier, plus a batsman's strong and weak areas of scoring. A shorter brief is sent to the players for them to study on iPads. Not all read it.

Another thing Leamon identified as being important was a small but crucial change in the playing regulations. At the 2015 World Cup only four fielders were allowed outside the fielding circle in the final ten overs. A second batting powerplay was usually taken between overs 35 to 40, resulting in a boundary blitz at the end of an innings. That changed in July 2015 as the International Cricket Council looked to give bowlers more protection. An extra fielder would be allowed outside the circle in the final ten overs, and the second batting powerplay was axed. It shifted the emphasis from the end of the innings to the start. Leamon called it 'taking down the new ball'. He also used a cycling analogy by comparing 50-over batting to a time trial. Riders gradually increase effort over the whole course, rather than riding slowly for three-fifths and then thrashing it at the end. So, Jason Roy and Jonny Bairstow had to attack the new ball, and going into the World Cup England had a higher strike rate in the first ten overs than any other team (6.24 an over).

The next target is the middle overs, where England look to continue the tempo. It is when spin is typically used to limit scoring. Leamon revealed England aimed to bat at a run a ball. Traditionally England batsmen struggle against spin, but Morgan, Root and Buttler are all good players of the turning ball. Root can find the gaps and run hard, while the others simply take the aggressive approach, either with innovative shots in the case of Buttler and Morgan, or more orthodox like Roy and Bairstow.

Against spin during overs 11 to 40 from the Champions Trophy in 2017 to the start of the World Cup, England scored at 5.4 per over, pretty close to a run a ball, and better than any other side, including those from Asia. In the four years from 2011 to the 2015 World Cup, England averaged 4.70 per over against spin between overs 11 to 40. Over the corresponding period between 2015 and 2019 this figure had risen to 5.88 – the difference between being World Cup no-hopers and favourites.

Records were smashed. The highest individual ODI score by an Englishman was reset twice, first by Alex Hales when he scored 171 against Pakistan at Trent Bridge in 2016 and then by Roy scoring 180 in that cathedral of Australian cricket, the MCG, in January 2018. England went into the

World Cup having scored more than 300 on 38 occasions. Their run rate was 6.24 an over, way ahead of South Africa in second place at 5.43. They set a world-record innings score of 481 against Australia in Nottingham (at a whopping 9.62 an over) a year before the World Cup and made three other totals in excess of 400 (as well as one of 399) between the two tournaments.

But how did they find the personnel? Partly, you have to go back to Mumbai, November 2012, long before their World Cup humiliation in 2015. While England were playing a Test series in India that they would eventually win, with Kevin Pietersen and Alastair Cook, two giants of English batting, leading their team to a famous victory, the Lions were also on tour.

While England stayed at the Taj Mahal Hotel in Mumbai, preparing for a pivotal second Test at the Wankhede Stadium, the Lions team were practising on the other side of the city at the DY Patil Stadium in Navi Mumbai.

Graham Thorpe, the one-day team batting coach for the past four years, was in charge and working with a young Buttler and Stokes. 'I was trying to get them to understand technique, but at one point they wanted to have some fun and started using a thin bat,' said Thorpe. 'I just watched as they hit it in all directions. That is when you have a choice as a coach. Do you discourage it and say "No, no, no, don't do that"? Or do you stand back, watch and realise there is a lot of talent required to do that so let them have some fun? That is the balance in coaching. There is a time when a good technique is required and a time to let players develop naturally and let them go and enjoy it.'

England also knew they had to bat deep. By picking bowlers who could hit the ball hard, they were able to attack at the end of an innings and had a higher boundary percentage in the final ten overs (15.23) than any other side over the two years before the World Cup.

'We have that strength in depth,' said Leamon. 'We have a tail that can clear the ropes. A lot of teams have a ceiling, get three down at an early stage and they struggle, but England can keep going, which is sometimes why we were bowled out. You can be conservative and plod to 240, but you will still lose. When we were two years out from a World Cup, why not keep attacking to train the brain to react with aggression when backed into a corner? If your ultimate goal is a tournament two years away, make sure it is second nature to play that way rather than be conservative and still lose.'

Liam Plunkett is one of the cleanest hitters of a ball and once smacked the final delivery of an ODI against Sri Lanka for six at Trent Bridge to tie a game (how England must have wished he could have done more than his one stunning four in the 2019 final), Adil Rashid's wristiness and unorthodox scoring areas were backed up by 11 first-class hundreds, while David Willey had opened in white-ball county cricket.

'With a high-tempo and high-risk game you have to give them the freedom to overdo it at times,' said Strauss. 'There have been occasions where we have had justified criticism for going over the top. If you are not willing to go over the top, then you will be self-limiting, play the percentages and try to get a score on the board. That is almost exactly what the opposition wants you to do. The group had to be very strong and say you can play that way, and if it goes wrong, keep doing it, and we will get better at it over time.'

Just days before the World Cup started, one veteran of previous failed campaigns had a simple message about England's strength with the bat. 'There is not a former player I can think of who would get in this one-day batting line-up,' said Stuart Broad.

Coaching such big hitters is a dangerous game. Bayliss soon took to wearing a helmet when giving throw-downs to Buttler and Stokes (before it became mandatory under ECB concussion policy), and Thorpe had metal stanchions removed from net areas fearing dangerous ricochets.

Coaches give throw-downs from behind a net shaped like a capital A, and it is rare to see a bowling machine these days. The coaching prop of choice is a long, pliable stick with a cup on the end that dog walkers often use to throw balls. Graham Gooch was the first to use it when he was England batting coach, and now it is ubiquitous in cricket at all levels. Bayliss has become a master at using one, but the quickest arm of all belongs to Mark Ramprakash, who spent four years as a batting coach within the England set-up. He could replicate inswing and outswing. Like golf-club shafts, sticks can have different levels of stiffness, which can change the pace of the delivery.

Some players have that Geoffrey Boycott love of an intense net session, others are more laid back. Some hit 20 balls and think that is enough. Joe Root wants to hit ten balls in a row perfectly. If he mishits the eighth ball, he'll start again. Jos Buttler wants to make sure he hits the last ball perfectly. If he does that, he walks out of the net. At times the coaches have had to stop some players from over-training.

'Understanding when they have had enough is vital,' said Thorpe. 'I tell them you only have a certain amount of hits in your body. Make sure that excitement and mental energy is there for match days.'

Power is one thing, but players need options. They have to adapt. England went into the World Cup thinking bat would dominate ball. The ECB even recalled scorecards to be sold at grounds and had them reprinted so supporters could score up to 500 (previously they stopped at 400). How wrong they would be.

'Hand speed is one thing, but players need the ability to be able to keep their options open,' Thorpe said. 'Some younger players might think "I'm going to smash it over row Z", and that is the only thing in their mind. But what happens if the ball is not in that position? Can the positioning of your body still allow you to hit the ball in three or four different areas? That is what a lot of these guys can do.

'They position their bodies so they have three options to every ball. They might be thinking about hitting it straight back over the sightscreen, but if it is a slower-ball bouncer, they still maintain a strong position, not over-committed to the shot, so they can pull it with power over mid-wicket. Or they might get a wide yorker so they have to break [twist] their wrists and slice it back over point. There are lots of scenarios to each ball they will have in their head. Ultimately playing games and doing it when the pressure is on is the gauge for them.'

England would mess up run chases and misread pitches, most notably in the Champions Trophy semi-final against Pakistan when they set a target of only 211 on a used surface and lost by eight wickets. They also came unstuck on a greentop against South Africa at Lord's and slumped to 20 for six in May 2017. A sour Morgan blamed the pitch, saying it was not good enough for one-day cricket. 'I don't think it was a one-day international wicket, to be honest,' he said.

In Adelaide in January 2018 they were eight for five (yes, eight for five) in swinging conditions before rallying to 196 and only losing by three wickets. Questions would dog the team throughout the four-year cycle between World Cups about whether they could be more than just big hitters on true pitches.

Strauss's job, in his role as team director, was to shape the ECB's strategy in the boardroom to redress the balance between white- and red-ball cricket. On his watch, one-day cricket would no longer be the poor cousin of Test cricket. More white-ball 'incremental' contracts would be offered to give England control of their players, and they were worth more money, rising to £175,000 or matching the player's county salary if that was higher.

Attitudes to the IPL would also change. Suspicion would be replaced by an acceptance that playing in India would not only make an England cricketer wealthier, but the players could act as sponges as well, absorbing information in a melting pot of ideas, with the best players in the world concentrated in one tournament. Without ever saying it publicly, the ECB accepted Pietersen had been right all along. The IPL should be embraced, not rejected.

'The great thing about going to those tournaments is that you go as an overseas player, so you're under pressure to perform and win games of cricket,' Strauss said. 'That's exactly what we want our players to do. Thirty-eight of the 44 players involved in the semi-finals of the World Cup [in 2015] had IPL experience. We should seek further opportunities to get our guys in there.'

The emphasis on Lions tours would shift from first-class cricket to 50 overs. Strauss introduced the North v. South concept, a series of 50-over games played in the UAE and West Indies. Players qualified for selection through the Professional Cricketers' Association's most valued player rankings, another nod to statistics-based analysis, rather than old-fashioned selection. The top four England-qualified players from each region in the Royal London One

Day Cup ranking plus the leading spinner qualified.

Morgan would be given absolute power to shape strategy, with Bayliss and his deputy Farbrace in charge of creating an environment in which players could flourish in the knowledge they would not be punished for holing out playing an attacking shot.

Gone were the days when England would try to make one-day players out of Test cricketers. 'The starting point was we have to play in a different style,' Strauss said. 'We had to have a more aggressive and more attacking mindset. We had to be less fearful of failure and [implement] a system that judges players not on how many runs they have scored but on are they playing the right sort of game to help us scare the big teams in the rest of the world?

'To see that through, we had to have a captain who bought into that and played that way naturally himself. We had to have a coach who was very experienced in white-ball cricket and understood what it took to win big events, whether they were T20 competitions or global events. That was my motivation, and from Eoin's point of view he fitted very well into that as a captain who is clear in terms of how he wants to play the game, and a guy who could be a role model for that way of playing.

'The batting department is an embarrassment of riches, and that healthy competition for places is something we have never had in English white-ball cricket before. Usually if you were averaging 30-odd at a strike rate of 75, you were part of the furniture, and these days you would be hard pressed to be picked if that is your performance level, so the shift upwards has been significant.

'The other point to make is that once those guys were given the opportunity to play, it was made clear to them it would be about exploring where the boundaries are, metaphorically and physically. Let's see where we can go. Maybe we can take 20-over cricket into 50-over cricket, and on the back of that we have seen some outrageous scores of 400-plus.'

Success came early. England stunned themselves by reaching the final of the World Twenty20 in India in April 2016, losing to West Indies in one of the great last-over assaults by Carlos Brathwaite. England were broken by the defeat.

Morgan looked at his players in the dressing room at Eden Gardens and delivered a short, simple message that would resonate further down the line at Lord's when another World Cup was on the line. According to one eyewitness, he just said: 'Never think you have won a game. Use moments like this to drive yourself forward to make yourself hungrier.'

A good barometer of a one-day team is its fielding, and England had to improve, be fitter and more athletic if they were going to compete in a World Cup. In Stokes, Buttler and Bairstow they had three natural athletes. Buttler and Stokes drive each other forward. They can be seen on tour running laps of the outfield after net sessions or matches.

In the West Indies, in the lead-up to the World Cup, the strength and conditioning coaches set the players a target of running two kilometres on a treadmill in under seven and a half minutes, because short sprints are so important in one-day cricket. Marathon runners know that short intervals are just as good as long runs at building stamina, and England would need lots of that in a World Cup. Stokes and Buttler led the treadmills charts on six minutes 36 seconds.

Jonny Bairstow once reckoned he did 17,000 squats in one season as a keeper playing Test cricket alone, let alone one-day and county matches, on top of walking or running 16 kilometres a day in the field.

Fitness sessions for the one-day side also targeted running between the wickets, specifically the quick two. Bairstow was the fastest in the World Cup squad, timed at running a two in 5.83 seconds.

The ECB's psychological testing, completed in 2017 in association with Bangor University, started first with county sides and was then rolled out to include the England team in 2018. The tests measure 26 personality and psychological skills, using questionnaires and an online decision-making task combined with heart-rate monitoring to work out how players cope with stress and behavioural reports to show how they respond to pressure in match situations. David Young, the ECB's head of performance psychology, told the *Daily Telegraph* the testing showed some players were more susceptible to threats, others to rewards. Those who feared threats did not like being hit for boundaries or getting out. Those attuned to rewards concentrated on runs and wickets.

As for fielding, it is a blend of strength and accuracy. As a boundary rider, Bairstow's throw is among the fastest in the world, clocked at 81mph. England use several different weighted balls in practice to help him achieve this.

'The general rule we are told is that if you have a throw of 80mph across 60 yards, and the ball goes straight over the top of the stumps, then you will run out a batsman taking on your arm,' Bairstow wrote in his *Daily Telegraph* column during the World Cup. 'As a batter, as soon as you see the ball up in the air being returned by the fielder you are second guessing whether you can make it or not. If that throw is on the money, you are going to be run out.

'One of the things we talk about in the field is being aggressive, whether that be in the ring at backward point or on the boundary. It is about getting the ball in your hands and out of your hands as quickly as possible without pausing. It takes time to perfect it. If you look at footage of Adil Rashid fielding three years ago and compare it with now, there would be a stark contrast. Now he sprints at the ball, picks it up and releases it in one movement. That is down to hard work.'

It was at Trent Bridge during a one-day international against Pakistan on 30 August 2016 that Buttler decided England's fielding had to improve. As wicketkeeper, as well as vice-captain, he felt it was his job to speak up and say the team's fielding was too conservative.

Coaches would hit balls along the ground to boundary fielders, where they would take a moment to steady themselves so they would be balanced before throwing the ball back to the keeper or bowler. Buttler took charge of the session from the coaches and said the players had to match their intent with the bat and ball in the field too. Instead of taking that extra second to be balanced, players should pick up and throw in one motion.

'Jos's attitude was don't be safe throwing the ball. The batters take risks, the bowlers look for wickets, so match that same intent with the fielding,' said Farbrace. 'That was a good sign. The players were starting to take charge and not wait to be led.'

During the World Cup, Leamon spotted that a fielding tweak was needed. With Wood and Archer bowling at 90mph, Leamon noticed that fine leg and third man were being beaten on the inside by the pace off the bat, so they were moved finer. This had been a favourite refrain of former England coach Duncan Fletcher, who had often been heard shouting to his fine leg and third man fielders: 'Never get beaten on the inside!'

England's bowling reflected English conservatism: right arm over, fast medium and finger spin, be it off spin or left arm, were about as adventurous as it got. How they missed in Australia and New Zealand in 2015 the variety of left-arm pace provided by Trent Boult and Mitchell Starc. Strauss and Morgan decided they needed left-arm pace and a wrist spinner who could beat both edges of the bat, and that their attack would include two slow bowlers.

Morgan knew it too. James Anderson and Stuart Broad were fine servants of English cricket, but Morgan knew they would not be able to cope with playing all formats as they entered the final years of their careers. Instead England invested in new blood and went back to an old face, Adil Rashid, someone with talent but who had lacked the trust of England captains.

David Willey was identified as England's left-arm option, a bowler who could swing the white ball in the early overs and take wickets. His pace was never comparable to those at the top of the international game, and it was quite a turnaround for a cricketer who had played at county level primarily as a batsman who could bowl some useful overs. Suddenly he was opening the bowling for England.

Other candidates were thin on the ground. Reece Topley struggled with injuries, and Harry Gurney had been picked for ten games and dumped before the 2015 World Cup. It would have to be Willey. He played 46 one-day internationals from 2015 until the start of the World Cup, taking 52 wickets at 36, and was trusted by Morgan in some tight situations. It was to his enormous credit that he took the news of being left out of the World Cup squad so graciously, having been moulded for the new-ball job for four years. However, once Jofra Archer's pace became available, and Mark Wood settled on a longer run-up that kept him injury-free for longer, it was inevitable that he would be squeezed out.

But while pace would be king at the World Cup, spin was England's main weapon for the four years leading into it. Rashid played six ODIs in 2009, was belted around in his final game by South Africa at nine an over and was not picked again until 2015 when Morgan began his reinvention of the team. The spinner repaid his captain in bucketloads.

Between the World Cups, Rashid took 129 wickets at 29.68, more than any other international bowler. Over the same period, he played 19 Tests and struggled, lacking self-belief. But when wearing the blue one-day shirt, and with more boundary protection in white-ball cricket, he was transformed. Morgan played a huge part in that.

'As a spinner you need backing, and the biggest thing is if you do get hit for a couple of fours, the captain does not take his cap off, throw it down on the floor and kick it,' Rashid's fellow spinner and great friend Moeen Ali said. 'You need the captain to say "come back the next over", and Morgy does that. There are also times when you are bowling well, but it feels like the batter is lining you up, and he takes you off. You never question that. I have had times when I've been bowling well and Morgy has come up to me and said you are not playing this game because we want one spinner, and we are picking Rash. It has been the other way round too, and I have played ahead of Rash, but you know what Morgs is doing is for the best of the team. You as a player accept that. We both agree he is the best captain we have played under.'

Rashid's job was to cut through the middle order, forcing the opposition tailenders to take risks later on, gifting wickets for the death bowlers.

'Rashid was phenomenal. He quietly contributed, while some of the bigger names have taken the plaudits,' said Strauss. 'Some of the success was down to an incredibly strong batting line-up that outperformed everyone else in the world by a long way, but then our ability to keep taking wickets in the middle overs was vital, and a lot of that was down to Adil.

'In the old days, even when we had a bowler as good as

Graeme Swann bowling in the middle overs, we found it very hard to apply pressure, especially when there were two set batsmen. We were not asking them searching questions. Adil asks a lot of questions, and has grown massively in terms of stature and confidence. He has real clarity about the role he is playing in the team.'

By the end of the World Cup, Rashid had played 99 ODIs. The next closest leg spinner on the appearances list for England is Ian Salisbury, who played four ODIs. Rashid was a trailblazer and his success represents the first time England has cast off its suspicion of leg spin.

Most of England's success between World Cups was based on dominant batting. But the series wins that gave Morgan the most pleasure were victories in Australia and New Zealand in the winter of 2017–18. In Perth, Tom Curran took five wickets to win a tense match and seal a series victory. In New Zealand, Chris Woakes was brilliant, giving an indication of the value he would provide in the World Cup. A few months later, England were ranked no. 1 in the world. 'The bowlers put down a marker to say that we are striving to get better and were the strong point of that winter,' said Morgan. 'That made us a more rounded side.'

On the field, England were flying. Off it, they were embracing the latest research. Sports science is a growing area of influence on cricket. Trends come and go. Ice baths are now a thing of the past, for example, much to the relief of fast bowlers. But at Loughborough, the home of the ECB academy, the sports science team started researching what would be called the 'four pillars' of success, aimed at winning the World Cup.

The pillars are talent; technical excellence; performing under pressure; injury prevention and physical performance. Researching talent goes without saying, obviously, for a sport carried by the abilities of its elite players. Technical excellence is an ongoing process too. But handling pressure and staying injury-free are far more relevant during tournament play such as a World Cup. The ability to stay cool in the most stressful of situations was evident in the Super Over, and the final ball run-out of Martin Guptill.

England inevitably had aches and pains during the World Cup. Morgan broke fingers and had a back spasm. Jofra Archer carried a side strain through the last three weeks, needing several injections, and Mark Wood suffered a rib injury in the final. Jos Buttler popped a muscle in his hip against Bangladesh, and Chris Woakes carried a chronic knee injury that needed managing. Jason Roy's hamstring tore against West Indies early in the group stage, but he was back on the park far quicker than expected, riding to England's rescue when their semi-final place was in jeopardy.

To mitigate against injury, England now use movement-sensor technology, basically GPS monitors strapped to a player's back, which details their movement in games and net sessions so workloads can be managed. 'We're not doing one size fits all,' Raphael Brandon, the ECB's head of science and medicine, said. Close fielders cover 9km in a match, boundary riders around 15km, so some of them train less to guard against injury. Woakes, for example, fields on the boundary so covers more ground than a ring fielder like Stokes. Boundary riders do more sprinting in training than the close-in fielders such as Morgan. A century for a batsman such as Root involves 10km of running when fielding is added, although of course it depends on how many singles, twos and threes he scores.

The players need fuel. It used to be a common sight to see them eating bananas during drinks breaks or while fielding on the boundary. They now prefer to use energy gels which can be more easily digested and are commonly used by endurance athletes. Before batting in the Super Over, Stokes had an energy gel, made by One Pro Nutrition owned by Matt Prior, the former England wicketkeeper. He had also been advised to eat more carbohydrates during the World Cup after complaining of cramps. Carbohydrate increases the muscles' glycogen stores, which helps to prevent cramping.

All of this backroom work, according to Brandon, was designed to 'shift the odds' in England's favour.

During the World Cup, Leamon told the *Telegraph*'s Tim Wigmore that once the tournament started he focused on oppositional analysis. He worked out which venues suited England most. His numbers told him playing Australia and New Zealand at Lord's was not a great combination, because the pitch is rarely flat, which does not suit England's batsmen. Australia beat England at Lord's in the group phase to throw their whole campaign into crisis, and the final against New Zealand was played on one of those Lord's pitches England hate.

England would have to be nimble on their feet and also in their minds. Four years of hard work on the field and behind the scenes put them in the best position to win the World Cup. But it would take more than that. England had to be flexible, and willing to rethink some of the tactics that had served them so well.

Morgan likes listening to podcasts. One of his favourites is by Dave Novak, the former chief executive of the Yum! Brands that include KFC and Pizza Hut. Once a week he interviews a guest with experience of business and sport. One episode Morgan listened to in the lead-up to the World Cup was a chat with Jack Nicklaus.

Morgan loves golf and played almost every day during the World Cup until his back spasm. He took on board Nicklaus's advice about leaving nothing to chance. 'Being prepared is the most important thing in life,' Nicklaus told Novak. 'If you are not prepared, you are not going to perform. My consistency came because of my desire to focus on what was important. It is so easy to be properly prepared.'

When Morgan sat in the Barrington Centre the day before the World Cup started, he knew his team had prepared. They were ready, but the next six weeks were going to test every aspect of their skills and character, culminating in the tensest examination any England cricketer has ever experienced.

FIVE
ENTER JOFRA

GAME ONE –
ENGLAND V. SOUTH AFRICA

THE OVAL, LONDON

Thursday, 30 May 2019

'Trust me, you won't want to miss any of it.' It took only half an hour for Prince Harry's speech at the Oval, officially opening the 2019 World Cup, to be proved correct. The words were barely out of the royal mouth before Jonny Bairstow edged behind the second ball of the tournament, setting Imran Tahir haring off on one of his wild wicket celebrations that lasted longer than the prince's speech.

'Ha, ha, ha, look at him go. Imran Tahir – early celebrations in this World Cup,' said a gleeful Graeme Smith commentating for Sky Sports. He may as well have said 'here we go again', because that is how it felt for England fans as another World Cup campaign started limply.

English pessimism could be sniffed on the south London air before the tournament was even an over old. Memories came flooding back of the opening ceremony of the 1999 World Cup when the fireworks failed, and England's campaign spluttered and fizzled out like a damp sparkler.

Bairstow's dismissal proved that no matter how diligently you prepare for something, it can all still go horribly wrong when the serious business begins. However, the fatalism was misplaced. England would not be left standing alone at the altar on their big day. They were the stars of the opening game of the World Cup after showing their class and flexing their muscles to beat South Africa by 104 runs, thanks to a combination of canny batting and express-pace fast bowling.

Ben Stokes seized the moment, with a catch of such stunning proportions that it provoked a flood of copycat videos posted online of people trying to replicate his feat. It was the filling in a Stokes sandwich that included a score of 89, his highest score since his arrest in Bristol, and two wickets to close out the match. Great all-rounders stamp their mark on big tournaments; Stokes was man of the match on the first day.

With the ball, Jofra Archer bowled rockets, taking 3–27 and hitting Hashim Amla a nasty blow on the head that forced one of the world's great batsmen to retire hurt. Archer had been unleashed, and Amla would not be the only opponent counting the bruises over the next six weeks, or even the rest of the summer.

'It will take time for international teams to get used to his action, because he is a bit nippier than you think when he hits the crease. It is why he is an X-factor bowler,' said Faf du Plessis, the South African captain, after the game. He was right. Archer's bouncer would be the ball of the World Cup, a delivery that was hard to read and could be used as a wicket-taking option as well as a method to dry up runs.

A week earlier, du Plessis was among the World Cup captains perched on some battered old sofas in an east London warehouse used to film, among other things, *Dragons Den* for the pre-tournament press conference. It was generally knockabout, light-hearted stuff that only veered into seriousness when a Pakistani journalist asked Virat Kohli why India will not play his country. With the question batted away dismissively ('my personal opinions do not come into it'), Kohli turned to the subjects of Archer and England.

Every opposition captain follows a familiar patter when playing England: hype them up so they can knock themselves down. The word on the street is England rarely handle being tagged as favourites well. Kohli also described Archer as an 'X-factor' bowler, but he wisely suggested some people were getting carried away by predicting a high-scoring tournament. 'They [England] seem to be obsessed with getting to 500 before anyone else,' he said. 'They smash it from ball one and for the full 50 overs. It could be pretty high scoring, but I don't see too much high scoring in the latter half of the tournament. Some teams might get on a roll, but you'll see 250 defended as well because of the kind of pressure that comes with it. Generally, teams will find a way, but I see pressure playing a massive role.'

Pressure. The P-word. Kohli lives his life in a bubble few can understand and carries the heaviest weight of expectation of any cricketer. But he has World Cup-winning pedigree so speaks with authority on the subject. He was right, the pressure of a World Cup is different from anything else players experience elsewhere in their careers, and England were about to find that out.

Behind the scenes, in the hours leading up to their first game, England were tetchy. The pressure was starting to take hold. They were ruffled by the pitch, which was a far cry from the Oval batting belters they were used to playing on. They immediately sensed an ICC stitch-up and thought grounds-men were working under instruction to produce pitches that would suit India. It was a suspicion that never left them throughout the World Cup. The pitches would be dry and slow, but England had to adapt and not look for others to blame. They adjusted in the opening match, putting away the big shots to grind out a winning score of 311.

England had romped to the top of the rankings and were fresh from beating Pakistan 4–0 in a five-match series. Defeat in a warm-up match to Australia at the Rose Bowl was noth-ing to worry about, despite a Steve Smith hundred, because of the decision to rest key players, and England bounced back by thumping Afghanistan by nine wickets in their last practice game two days later at the Oval.

The series against Pakistan sorted out the final selection issue. Archer bowled his way into the squad within just four overs of the opening game, providing the only highlight in a match washed out by rain. He had Pakistan batsmen hopping around as he reached 90.46mph in his first over. Morgan posted three slips and even a short leg, a Test match field, as Archer's pace gave the England captain a potent new force to exploit. The only previous time Morgan had posi-tioned a short leg was to leg spinner Adil Rashid.

Bowling tight lines to both left- and right-handers, Archer only conceded six runs, four of those from his last ball. Not many Pakistani batsmen were happy to get on the front foot, and his wicket of Fakhar Zaman was an edge off the splice of the bat that reared up off the pitch. Archer would play in the World Cup. England simply had to pick him. There was no other choice. Dropping David Willey was a hard call for the selectors, but they knew in Archer they had a potential World

Cup-winning bowler on their hands, and one with the added advantage of being at the start of his career, so not many batsmen had faced him before.

It all appeared to be so natural for Archer. The lithe, athletic run-up brought back memories of Michael Holding running in at the Oval in 1976. Archer has the same deceptive approach to the crease and generates pace from a snap of the wrists. Batsmen say the hardest fast bowlers to face are those who are tricky to read as they run up. Archer's bouncer is difficult to pick, because his length is hard to define from the hand. It rears up at throat or nose and batsmen have little time to adjust. They have a fraction of a second to decide whether to defend, get out of the way or play a hook shot, which is hard to control when the ball is coming down at 90mph. It is no wonder Archer rated his bouncer so highly as a wicket-taking ball, a potential dot ball, and to intimidate.

'He is the fastest I have ever faced,' said an awed Moeen Ali after batting against him in the nets. The bouncer made the pitched-up yorker more lethal too, because batsmen were hanging back waiting for the short ball. Pace had been the missing piece in England's ODI side. It had now arrived.

Archer's reputation had been forged in Twenty20 leagues in India and Australia. Shane Warne worked with him at the Rajasthan Royals. 'His yorker is brilliant,' he said. 'He has that angle and bowls at 90mph-plus and you can't hit it. Everyone has tried in the last two years in the IPL, but when he gets it right, they have no chance. England have never won the World Cup, so he could be the icing that gives England their best chance of doing it.'

There were gripes when the ECB rewrote their rules, changing the residency qualification from seven years to three to conveniently make Archer available for the World Cup, as much to his surprise as anyone else's. And David Willey,

Mark Wood and Chris Woakes all claimed to have been mis-represented when they were each quoted before World Cup selection saying that picking him could upset the team's bal-ance, but they were victims of some spicy online headlines (rather than being misquoted). They were just team-mates sticking up for each other, not wanting anyone to miss out, although there were legitimate concerns from some pundits that introducing a new face so close to the World Cup could upset a carefully pieced-together team dynamic.

In the Caribbean in March Willey had asked 'whether someone should just walk in at the drop of a hat because they're available. Whether that's the right thing, I don't know.' Woakes, hardly one to court controversy, claimed his comment that picking Archer 'probably wouldn't be fair, morally, but at the same time it's the nature of international sport' was taken out of context. Wood, who has an impish sense of humour and witty turn of phrase, compared picking Archer to Newcastle United signing Faustino Asprilla in 1996 when they were top of the Premier League only to see him fail to fit into the squad and their title bid falter.

All three personally contacted Archer to clarify what they'd said. 'Since I've been here, I didn't feel any malice at all. It's a really welcoming bunch of lads. I'm happy,' said Archer after his ODI debut in Dublin. When asked if any players had approached him to explain their comments, Archer said: 'Yes – Dave, Wood and Woakesy.'

When Archer was picked in the squad for the one-off ODI against Ireland and the Pakistan series, but not the provisional World Cup XV announced a month before the tournament started, the selectors also called up his friend Chris Jordan, the man responsible for bringing him over to Sussex from Barbados in the first place. Jordan, a fellow Bajan, is a very popular figure in the England dressing room, and he helped a shy Archer integrate into his new team. He even presented him with his Test cap against Australia five weeks after the World Cup, the first time a debutant has specifically requested, and been granted, a certain individual to do the honours.

Before the World Cup, some of the players knew Archer already, with Ben Stokes and Jos Buttler having played alongside him in the IPL for Rajasthan Royals, but Jordan helped to smooth over any doubts in those weeks leading into the tournament. Archer also quickly built up a close friendship with Moeen Ali and Rashid. He rarely drinks, loves gaming, particularly playing Fortnite, and is quiet and laid back.

The management knew little about him, having not seen him graduate through the England age ranks. The team's sports psychologists offered to help settle him in, but Archer is a confident individual and just wanted to be left alone.

Jordan told *Wisden* before the World Cup 'I view him as a brother'. They met in Barbados in 2013 when Jordan had returned to the island as an overseas player, having decided to make his career in England. Archer tried to knock Jordan's head off with the first ball he bowled to him in the nets at the Kensington Oval.

'His first ball is a very quick bouncer,' Jordan wrote, describing the incident in a diary for Sky Sports. 'It's whistling past my ears, and I look back at Shai Hope [wicketkeeper] climbing to take it above his head. Had it been on target, it definitely would have cleaned me up. He [Hope] ran back to the stumps, had a little giggle and said: "I told you so".'

Archer's World Cup debut at the Oval completed a remarkable rise for a young cricketer who at one stage wanted to be a wicketkeeper–batsman and cited England's Craig Kieswetter as an early role model. Growing up in Barbados, Archer had liked Kieswetter's strokeplay when he went to

113

the Kensington Oval as a schoolboy to watch England win the World Twenty20 in 2010, and he wanted to be a swashbuckling batsman–keeper rather than a knock-your-block-off quick. When he was picked for England, he decided to wear the number 22 on his Test and ODI shirts, the same as Kieswetter.

As a child Archer would play cricket every day with his step-father Patrick Waithe, bowling with a tape ball, but it was at Christ Church Foundation School, a short walk from the Oistins beachside fish market on the Barbados south coast, that he discovered he could bowl fast, which is fitting given Joel Garner is also a fellow alumnus.

Over one summer Archer went from being a 'timid, frail young boy', according to his early coaches, to being able to bowl over 80mph once they had ironed out his action to avoid injury. 'When I first came here, Jofra was a wicket-keeper who used to bowl leg spin and bat. When he came back from vacation in 2010, he had grown quite a bit, and I asked him about bowling and trying to be a fast bowler,' Nhamo Winn, the Foundation School cricket coach, told the *Daily Telegraph*. 'We tried off a couple of paces. It went pretty well. He had all the attributes of being a fast bowler. His approach to the crease was good, and he had a quick arm action. Within about six months, he was bowling close to 80mph.'

Before the World Cup there was a mixture of disappointment and worry at Foundation School. Disappointment that Archer chose England after losing heart with the politics of West Indies cricket when he was left out of the 2014 Under-19 World Cup squad. The worry stemmed from seeing West Indians from previous generations gamble on England but suffer at the hands of fickle selectors.

'For me, personally, I would have preferred him, in terms

of longevity, to play for West Indies. Here selection is very different. In England whenever you are off the boil there is a high chance you will be dropped. In West Indies you tend to play for a longer period, so I figure for his talent he would do well for West Indies,' said Denis Osbourne, the school's physical education teacher for 25 years.

However, Archer, who has had a British passport from birth through his father, was adamant he wanted to play for England as soon as he joined up with Jordan at Sussex in 2016.

At one point, Archer's action was questioned because opposition teams were surprised by his pace. His coaches were also concerned he would pick up injuries unless he tinkered with his technique.

'He was really frail at that time,' said Winn. 'And he was a little timid because he was frail. Understanding the importance of strengthening his body, sometimes that was a challenge. He was always ready for any activity that relates to cricket, but he only understood the importance of training after picking up injuries. Whenever I speak to him, I remind him that he is playing a lot of cricket and the engine room, which is your body, has to be strong. You have got to look after your body.

'At one point his injuries at such a young age were really concerning. Also, when Jofra started bowling fast, people questioned his action. What we did here was slow it down and break it down frame by frame to make sure it was within the degree allowable. We continued to work on it, then his accuracy, his pace and ability to bowl yorkers grew. He got nine wickets in one innings in an intermediate game at the beginning of his bowling career. Everything comes natural to him.'

South Africa, and Amla in particular, discovered that fact

on 30 May 2019, not at the Kensington Oval but the Kennington Oval, as Archer launched England's World Cup campaign in style.

The loss of Bairstow that day to the second ball momentarily stunned England. Du Plessis's tactic was actually meant for Jason Roy, but he got off strike first ball, and Bairstow ended up as collateral damage, collecting the first golden duck of his life. Bairstow, who a few minutes earlier had looked visibly emotional at the singing of the national anthems, pushed hard at a regulation leg-break that clipped his outside edge and was caught by keeper Quinton de Kock.

Teams would open the bowling with spin in England's first three matches of the tournament, but the tactic was deployed less as the World Cup progressed as the importance of new-ball pace bowling became apparent. Root's first two balls from Tahir were googlies, the second of which he inside-edged on to his pads and could so easily have hit the stumps. That really would have punctured the party.

The week had started for Root and the England players with a kit launch in another east London warehouse film set. There the light-blue strip was revealed that England would wear in the tournament. It was a homage to the 1992 team that had reached the World Cup final, and attending the event was Neil Fairbrother, agent to Root, Buttler and Stokes. The kit he wore in the 1992 final was on show in a glass case, like a museum piece, with supporters taking selfies next to it. In a small side room Fairbrother's client Root explained his role in the ODI team.

'The balance I have to strike is knowing how to pace batting personally and not feel like I'm leaving someone else too much to do, or similarly not going too early and leaving the guys in a difficult position where they have got to bat too long before they can give it a good clout at the end,' he said.

'Sometimes you look at them and think: "I wish I could do that." I wish I could feel in a position where I could join in, but it's part and parcel of your role in the team.'

Root was in his element against South Africa. The team needed his steadying influence. The ball stuck in a soft, dry pitch, and this was a World Cup match that needed calm heads and not a gung-ho spirit. Root and Roy steadied the nerves with a second-wicket stand of 106 from 18 overs, as South Africa failed to press home their early advantage. The scoreboard is never static when Root is batting, and menace always lurks beneath the surface when Roy is at the crease, even if he is trying to play within himself.

The loss of Dale Steyn with a tournament-ending shoulder injury leading into the match took the edge off South Africa's attack. Kagiso Rabada and Lungi Ngidi recognised slower balls were the way to go, but South Africa did not attack Root and Roy with close-in fielders and let them easily settle into running well between the wickets and carving out a score.

Du Plessis had won the toss and elected to bowl on a sunny day, so it was a surprise he did not show more ruthlessness with his field settings. Instead Roy made 54 from 53 balls and Root 51 from 59 deliveries without ever really extending themselves. They fell within four runs of each other as South Africa pulled England back into line. Roy was furious with himself after top-edging to mid-off, and Root steered a catch to backward point. It was a soft dismissal and blew a golden chance for him to make a hundred.

But another century stand, also 106 between Morgan and Stokes, eased England towards a competitive total. Morgan recognised he could not slap it around and instead was patient in making 57 off 60 balls. He did hit three sixes, the only ones of the entire innings, with two off consecutive balls from Ngidi. The first was smacked high over wide long-on, the second a pulled short ball lifted over fine leg. Aiden Markram's gentle off spin was treated with too much respect until Morgan slog-swept him over mid-wicket for six.

At the other end Stokes could not get going. His rhythm with the bat had been off for a while. He'd had a poor IPL and looked out of touch in the Pakistan series until the fourth match when he moved up to no. 4 and made an unbeaten 71 at Trent Bridge. He was still looking rusty and knew he needed time at the crease. His maturity shone through, though – a younger Stokes would have let the frustration overcome his better instincts and gifted his wicket. This time his head was down, and he grafted for his team.

With Morgan caught brilliantly by a diving Markram off Tahir at long-on, and Buttler lasting just 16 balls, England went into the final nine overs relying on Stokes to see them home and make up for the loss of their two unorthodox hitters. England scrambled 64 off the final 52 balls of the innings, hardly the kind of late barrage they had come to inflict on sides, but with Archer lacing his first ball for four, and Stokes holding it all together, it felt like they had enough to defend with 311 on the board.

'We fought ourselves individually and as a batting unit throughout the innings,' said Morgan. 'The wicket did not allow us to execute Plan A, which is scoring a big total, but our maturity showed the improvement we have made over the last two years.'

It would prove to be plenty of runs once Archer had the ball in his hand and was bowling at 93mph. His first five overs were electrifying, bringing two for 20 but so much more besides. Amla was on five when he was late on the 90mph bouncer from Archer that smashed into the grille of his helmet. He had treatment on the field for several minutes and was given a replacement helmet but eventually shuffled off to have concussion tests, including computerised testing, in the dressing room. He would miss South Africa's next match and retired from international cricket after a poor World Cup.

He was replaced by Markram, who punished Archer for a rare bad ball, driving him through the covers for four, but the next delivery was sharper, and he nicked to slip. In Archer's next over, du Plessis was also beaten for pace trying to pull a short ball and was caught off a top edge.

South Africa were 44–2 but really 44–3 given the state of Amla and in deep trouble. England fielded brilliantly, with Roy stopping two certain fours at backward point, diving both times to pull off excellent stops to back up Archer's pace. The rope was tightening around South Africa. England's analysts later calculated they saved 35 runs and ranked it their best fielding performance in four years.

De Kock and Rassie van der Dussen rallied South Africa but needed some good fortune. De Kock was bowled by Rashid, but the zinger bails used in the World Cup failed to dislodge. On 25 in the 11th over, de Kock had played himself in when he went for a fine reverse sweep off Rashid only for the ball to hit the stumps, which lit up, and ricochet for four. England did not bother chasing the ball to the boundary because they thought they had bowled de Kock, but it was the first of several examples in the early stages of the World Cup of the bails refusing to drop. Meanwhile, van der Dussen was feeling his way in when he got a thin edge on a Moeen offbreak, but Buttler dropped the chance, and to sum up a poor over for the England keeper, three balls later he let four byes through his legs.

Van der Dussen and de Kock were opening up when Morgan turned to his most reliable bowler of the previous four years: Liam Plunkett. His slower-ball rib ticklers were perfectly suited to this surface. De Kock tried to flog one out of the ground but mistimed it and was caught at deep backward square leg, becoming the first of a line of top-order batsmen Plunkett would dismiss in the tournament.

Then, J.P. Duminy took leave of his senses in the 26th over when two balls after slapping Moeen over mid-wicket for four he tried to loft him over long-off for six only to hole out to Stokes. Dwaine Pretorius was run out two balls later and then Morgan sensed his chance, bringing back Archer to finish it off. He produced a wicket maiden in his first over, with van der Dussen lobbing a catch to mid-off for 50 off 61 balls.

South Africa were 167 for six and sinking fast. Andile Phehlukwayo hit a couple of nice fours but gifted the match its stand-out moment. He connected beautifully with a slog-sweep off Rashid that was heading for a flat six. Stokes on the boundary misread its flight and attacked the ball too early. He was out of position but somehow leapt up, and, even with his body past the perpendicular, was able to stick his right arm out and pluck the ball out of the air.

'No way. No, no way. You cannot do that, Ben Stokes,' yelled a stunned Nasser Hussain on commentary for Sky. 'Ben Stokes, that is remarkable. That is one of the greatest catches of all time. You cannot do that.'

Stokes looked shocked himself as he turned to the crowd holding the ball up. 'I had a panic on. To be honest, I was in the wrong position. I was ten yards further in than I should have been. If I had been in the right position, it would have been a regulation catch,' he said. 'I mean, that feeling for about five seconds when I was facing the crowd and every-one was cheering was phenomenal.'

Morgan knows his players' mentality. He turned to Stokes as a wounded Amla came back to the crease. 'Morgs asked me before I bowled my first ball of my spell: "How is your heart going? Have you settled down now?" I said: "Yeah, I'm all right now."'

In his own words Stokes 'burgled' the last two wickets, taking two for 12 off 2.5 overs as South Africa were bowled out for 207 with 61 balls to spare. There was no other choice for man of the match. 'He had a full day out today, did Ben,' was Morgan's response.

'There had been a lot of nerves kicking around,' admitted Stokes. 'I had not felt like that in a long time when I came to the ground this morning, so it is always nice to get the first game out of the way. To come away with a win is a fantastic start.'

But it was more than that. England came away with two points and a new fast-bowling star. 'Honestly, it was a great atmosphere,' said Archer. 'Everyone exploded when my name was announced, and it was a great feeling. It gave me that little bit extra.'

In the assembly hall at Archer's old school is an honours board entitled Beacons of Excellence. Hanging are portraits of two former pupils who became prime ministers of Barbados and a black-and-white photograph of Garner in his pomp. A blank space awaits, to be filled by the next notable student. Archer had gone a long way to ensuring it will be his photo hanging there one day.

SIX
FUMBLES, FINES AND FRUSTRATION

GAME TWO –
ENGLAND V. PAKISTAN

TRENT BRIDGE, NOTTINGHAM

3 June 2019

It was raining at Trent Bridge on the day before England's match against Pakistan. Practice was curtailed, but out on the ground one player was oblivious to the wet. There was Jos Buttler, running furiously around the boundary edge on his own before doing some intense catching practice with Bruce French, the wicketkeeping coach.

It was a familiar sight. Buttler was one of the fitter members of the squad, along with Ben Stokes and Jonny Bairstow, and was often seen going that extra bit further, practising that little bit harder, which was not easy amongst a group that trained so hard anyway. It was not a reaction to his performance in the opening match against South Africa, even if he did not have a particularly good day at the Oval: only 18 runs and a below-par performance behind the stumps.

Despite England's victory, Buttler's off day had not gone unnoticed. So much was expected of England's wicketkeeper and vice-captain at this World Cup. He had dealt so routinely in moments of genius in its build-up that he entered it as England's most feared player, the batsman who could truly destroy an opposition in the blink of an eye. He had done just that in one of the pre-tournament matches against Pakistan, at Southampton, when he made a century off just 50 balls, England's second-fastest ODI hundred (he has the record, of course, in 46 balls).

Buttler made another century here at Trent Bridge, his ninth in ODIs, off 75 balls, which is sedate by his standards, but it was still England's fastest in a World Cup at the time. That Joe Root made a century too and England still lost, failing by 14 runs in pursuit of Pakistan's 348 for eight, says much about Pakistan's excellence on the day, as well as England's sloppiness in the field. It was only the second time in his nine ODI centuries to date that Buttler had ended up on the losing side. The other occasion was when he made 121 in vain against Sri Lanka at Lord's in 2014.

It was a remarkable result given that Pakistan had lost their previous 11 ODIs and had been beaten 4–0 by England in the series immediately preceding the tournament. Trent Bridge is England's favourite ODI ground, where they have set two world records with the bat (indeed, this match was played on the same pitch on which they had made their highest score of 481 for six against Australia in 2018), and it was here only three days before that Pakistan had been bowled out – bounced out, in fact, by the pacemen – for just 105 by West Indies in a match that barely lasted three hours.

The reasons for this turnaround? Well, this was a very

different Pakistan side from the one thrashed by England in that warm-up series. It now included the two left-arm quicks Mohammad Amir and Wahab Riaz, as well as the leg spinner Shadab Khan. Amir had been suffering from chickenpox, and Shadab had just recovered from hepatitis, while Pakistan had simply been looking at younger alternatives to Wahab until he produced some brilliant form during the Pakistan Super League and the selectors changed their minds about him. All three are high-quality performers, and all three are the type of bowler any ODI side would crave.

The defeat by West Indies was embarrassing. This was a side who were Champions Trophy winners in 2017 after all. Using the word mercurial in relation to Pakistan cricket has long been a cliché, but it is true. They remain supremely talented, yet maddeningly inconsistent.

England had seen how the short ball had troubled the Pakistanis, so it was no surprise that they introduced the Durham fast bowler Mark Wood, replacing Liam Plunkett in the only change from the opener against South Africa. It meant Wood lined up alongside Jofra Archer for only the second time for England. That other match had been at Trent Bridge too, little more than a couple of weeks previously against Pakistan, and Archer and Wood had troubled the Pakistanis then, with Wood causing Imam-ul-Haq, the left-handed opener, to go to hospital after hitting him on the left elbow.

England captain Eoin Morgan was, though, understandably cautious in his assessment of all of this before the match. Short balls can disappear as well as dismiss. 'You still have to bowl extremely well,' he said. 'If you bowl short and it's off, it gets met in this day and age. If you are going to use the short ball, make sure it's in the right area.

'It is exciting having Wood and Archer together, but it's like saying can you add a Jason Roy 180 and a Jos Buttler 150, both of them off 70 or 80 balls. It might happen. If it does, that would be awesome. We just have to wait and see.

'The short-pitched bowling could be a trend. Probably over the last couple of years in the shorter formats of the game it's been leg spin. This might be a trend for the tournament. It might be the nature of the pitches.'

In a moment of serious prescience, given the way the pitches in the tournament turned out, with the one prepared for the final at Lord's being a classic example, Morgan said: 'Cross-seam into the wicket might be getting a better reaction than any other bowling. It's potentially coming off two-paced, which makes cross-bat shots a bit harder and means you have to take a higher risk.'

And all of this was, of course, not forgetting that Pakistan could target England with the short ball too. They had done so at Headingley – Root, James Vince and Morgan were all out hooking – in the final match of the warm-up series. 'We've got bowlers who can bowl 140kph-plus [87mph], so they can do the same thing to England's batters,' said their assistant coach, Azhar Mahmood.

Pakistan were ready for a battle, as was evident from the moment Morgan won the toss and bowled. The left-handed opening pairing of Fakhar Zaman and Imam-ul-Haq batted with great spirit and determination, and no little skill too, especially when Imam was lofting Chris Woakes over long-on for six and Fakhar was scooping the same fielder down to the fine leg boundary.

They took their side to 69 at the end of the ten-over powerplay and then on to 82 in the 15th over before a wicket fell. It was exactly the sort of start Pakistan needed. It exorcised the demons of the West Indies defeat, and it rattled England, who had tried the fast and short stuff, even posting a leg gully for Archer, without success.

125

It took the introduction of Moeen Ali's off spin to apply the brakes, which was a surprise. He snared both openers. First, Fakhar was smartly stumped by Buttler, and then Imam hit a catch out to wide long-off that was taken brilliantly by Woakes. Moeen's first spell of seven overs, in which he used the brisk cross-breeze cleverly, cost just 36 for those two wickets.

Babar Azam, batting at no. 3, played quite superbly for 63 at only just under a run a ball, the type of innings Root would play for England so often in the tournament, and with the same sort of class and composure. He really is some player. It took the return of Moeen to the attack to bring his innings to an end, as the spinner finished with three for 50 from his ten overs, easily his best figures of the tournament. He only took one more wicket after this.

The outstanding batsman, however, was Mohammad Hafeez, the 38-year-old who batted more like an excited teenager, running down the pitch to his very first ball and hitting Moeen over mid-off for four and then cruising to his half-century off just 39 balls. He deservedly won the man-of-the-match award.

He had a life on 14, though, when Jason Roy dropped a sitter at long-off. It was a shock given how well Roy had fielded at the Oval, and how good a fielder he is generally, and it was a game-changing moment. It was simply not Roy's day. He was later fined 15 per cent of his match fee and given a demerit point for using an audible obscenity after misfielding.

Archer received the same punishment for showing dissent after he was adjudged to have bowled a wide later in the innings. After starting the tournament with his three for 27 against South Africa, Archer had a chastening day and conceded 79 runs in his ten wicketless overs. He was not the first, nor indeed will he be the last, fast bowler to suffer on this ground, though, with its mostly flat wickets and odd mis-shaped boundary, especially short towards the right of the pavilion as we, the observers and spectators, look at it.

It seemed as if captain Morgan might suffer censure for a slow over rate too, which was not helped by leg spinner Adil Rashid only bowling five overs after he conceded 43 runs in that time (that drop by Roy off Hafeez did come, though, at the start of his second over, having gone for just four in his first over), as Pakistan's innings overran by 20 minutes beyond the allocated three and a half hours.

Morgan had missed England's pre-tournament ODI against Pakistan at Trent Bridge after England had been slow in bowling their overs in the previous match at Bristol – but it was his opposite number, Sarfaraz Ahmed, who was eventually fined 20 per cent of his match fee for Pakistan's rate later in the day, with his team-mates receiving 10 per cent fines.

England fielded dreadfully overall, though, despite Woakes taking a record four catches. They conceded 17 runs in mis-fields. For a side that has always prided itself on that aspect of the game, with Trevor Bayliss coming in and setting great store by it, and especially because they had fielded so well in the tournament opener at the Oval, this was uncharacteristic and unexpected. The pressures of a home World Cup were there for all to see.

It was started by, of all people, Morgan, who let through a four at cover from the fourth ball of Pakistan's innings from Woakes and, despite some excellence from Jonny Bairstow on the boundary – a familiar sight in this competition – the team's fielding did not really improve.

With typical honesty afterwards, Morgan blamed that poor fielding for the defeat. 'I don't think it was that bad a day for us, but fielding-wise it was,' he said. 'We have gone from probably one of our best performances in the field [in beating South Africa] to one that, whilst not extremely bad, has cost us probably 15 to 20 runs, which is a lot in the one-day game.

'Our batting and bowling go up and down, but our fielding must be a constant. I'm frustrated [by the loss] in that we could have done something about it. When the difference between the sides is in the field it is doubly frustrating.'

It was a fraught day in general, with a hefty Pakistan contingent in the crowd generating considerable noise. When Woakes caught Imam, he put a finger to his mouth to say shush to those opposition fans. It was unlike the usually phlegmatic Woakes, and it was unlike England to be ruffled.

'I think most of the time it is like friendly banter with the crowd, and that's good, but whether it was the occasion – there were a lot of Pakistan fans – or whether we got wound up by their batters, them smacking it, or whether we just got too heated in the moment, I don't know,' said Mark Wood afterwards. 'But it was unlike us. Normally we are a really good fielding side. We practise really hard, so I think it is just one of those things we need to address for the next game.'

Both teams were also warned by the umpires in the field about deliberately throwing the ball in on the bounce to rough it up, and Jos Buttler even asked to see the ball after he had been dismissed.

'There were discussions throughout the two innings,' Morgan said. 'The umpires came to me, mid-innings, and seemed to think that we were throwing the ball in on the bounce too much. They emphasised it would be the same for both sides. Jos was just intrigued to see the ball. When the ball is hit against the LED advertising boards it does scuff it up quite a lot, so he was just interested to see if one side was rougher than the other, natural or unnatural.'

There were clearly some suspicions in the England camp. 'I'm not going to get involved, or I'll only get myself in trouble,' said Root, tellingly.

'It's the umpires' job, and they were doing their job,' said Hafeez. '[There were] a couple of incidents for both sides where the throw didn't come in one bounce, but in two or three bounces. We got a warning after 20 overs that if we threw in on two bounces, we would get a penalty, so I made a point of running in to hand them the ball. You don't want to have to do it, but they were just doing their job, and they did it right.'

Hafeez eventually made 84 from just 62 balls, and Sarfaraz chipped in with a perky half-century, leaving England a record World Cup chase to win.

England's reply did not start well. Pakistan copied South Africa's use of a spinner in the first match to open the bowling with the leg spinner Shadab, who was doing so for the first time in an ODI. Just as it had worked for South Africa, so it worked for Pakistan, as Roy completed his utterly miserable day by being lbw sweeping – a poor choice of shot given his relative strengths and also given the fact that the ball was very full and pushed through quickly.

He unwisely reviewed the decision too, which was predictably not overturned, and he was sent on his way with a volley of advice from the fielding side. He did not take kindly to that, and the umpires had to step in to cool matters. It really was that sort of day.

It was also another day in the World Cup when Morgan was tested severely by the short ball. Pakistan's immediate posting of a short leg to him rather signalled their intentions. He never settled, top edging a hook off Hasan Ali over the wicketkeeper before he was bowled by Mohammad Hafeez for just nine, so it was left to Root and Buttler to fashion the partnership that looked as though it might win the game for England.

They came together in the 22nd over with the score at 118 for four. It was already a tricky situation. A colleague of ours in the press box mentioned that Buttler could get a hundred and England might not make the 349 required. Surely not. Every side knows the damage Buttler can wreak. They all know that until he is back in the pavilion anything is possible.

Buttler was soon hitting the spin of Shoaib Malik over mid-off for four. Then he pulled Mohammad Hafeez's spin over deep mid-wicket for six. It even tempted his partner Root, who often has to stop himself from trying to outdo his more muscular batting colleagues, to hit the same bowler over long-on for six.

This was Buttler at his best, the 28-year-old from Somerset, with the softest of voices but often the loudest of statements with a bat in his hand, a polite and unassuming man who can surprise you, such as when you learn that he has the phrase 'fuck it' written on the top of his bat handle.

'That is the thing I can always come back to, whether it is about committing to a shot or about getting out first ball,' he says. 'I think it keeps cricket in a really good perspective for me, where it lands in the scheme of life. If you pick up a paper and start from the front, by the time you get to the sports pages you realise getting out for a duck is not the be all and end all.'

It was actually a shame that this tournament did not truly see him at his consistent best. 'Jos's contribution to the side over the four years is arguably the biggest,' said Eoin Morgan. 'Because he does things that nobody else in the world can do, and then backs it up with a common goal of trying to win games and being a better team.'

Buttler played magnificently well in the final, but, that aside, this was his finest knock of the competition. Was he too desperate for success? He certainly admitted after the tournament had ended that he had sought out the team psychologist, David Young, to help him cope with some of his thoughts around the possibility of England failing.

'We'd been favourites, so highly fancied by everyone, and there was the danger that four years of playing such good cricket was going to come to nothing,' he told the *Mail on Sunday*. 'Think about what people will say about us as a team, think about how they will call us chokers, everything else they will say.

'I remember seeing a comment about how it would be the biggest failure because of how much had gone into this World Cup. I was struggling with the thought of that.

'What was scaring me was if we lost, I didn't know how I'd play cricket again. This was such a once-in-a-lifetime opportunity, a World Cup final at Lord's. It felt like destiny, and I was thinking: "If it doesn't happen, I will have no motivation to pick up a cricket bat for a very long time." When I was talking to David, I knew the answers.'

It was clearly why Buttler was so angry upon being dismissed in the final. And he was angry here too, because he was out the very next ball after he had reached his century, slashing Mohammad Amir's cutter to short third man. It was not what England needed, just as it had not been when Joe Root was out only six balls after passing his own century milestone.

'You can't really describe the way he plays – it's a bit freakish, isn't it?' said Root of Buttler in this match. 'He's got the ability to do things other guys can't. He's a great person for me to bat with. I just try to give him as much strike as possible and let him go.'

But we had still been treated to a typical Buttler masterclass, with his batting being that alluring combination of muscularity (Buttler's forearms and biceps are surprisingly big), flexible wrists and fast hands.

Batting, in whatever format, is about good decision-making, and Buttler is recognised as one of the better decision-makers in the game. He remains so calm and has both the face and the mind of a poker player.

He had long been identified as an exceptional talent, as evidenced by this tale from Mark Garaway, who was the Somerset academy coach when Buttler was a youngster at King's College, Taunton. 'The first time I saw him he was 12, and we weren't supposed to include players on academy programmes until they were 14, but I rang Hugh Morris [the managing director of England cricket at the time] and asked if we could make an exception,' he said to *The Times*. 'Hugh asked why, and I said: "Because this lad will play for England." You don't get that sort of thing right all the time, but I was pretty sure on this one.'

Not a bad call that. Buttler truly is a remarkable batsman. His technique when power hitting is very much like that of a baseball hitter, going deep in his crease, moving back to then come forwards (but never letting his head go too far back), and his front leg is cleared out of the way so that he can either hit easily on the leg side, scythe away on the off side or even hit straight down the ground with a flat bat.

A right-hander, Buttler has a strong bottom-handed grip, which Garaway once attempted to change. 'We felt he might be able to keep the bat face on the ball a bit better,' he said. 'That was a painful process for Jos and reduced him to tears on quite a few occasions. It didn't feel comfortable for him and was compromising his strengths. But the thing I remember the most is that his mum, Patricia, knew that we were challenging him. When Jos was feeling teary, he'd look over towards his mum for comfort and she would avert her eyes. She was a tennis coach herself and understood the process. That's a big thing for a parent to do.'

It was decided that they would abandon the change, and Buttler reverted to his natural grip, with his bottom hand a long way around the handle. 'He uses the same grip now as when he was 12 or 13,' Garaway said. 'It suits his game perfectly. He's a very right-sided player. He lines the ball up with his right eye and takes aim with his right shoulder. The MCC coaching manual would rather you line up with both eyes and, as a right-hander, lead with your left shoulder. But fair to say it hasn't turned out too badly for Jos.'

Although he can be quite orthodox technically in the longer forms of the game, taking the ball late and staying more side-on, especially when defending on the back foot, often in white-ball cricket Buttler does not try to hit the ball with a traditionally straight bat through extra cover and mid-off, preferring to snap his wrists and get his hands through the ball with astonishing speed. The area through extra cover and wide of mid-off is his favoured scoring area, and it is a question often posed by former England captain Mike Atherton as to why opposing captains do not position their mid-offs much wider to Buttler.

But then again Buttler has often mocked traditional fielding positions. The ramp has become one of his trademark shots, something he first attempted at the Somerset academy, with the Sri Lankan Tillakaratne Dilshan and his 'Dilscoop' as his inspiration. 'I saw Dilshan doing it, and it just made sense,' he said. 'There are no fielders there behind the 'keeper. If you make cricket as simple as you can, it is about hitting the ball where the fielders aren't. There is never one there. You can go through an innings not playing it, but the opposition just knowing that you can play it can make them bowl differently.' And how does he practise it? 'You're almost best off going in the kitchen and practising flipping a pancake, that's pretty much what it is,' he said.

But the truth is that most mortal batsmen generally only attempt this shot when fine leg is up in the fielding circle. Buttler has changed that mindset. He will do it with fine leg back. And that is what he did here at Trent Bridge to Wahab Riaz, with Buttler using his trademark dummy of a movement towards leg before moving back across his stumps and scooping the ball over the wicketkeeper.

When Buttler was dismissed, 61 were needed off 33 balls. It was too big an ask without him. Hasan Ali's combination of slower balls and bouncers was too much for Moeen Ali, who made 19 but gave further worrying evidence that his batting was in decline. Since the start of 2018, he had been averaging just 16.77 in 35 ODIs, with a highest score of 46 not out. England wanted more from their no. 7. That century he had made off just 53 balls against West Indies in Bristol in 2017, on a day sadly remembered for the night afterwards rather than Moeen's innings, seemed long gone.

Very soon England needed 38 off three overs, then 29 off two, so that Wahab was able to saunter through the last over off a short run. It was a shock result, but, their fielding aside, England had not played terribly, even if they had been taught an early lesson about the difference between chasing big totals in much less relevant bilateral series and then hunting them down in this, the most pressurised of environments.

'The most important thing now for us as a group is not to panic,' said Root. 'We know what works for us as a formula and as a team, but other sides are allowed to play well. We've got to make sure we learn quickly. The temptation is to get a little bit tense. But one of our great strengths as a side is sticking to the way we go about things and being as smart as possible. And the beauty of this format is that I do believe the best four teams over the tournament will qualify for the semi-finals, and we've got to make sure we play some good cricket in our remaining games.

'One thing this side doesn't do very often is to make the same mistake twice, and I'm sure the guys will make sure it's a very different performance against Bangladesh.'

SEVEN
ROY LAYS HIS GHOSTS
TO REST

GAME THREE –
ENGLAND V. BANGLADESH

SOPHIA GARDENS, CARDIFF

8 JUNE 2019

Eoin Morgan was asked by the BBC after England's last net session before the game against Bangladesh whether he had spent his two days off since the defeat to Pakistan watching the World Cup. 'Nah. Personally I like to watch a lot of horse racing and try to get away from the game,' he said. It was a small but important insight into England's mindset. The captain had told his players to go home after the bitter loss to Pakistan and urged them to forget about cricket.

Morgan is close to Jason Roy and realised his friend needed more space than the others after his poor game at Trent Bridge. He allowed Roy to stay at the team hotel the day before the Bangladesh game and spend time with his baby daughter and wife instead of going through the usual batting and fielding drills. Throughout the World Cup, England booked separate rooms for family members to ensure the players had a good night's sleep before each game, but their very presence around the team lifted the mood. Roy admitted fatherhood had changed him, and forgetting about batting to concentrate on feeding and changing the baby's nappy allowed him to clear his mind.

Bangladesh were a tricky opposition for England, particularly on the back of a defeat. Bangladesh had beaten them at the last two World Cups, starting with a feisty match in Chittagong in 2011 when England lost their cool on a muggy night, and their famous win in Adelaide four years later that knocked Eoin Morgan's team out of the tournament. Bangladesh were packed full of experienced players, such as Shakib Al Hasan, Tamim Iqbal and Mahmudullah who had played in both those games.

'It's going to be a difficult game,' Morgan said. 'Bangladesh are a good side. I think people underestimate them. But we certainly don't.'

When the two sides last met in 2016 there were testy exchanges on the field involving Roy and Tamim. Ben Stokes puffed his chest out and tried to sort the situation out in his own way at the end of one game in Dhaka, finger pointing and telling Tamim what he thought. He later tweeted: 'Congrats to Bangladesh on the win tonight, outplayed us, what I won't stand for is someone putting a shoulder to my teammate at handshakes.'

It felt like Cardiff was about to host another ill-tempered showdown. In the end Roy let his bat do the talking this time, scoring a brilliant 153 off 121 balls, an innings that only ended when he gave his wicket away in the pursuit of hitting six sixes in an over off Mehidy Hasan.

England made what would be the second-highest score of the tournament, 386 for six, and set a world record in the process by becoming the first team to score seven consecutive totals of 300 or more in ODIs, beating the record of six held by Australia. They lifted their net run rate in the tournament from 0.9 to 1.3 and belted 14 sixes. It was the tenth time England had hit 14 or more sixes in an ODI, and all had happened since the previous World Cup in 2015. Prior to this game they had never hit more than seven sixes in a World Cup innings before. Roy managed five on his own, including those three in one over off Mehidy.

It was raining heavily when England gathered in Cardiff two days before the game. The benefit of a home World Cup is being able to sleep in your own bed between games and England had enjoyed time away since the loss to Pakistan, all dispersing to different parts of the country.

Mark Wood could not face driving from Nottingham to the northeast and back down to Cardiff so instead spent two days in London with his wife, visiting the Harry Potter studio tour.

When they assembled at Sophia Gardens on the Wednesday, they were allowed a light training session. In effect it was just a photo shoot with some local schoolchildren. Stokes and Liam Plunkett were the ones who agreed to join in with some fielding drills. When it emerged that the school was the Cathedral School, Llandaff, a local private school with excellent facilities, it felt like the ECB were getting the public relations game wrong. Surely there was a local state school that would have benefited more?

The day did give an insight into England's thinking, though. It was clear Plunkett would play. His bang-it-in-the-pitch style suits the normally slowish Cardiff surface (although, with plenty of grass left on them, they produced good pace in this competition) and forces batsmen to play to the much bigger playing areas square of the wicket rather than down the ground to the short boundaries.

One of the spinners would make way. It was obvious that Adil Rashid was struggling to keep his place, having bowled poorly in the first two games and the series against Pakistan. Moeen Ali was the best bowler in the Pakistan game at Trent Bridge and had a stronger case for keeping his spot. But Morgan made a big call that would have ramifications for England for the rest of the tournament. It would have been easier to drop Rashid and pick the more reliable Moeen, even though he was badly out of form with the bat. But Morgan knows Rashid thrives on a captain showing him confidence. He stuck by the leg spinner who had been such an important part of their World Cup planning.

Rashid's shoulder was giving him trouble, and he needed injections to get through the tournament, but Morgan axed Moeen instead. He figured a good day for Moeen is worth two for 40 off ten overs, whereas a good day for Rashid is four for 60. Rashid wins games. Moeen helps you not to lose. It was Moeen who would make way for Plunkett.

'When you play a series against India or Pakistan and you win it 4–1, you don't really think about the loss, you try to bounce back and win the next game,' said Plunkett. 'That's what we've got to do. It's different opposition, but we just need to come and play our cricket. I think that will hopefully be good enough to win the game.'

On the morning of the match, Paul Farbrace was working as a summariser for *Test Match Special* and gave insight into how Morgan would have reacted to the Pakistan defeat. He said the message would have been to not panic. Farbrace pointed out one of Morgan's strengths is the clarity of his team talks. He would have told the players to go away and think about their individual performance and how that fitted into the team result.

Farbrace also believed Morgan would have reminded the players to enjoy the World Cup and embrace the experience. That had been a message drummed into the players for the four years leading into the tournament. If they did not enjoy playing in a home World Cup then negative thoughts and worries were more likely to creep in. Put simply, they had to go home and chill out for a few days.

Farbrace was right. England were far more relaxed in Cardiff. They were also helped by some Bangladesh ineptitude: they won the toss but opted to bowl first when surely their best bet would have been to grind out a total of around 280 and then let their spinners strangle England. Instead they gifted England first use of the pitch, thinking the overcast conditions would help their seamers. The England players have spent their lives facing 85mph fast-medium bowling and tucked in, led by Jason Roy and Jonny Bairstow.

They were patient, scoring just 15 off the first five overs as they saw off the threat of Shakib's left-arm spin. He was the dangerman, and Bangladesh opened up with him knowing England had lost openers to spinners in the previous two games. Shakib was sliding the ball in 'on the angle at middle and leg, and Roy struggled at first. He recognised that trying to cut off the back foot was not wise, and, as he became more confident, he played straighter and survived the test.

The short boundary at the River Taff end, and the breeze at the back of England's two powerful openers, meant Bangladesh only bowled one spinner at a time, so Roy and Bairstow could score freely from the seamers at the other end. After 18 overs England had scored 38 off spin and 78 off the seamers.

Roy was in control. It was a brilliant performance. He

would help England lay two ghosts to rest. They buried their Bangladesh World Cup demons and wiped away memories of their Champions Trophy defeat to Pakistan in Cardiff two years previously. On a personal note, he moved on from Trent Bridge, and from being dropped in Cardiff for that Pakistan match in 2017. Then he was in miserable form. Now he was on top of his game.

Roy played within himself until he was settled. He did not sweep against the spinner, as he did in Nottingham, and, as he does when he is at his best, he hit down the ground with controlled aggression. There was one dodgy reverse sweep, but that was his only aberration. The rest of the time he bristled with intent but played orthodox, strong cricket shots.

This maturity was typical of his mindset since getting married 12 months earlier. With his personal life settled, Roy changed on the field too. Gone was the brashness that was really just a vehicle to cover up his own insecurity. Instead he exuded measured confidence. Arrogance, yes, but the right arrogance, the kind that speaks volumes about a player finally recognising his strengths. Some never manage to work it out. Others do it at just the right time in their careers. Roy was one of those.

He moved to England from Durban aged ten and went to Whitgift School on a sports scholarship. He was often compared to Kevin Pietersen (they constantly called him the Young KP), but his early coaches prefer the comparison with the Curran brothers. 'I saw him play for Surrey Under-11s just after his family had moved to England and he had joined a state school,' Neil Kendrick, the former Surrey and Glamorgan left-arm spinner who is head of cricket at Whitgift School, told the *Telegraph*. 'He was so athletic, with such a natural sporting ability, that we chatted to the Whitgift headmaster, and he came over on one of our sports

141

scholarships. We just had to steer him in the right direction.'

What Kendrick enjoyed about Roy's innings in Cardiff was how he kept control of his emotions. 'The biggest thing I worked on with him was to get him to knock it around in the middle overs,' he said. 'He used to get so many brilliant 40s and 60s.'

The England management had noticed Roy's change of personality in Sri Lanka in November before the World Cup. There he struggled in two games in Dambulla, scoring 24 and nought. But he worked out for himself that his problem was his trigger movement (the movements a batsman makes to ready himself before the ball is bowled). He realised on the slow Sri Lankan pitches, and against bowlers of no great pace either, he was better off staying still and hitting from a solid base. In his next two innings, he scored 41 and 45 and looked far more confident.

Roy has a simple technique. Defensively he might not be the best, because he is always looking to go hard at the ball, but he hits it straight and cleanly. Graham Ford, his former coach at Surrey, believed that when Roy struggled it was because his back-lift became skewed. It would come from outside leg stump and behind his body. It was this small kink that was the problem in the Champions Trophy when a rotten run of form cost him his place. In the nets before the crucial game against Australia he was so bad that the England coaches knew he would be out for a low score that day. He was leg-before to Mitchell Starc for four to the second ball of the match, over-balancing and playing across the ball.

The day he was dropped for the Pakistan Champions Trophy semi-final, he went back to Surrey and smashed 92 against Worcestershire in a 50-over game. It did not take long for the old Roy to return. From being dropped in 2017 to the start of the World Cup, he averaged 48 and scored four hundreds, including his record-breaking 180 in Melbourne.

'I think my form since that competition and coming back into the team has shown where I've changed my game a bit, mentally and physically,' he said. 'I was in a bad place before the Champions Trophy, got dropped, rightly so, and then brought back into the team and adapted from there.'

If it happened again, he said, he would 'probably be a bit more relaxed about it. Identify where I'm going wrong quicker. I was in that frame of mind I wasn't able to identify where I was going wrong. Now I know where I was going wrong.'

Roy believed he burnt himself out in 2017 by playing in the IPL before the Champions Trophy. He did not make the same mistake with a World Cup looming, preferring to stay at home instead with his young family. At the start of the season, he credited his new family life with changing his cricket, a view shared by his team-mates, who saw at close hand how he'd matured, becoming more professional in training.

'Life changes a little when you get married,' he told the *Independent*. 'I'd been with my partner for eight or nine years, and it's nice to wake up the day after the wedding and call her your wife, but a child just flips your world upside down.

'The moment I decided I was going to propose, I realised there are no better things out there. It changes your perspective on things. From that point, everything off the field is better and more solid, and you find that things on the field get better too because of it. You have more focus. You train harder – now, training hard wasn't ever really a problem for me, but it kind of eliminates distractions, you know.'

There is no doubt that pairing him with Bairstow helped. England insiders say Roy is brilliant at handling Bairstow, who can be prone to mood swings. Bairstow reacts well to praise, and Roy is always telling him how good he is playing in the nets, even if that is not always the case. Morgan trusted him to handle Bairstow and get the best out of his partner.

When Roy and Bairstow gave England a platform, Bangladesh were there for the taking. They put on 128 for the first wicket before Mashrafe Mortaza found some extra bounce and Bairstow nicked behind.

Root started with 12 singles and never looked right as he made a patchy 21. When he was out in the 32nd over, Morgan made a big decision. He sent in Jos Buttler ahead of himself. It was a good move. Buttler had time to adjust to the pace of the pitch, instead of having to tee off from his first ball. He was batting on the back of a fine hundred in Nottingham, his confidence was high and, with so many power hitters still to come in, he could take his time before launching the Bangladesh bowlers into the river.

Roy made his hundred off 92 balls, a steady accumulation in this era. As he reached his century, umpire Joel Wilson discovered why Roy was such a good rugby player and as a 17-year-old was offered a contract by Harlequins. Roy accidentally collided with Wilson as he ran to the non-striker's end. Wilson was flattened and had to have treatment and a concussion check.

Reaching three figures freed up Roy. He then went on the attack. His next fifty came off only 28 balls, including four sixes and two fours. Shakib was brought back to stem the runs, but by then Roy was back to his strutting best. He hit Shakib for 16 in five balls, dancing down the pitch twice to hit him over the top for consecutive straight sixes. By the end of his innings, Roy had scored 68 runs against spin, at a strike rate of 151.

He walloped Mehidy for three consecutive sixes and was suddenly eyeing the chance for six in an over. He was not going to miss out on that. He tried to give the fourth the same treatment, but instead it looped up and he was caught at extra cover, ending the chance for a first double hundred by an England player in ODI cricket. There were still 15 overs to go. Roy could have faced another 50 balls and easily gone past 200 but had opted to go down taking the attack to Bangladesh.

'It was great to go out there and right our wrongs,' said Roy. 'Jonny and myself built the innings well. We did not know how the pitch would behave, so we sat in.'

England actually stuttered for a while after Roy's dismissal, but Buttler played a gem of an innings. He slapped 64 off 44 balls, including four sixes. But in hitting one six into the river, he injured his right hip. He had been hit on the bone batting against Pakistan earlier in the week, and when he extended himself trying to hit down the ground, he felt something go. He needed lengthy treatment on the field and was unable to keep wicket later in the day. It was a remarkable shot, a straight six hit off the back foot with huge power, and it was no wonder it took a toll as he swivelled his body with such force. Plunkett blasted 27 from nine balls and Chris Woakes played a nice cameo, making 18 as England added 45 off 17 deliveries at the end to lift their total way beyond Bangladesh's reach.

'Today that opening stand really did lay a solid platform,' said Morgan after the game. 'I don't think it was that easy up front. I don't think the ball came on to bat a lot. The first four or five overs proved that; we didn't really go anywhere. We were trying to score runs, but we didn't go anywhere. I thought Jason and Jonny were outstanding. They assessed the conditions well. They waited for the bad ball, waited for themselves to impose themselves in the innings, and 128 is a considerable standard.

'To be honest, it's a luxury [having Roy in the team]. People in general talk about scoring hundreds. He's an exception to the rule that just goes on and gets big scores, and it can range from 140 or 180, and the rate he gets it at, he's just so difficult to defend against.

'He scores all the way around the ground. He takes really good bowlers down as well. He hits good balls for boundaries. So, he's great to have in the side, particularly when he's in this form. If you look at the guy as he's matured from a county cricketer into the full-blown international cricketer he is now, the temperament he shows at different stages of his innings and how he goes about picking off his boundaries and the areas in which he scores – I think from the start of his international cricket [career] to right now, I think there's a considerable difference.'

This was an important innings for Roy for another reason. His patience was timely with the Ashes looming. Trevor Bayliss had long thought he could be a Test batsman but had been unable to persuade other selectors to back him. 'If Jason continues to play the way he is, the Ashes are within his reach,' Farbrace said. 'He has developed his game. He has matured as a person and a player. He's capable of playing Test cricket.' And Roy would play in the Ashes after making his Test debut against Ireland a few days after the World Cup final, but lasted only four matches against Australia before he was dropped.

Despite his miserly start, Shakib in the end conceded 71 runs, and Bangladesh only bowled 22 overs of spin – not enough against England. Beating them with seam was never going to work.

England, by contrast, had firepower in their pace bowling

and went after Bangladesh. Mark Wood and Jofra Archer both reached speeds of 95mph, and all five of England's seamers were a handful. Woakes conceded 64 but bowled mostly into the wind, so allowances had to be made. Plunkett too had to dig deep and run into the gale for eight overs, leaving the 'young' quicks, as he called Wood and Archer, the luxury of bowling with the breeze behind their backs.

'Morgs asked me if I was all right with it, but I said: "I'm not sure I've got a choice but thanks for thinking about me,"' said Plunkett. 'It was swirling, but I felt in rhythm and that I did a good job bowling my eight overs into the wind.'

Shakib played wonderfully in making 121 off 119 balls, taking on the quick bowlers and hitting Rashid for 31 off 25 balls, but despite stands of 55 with Tamim, 106 with Mushfiqur Rahim and 49 with Mahmudullah, Bangladesh never really looked like pulling off a stunning run chase.

Archer bowled Soumya Sarkar with a beauty that nipped off the seam and crashed into the top of off stump in the fourth over. Tamim was uncomfortable as England roughed him up with the bouncer and was out in the 12th over trying to be aggressive to relieve the pressure, top-edging a pull off Wood to extra cover.

Mushfiqur and Shakib brought all their experience to bear by steadying the innings, but with the run rate climbing they were simply delaying the inevitable. Mushfiqur did not pick a cross-seamer from Plunkett and was caught off a leading edge by Roy at point off the last ball of the 28th over.

Four balls later Mohammad Mithun had a big heave at Rashid and was well caught by Bairstow, keeping for the only time in the World Cup. When a Ben Stokes yorker bowled Shakib off his toe, it was all over for Bangladesh. They only had their net run rate to play for, knowing that it could be important if places for the last four became closely fought in the latter part of the group stage.

It was left to Archer and Stokes to wrap it up for England. Archer had Mehidy caught behind and finished the game off with a nasty bouncer to last man Mustafizur Rahman, who fended at it in self-preservation mode but only looped up a catch to Bairstow.

Job done. Equilibrium restored. England could now enjoy two days off before starting preparations for the game against West Indies in Southampton, and without having to think about bouncing back or restoring pride. At the Rose Bowl, Roy would again be the centre of attention, but this time for a different, more worrying, reason.

EIGHT
ROOT, THE WALKING GLUESTICK

GAME FOUR –
ENGLAND V. WEST INDIES

ROSE BOWL, SOUTHAMPTON

14 June 2019

I n the four years between World Cups, Eoin Morgan had become a skilled press-conference operator. He had learnt how to find that happy balance between being honest whilst recognising there are always things that have to be kept within the confines of the dressing room, and remaining chipper, measured and interesting in his responses even when the questions so obviously tested those qualities. But it was still a surprise when he volunteered a snippet of news before England's match against West Indies at Southampton.

The weather had been poor in the build-up, and on the day before the match England practised in the indoor school on the first floor above the atrium of the Rod Bransgrove pavilion. The indoor school is also where the press confer-ences take place, so there was a lengthy wait outside for the press, with even one of the England coaches bemoaning the fact that the players were practising for so long on the indoor surface.

When Morgan did speak, he revealed that fast bowler Mark Wood was struggling with his ongoing ankle problems. Wood had bowled quickly against Bangladesh in Cardiff five days earlier but had been unable to test his left ankle since, and given that he had already had three operations on the joint – and had only bowled 31.1 overs in the season at that point – some caution was justified.

The initial questions had been about Jos Buttler, who had hurt a hip in the Bangladesh match (but was fully recovered and was again seen on the outfield practising his wicket-keeping in the rain), and Moeen Ali, who had not been selected for Cardiff but had left the camp to be with his wife Firuza, who was about to give birth. 'Mo's wife gave birth to a baby girl, all healthy and well, so it's great to see him back,' announced Morgan.

But then the captain said: 'Mark Wood is going to have a fitness test in the morning. Nothing too serious. It's just he pulled up a little bit sore after the game in Cardiff, so he is the only concern at the moment.

'We haven't bowled for a few days, so it depends how he feels when he bowls. If it's still sore, we probably won't take a risk. It's just soreness, not an injury. But, with all fast bowl-ers, you have to manage them throughout the tournament. We've seen how valuable fast bowlers have been.

'I'm not worried. I'm quite positive about it. If he doesn't play, it's not a big worry. We'll have to rest other guys and manage him the same as Pudsey [Liam Plunkett], [Chris] Woakes and [Jofra] Archer.'

But it was a bit of a worry, and just the fact that this conversation was taking place at all was a reminder of how, sadly, Southampton became synonymous with injury that summer. For it had been here in a warm-up match against Australia, which England had lost, that Wood had left the field after bowling just 3.1 overs. It had been the same ankle problem, and he was sent for a scan. 'Wood's World Cup over' was not what anyone wanted to write, but it would be wrong to say that it wasn't mentioned or considered.

Thankfully, the results of that scan were fine. However, it was in the same match that Liam Dawson, the reserve spinner, had gashed the ring finger of his right (non-bowling) hand, and Jason Roy had been hit on the arm when fielding and on the hand when batting. Roy was administered painkillers while still on the field, and England were lucky that it was not an 11-a-side match, as players were permitted to go on and off.

Once the match started here in the tournament proper, they suffered two much more worrying injuries. First, Roy tweaked a hamstring in the eighth over of the match, chasing back to retrieve a Chris Gayle slap over cover and pulling up immediately, clutching at the back of his left leg. He left the field and took no further part in the game. It was concerning, because Roy had been struggling with injuries in the build-up to the competition. He had missed seven weeks with a hamstring injury at the end of the winter tour of the Caribbean and then missed a further few weeks at the start of the English season with a back complaint. He had also missed England's one-off ODI against Ireland, a T20 against Pakistan and then the first ODI of the warm-up series against the same opponents.

Then in the 40th over of West Indies' innings Morgan's back seized up as he moved to back up a throw at the bowler's end. He was in obvious discomfort, and he too left the field gingerly, taking no further part in the match. He had to do his post-match press conference standing up, with his back still in spasm.

'When any two players go down, it's a worry, but we're not at panic stations,' Morgan said. 'We'll do a risk assessment before the Afghanistan game [which was four days later]. I have had back spasms before, and this is another. It takes a few days to settle down. It's unclear [how bad it is].'

England had been unchanged from the Bangladesh match in Cardiff, meaning Mark Wood did play after all, which would not have pleased England's opponents. Wood, having lengthened his run-up before Christmas, had terrorised them during the winter tour of the Caribbean. He had bowled a spell in the third Test in St Lucia in which his speed had peaked at 94.6mph. He was so rapid that Scyld Berry, the *Telegraph's* cricket correspondent and the old sage of the press box, had reckoned it to be the fastest he had ever seen by an England bowler.

'It cannot be ranked the greatest spell of fast bowling ever for England – because the series had been lost – but Mark Wood's spell before tea on the second afternoon of the third Test was probably the fastest,' wrote Berry.

It was certainly fast, and that was certainly some claim by Berry, even if it took Jofra Archer just one Test at Lord's against Australia to bowl even faster, bowling the fastest over by an England bowler (an average of 92.79mph) and the swiftest ball (96.1mph) on debut.

Wood was England's leading wicket-taker across all formats on that Caribbean tour, taking 16 wickets at 19 apiece, and he was now, even with the emergence of Archer, considered invaluable in the ODI side.

It had not been so earlier that winter in Sri Lanka when he

was a peripheral presence, a far cry from the 2017 Champions Trophy when he had been Eoin Morgan's go-to bowler whenever England were in need of a big wicket. Wood was even sent on a Lions tour of the UAE to sort himself out. 'By the time of Sri Lanka, I was probably the guy [in the ODI squad] with the target on my back,' Wood told the *Sunday Times*. 'I had to step up and perform. Trevor [Bayliss] challenged me to show some toughness, and I felt I did that. I bowled well, in unfriendly fast-bowling conditions, against a good Pakistan A side.

'I was away from the spotlight, there weren't cameras judging my every delivery and I got into a groove. I worked hard on my run-up. After I got back from Sri Lanka, I'd been down in the dumps, but Kevin Shine [the ECB's lead fast-bowling coach] got me to love the game again. I was having fun, trying new tricks. It was like when I first got into the England side, almost carefree. That led to the good performances in the West Indies.'

Wood had not actually been selected for that Caribbean tour but was summoned when Warwickshire's Olly Stone was sent home with a stress fracture of the lower back. And Wood took his chance. 'I was in a good place,' he said. 'I'd got married in December and had time off. There was the adrenalin of being back in the side. I was happy with what I produced. Off the back of the Test and the ODIs, I felt like a proper England player. The West Indies was great timing in terms of my career.'

It certainly was. England needed him back at his best, and the squad would certainly not be unhappy with his jovial presence. He might be from the same Northumberland town, Ashington, as former England bowler Steve Harmison, but they are very different fast bowlers. Harmison was tall, lithe and bouncy; Wood is short, whippy and skiddy.

As a character, Wood is a bit of a one-off, a smiling presence who is always a pleasure for the press to deal with. This is a man who even has his own imaginary horse. 'I tend to be a bit of a joker on the field,' Wood told the *Guardian* before his England debut in 2015. 'There are times when it gets boring in the field, so I bring out the imaginary horse and try to joust my team-mates. I don't know how the England boys will take it, but I'll have a go. I like to have a trot and feed him apples – he loves Granny Smiths.'

A Labour supporter, Wood once delivered election leaflets for the local MP, Ian Lavery, and he is a lifelong teetotaller, making him the designated driver whenever the England lads want a night out.

Goodness knows what Archer made of him at first, but Archer's arrival certainly did not send Wood into his speed shell. Instead he simply relished the competition to be the quickest of the pair. Both had already been clocked above 95mph in the competition at this stage, with Wood reaching 95.7mph in that victory over Bangladesh in Cardiff.

'It pushes us for sure,' said Wood. 'It is friendly competition, but with a point to it. You're pushing each other to be the best you can be and to be as quick as you can be. You have banter about it, but you're helping each other. I'm trying to bowl 0.1mph quicker than Jofra and he's trying to bowl 0.1mph faster than me.

'When you come off and the analyst says: "Jofra was quicker today," and you think: "Right, I've got to put the throttle down here," and then the next time he says: "You were quickest," you get a little buzz.

'All the while, though, I'm thinking: "But Jofra's just flicking his wrist, and it is coming out like a rocket." There might be a bit more in the tank if he really wants it. He's just toying with me at the minute. I have to nearly break my back to get it as fast as him.'

This was the first time that the Barbados-born Archer would play against the side that he could have represented. Dublin-born Morgan, having played against Ireland, knew all about that. 'I think it is a moment where you reaffirm your decision,' he said. 'Leading into the game, there is a different feel until you get out there. He won't know how it feels until he plays the game. Being in that position myself, it does feel very different playing against a side you could potentially have played for.'

Just as there had been before the match against Pakistan at Trent Bridge, there was much talk about pace, and even a question put to West Indies captain Jason Holder about the large size of the West Indian team. Holder joked that it was not going to be a fist fight.

But for England it did look as if it might be a serious test. Their ODI series in the Caribbean had been drawn 2–2 (with one no result) after England were bundled out for 113 in the final match on a bouncy pitch in St Lucia, with Oshane Thomas taking five for 21.

'From the first game they played in this tournament [against Pakistan], back through the games we played in the winter, the big games where they made big contributions all had to do with their fast bowlers,' said Morgan. 'Their seamers are taller, hit-the-deck bowlers. They offer a different challenge.'

And, of course, with the ball there was the challenge of facing the 39-year-old Chris Gayle in probably his last international appearance against England. He had averaged 106 against them in the ODI series that winter, even though he had often taken time to get going. 'We have looked at previous series where we've played at home and plans that have

155

worked, and also recently in the Caribbean on flat wickets where he's hard to contain,' Morgan said. 'We've planned for that as well. In the West Indies, he played extremely well, but for a long part of his innings he didn't go at more than a run a ball. When guys are doing that, it's not necessarily hurting you as a team.

'So, it's important to stay engaged with the scoreboard – when he hits three sixes in a row. It might not feel like it, with the crowd going bananas, but you look at the scoreboard and think: "Does it reflect the game?"'

With all the rain that had fallen before the match, it was a good toss to win, and Morgan had no hesitation in inserting West Indies. Chris Woakes was again quite superb with the new ball, bowling two maidens in his initial five-over spell that only cost 16 runs and included the wicket of the left-handed opener Evin Lewis, bowled by a yorker.

But West Indies' innings was always going to be about Gayle, and he always rather likes that. Gayle again made a slow start, with his side having made just eight for one from five overs. In the fourth over Archer had bowled a quick bouncer (91mph) that had flown over his right shoulder, bringing an instinctive flinch from the mighty left-hander, whose attempted pull shot two balls later so nearly brought his demise, the ball flying down to the fine-leg boundary off an inside edge.

In the sixth over Gayle decided it was time to take on Archer, hitting him for two consecutive fours. The new England paceman, showing no nerves whatsoever in facing his countrymen, responded by rapping Gayle on the gloves with a quick short ball. It was certainly an absorbing contest.

Woakes really ought to have dismissed Gayle in the seventh over, when an attempted heave to the leg side flew down to third man, where Mark Wood dropped the catch diving forward. Woakes is good-natured and not exactly given to histrionics, but he was upset. Wood's brave effort was actually admirable, but he had moved for the ball too late. It seemed a big moment.

In Woakes's next over, Gayle slapped a short ball for four over mid-on and then waited for the response of a fuller-length ball and duly slotted it into the stand at long-on for six. West Indies were 38 for one after nine overs, and Gayle had scored 32 of them. This truly was just about Gayle.

But he had only made four more when he pulled a short ball from Liam Plunkett to Jonny Bairstow at deep square leg. Plunkett had confirmed his reputation for taking the big wickets, and had done so with his trusty method of banging the ball into the pitch in the middle overs, aided here by Southampton's long square boundaries.

Shai Hope, the no. 3, was the ideal example of how the other West Indian batsmen struggled once Gayle was gone. He just could not get going. His 11 runs took 30 balls before he was trapped leg-before by Wood. It needed a review, but it was plumb.

Wood's first spell of four overs cost only six runs before Nicholas Pooran and Shimron Hetmyer, the two exciting left-handers, put on 89. Pooran looked the more certain of the two, with Hetmyer often not getting the reward his big shots demanded before he succumbed, caught-and-bowled, to Joe Root's off spin.

It was the start of a rather satisfying day for Root. It was his first ODI wicket since January 2018. With leg spinner Adil Rashid still not quite at his best, having conceded 61 in his ten wicketless overs, one could see why Eoin Morgan decided to call on him.

Root soon had a second wicket, from another return catch, this time from a knuckle ball in rather farcical circumstances, as the ball would have been deemed a wide down the leg side had Jason Holder not used his long arms to reach it and get a leading edge that gently lobbed back to Root.

'I've just been trying some things, as you do when you don't have the skills some of the others have,' Root said afterwards. 'It's a work in progress – there were five wides as well.'

Root celebrated that second wicket with a double-finger-wagging, hip-swaying jig that was a tribute to Ian Botham's antics in the 1992 World Cup, when England had reached the final in Melbourne. Root was only 15 months old then, but the England squad had been watching reruns of that tournament during rain breaks in the Pakistan warm-up ODI series earlier in the season, and Root and Chris Woakes had decided they were going to try the celebration at some stage.

And they did try it, with Woakes first doing so when Root took a catch off his bowling in the Pakistan series at Headingley. And now Root decided to try it as well. 'I had to make a bit of an idiot of myself,' said Root with a laugh. He did not, however, take another wicket in the tournament, bowling just more six overs to add to the five he bowled here.

West Indies, disappointingly, had little else to offer. Andre Russell made 21 from no. 7, merrily slogging a few before being dropped by Woakes and then hitting Wood to the same fielder out in the deep on the leg side.

Pooran needed some support, but his excellent innings of 63 off 78 balls was ended when trying to avoid a nasty short ball from Archer. He only succeeded in gloving the ball through to wicketkeeper Jos Buttler.

Archer and Wood were both superb at the end of the West Indian innings, claiming three wickets each in total, with Archer finishing with three for 30 in his nine overs, including a maiden, and Wood trotting off with the remarkable figures of 6.4-0-18-3. There were still five overs and two balls to be bowled in the innings when West Indies were all out for 212.

Root opened instead of Jason Roy, and, in truth, it was a stroll to victory with 16.5 overs remaining, with Root making a masterful unbeaten century that took him to the top of the tournament's run-scoring chart at the time, with 279. That is a serious thrashing in an ODI, and it really was that one-sided.

West Indies clearly thought they could bomb England out with the short stuff from their quicker bowlers, but that appeared to be their only plan. They just bowled either short or full, which Jonny Bairstow and Root feasted upon. They both cut, pulled and drove with ease. A couple of Root's cover drives to the boundary were simply beautiful, and an on-drive off Oshane Thomas by Bairstow was emphatically powerful.

The running between the wickets was sharp as well. These two Yorkshiremen have always had a good understanding in that regard. Bairstow is lightning fast, and while Root would never claim to be that, he possesses excellent instinct and anticipation. They make it look easy.

After ten overs and the first powerplay, England were 62 without loss, compared with West Indies' 41 for one at the same stage. Even without Roy, it was another fine start by England, the fourth time in four matches that they had passed 60 in the powerplay.

'It was just nice to get some batting in the powerplay, to be honest,' said Root. 'It was nice to have the fielders up and hit some good shots. There's not much difference to playing at three, and you just try to play the situation.'

Here was confirmation again of how good England had become in those first ten overs when only two fielders are permitted outside the fielding circle. Power and decision-making are key.

James Vince, England's reserve opener in the tournament, was asked at the start of the summer if the England team set any targets in that period, something it turned out he'd spoken to Morgan about when he was summoned to open against Ireland in Dublin in May. 'I did actually chat to Morgs in Ireland about our approach and whether there are set targets,' Vince said. 'There's not too much science about it. At the top, it's our job to assess conditions, and if we think it's a good wicket, [we have] to play with freedom and take the game forward – to be brave. That's pretty much the message.'

Bairstow had a horrible moment on 27 when he was hit by an Andre Russell bouncer. Both men, the batsman and the bowler, fell to the ground. Russell did not look fit all the time he was on the field, and this delivery appeared to have exacerbated a knee problem so that he hobbled from the field.

Bairstow underwent and passed the mandatory concussion test, but was eventually out to a short ball, attempting to uppercut Shannon Gabriel but only finding third man. He was gone for 45. With Roy and Morgan injured, England decided to promote Chris Woakes to no. 3, and West Indies continued with their short stuff, posting a short leg immediately. Even if he had never previously batted above no. 7 in an ODI, Woakes made a neat 40 off 54 balls, before being dismissed with 14 required for victory.

But Root was still there at the end, undefeated on exactly 100 from 94 balls. It was his 16th ODI century, his second of the tournament. 'Joe is the glue that holds everything together,' said Morgan. 'He's such an important player for us. It's exceptional to watch.'

Root was so often described as the glue of England's batting in this tournament that he should have been sponsored by Bostik. But it was true. Root was the player who often held England together. In days gone by, he would have been described as an anchorman, but he is more than that. He scores a lot more quickly than an anchorman might. Yes, he is first and foremost a Test-match batsman. The longer game is his more natural habitat. That is the format for which he will doubtless be remembered most. But Root has kept pace with the modern one-day game.

'I think Joe is probably the most complete batsman I've ever played with,' said Stuart Broad. 'He is a brilliant team man in the way he plays, but he's got every tempo and every shot in the book.'

It might be a surprise to some to learn that Root's strike rate in ODIs (87.37 at the end of the World Cup – he had ticked along at 89.53 in the tournament itself) is higher than Kevin Pietersen's (86.58) was during his career. It is also higher than that of Marcus Trescothick (85.21), who was for so long deemed the doyen of England ODI dashers.

Comparisons can be harsh, of course, because the ODI game has altered so much in recent years. Bats are definitely bigger these days, while boundaries are often smaller, and the shots played, because of Twenty20's influence, are of a range previously unconsidered. Range-hitting, for example, is now a crucial component of most practice sessions. But at the end of the tournament, Root's ODI average was 51.36, which meant that he counted as one of only nine players – including England's Jonathan Trott – to average 50 or more in the format from a minimum of 20 innings. Of those who played in the 2019 tournament, India's Virat Kohli and M.S. Dhoni, and the Pakistan pair of Babar Azam and Imam-ul-Haq were also on that list.

Root has also scored more ODI centuries than any other England player. For so long Trescothick had held that record with 12. He played his final ODI in 2006, and it was not until 2018 that Root passed him. At the end of the World Cup, Root's 16 hundreds placed him equal 22nd in the all-time list in this format (New Zealand's Martin Guptill had 16 too, as did his compatriot Nathan Astle and Australia's Adam Gilchrist).

England now score a lot of ODI centuries. In the 2019 World Cup they eventually scored seven, a tally equalled by India (Rohit Sharma getting five of them). Australia scored five, Bangladesh three, and each of Sri Lanka, New Zealand, West Indies and Pakistan scored two. The crucial statistic here is that in the previous 11 World Cups, England had scored a grand total of 11 centuries. The most they had scored in one tournament was two (on four occasions, in 1975, 1983, 2007 and 2015).

The England team under Eoin Morgan and Trevor Bayliss apparently never talked about scoring ODI centuries at all. The subject was never openly discussed, because it would not have fitted in with the idea of selflessness established by their team philosophy. Sauntering to a milestone while ignoring the team's greater needs would clearly not be looked upon kindly.

So, the increase in the number of ODI centuries was simply a natural spin-off of the team's more aggressive approach and some very good players executing it.

There has often been talk about Root's place in England's Twenty20 international team, and indeed he was dropped from that side – much to his chagrin – for a match against India in 2018. He could not find a deal at an IPL franchise either, even though he badly wanted one, and when he went to the Big Bash in Australia, he hardly set the tournament alight. But the truth is that he has not played that much Twenty20 cricket. When he does so regularly, he still does it rather well. Just witness his innings of 83 from just 44 balls to win the game for England against South Africa in the World T20 in 2016.

'It was as good a T20 innings as we have seen in the last few years,' said assistant coach Paul Farbrace in 2018 when the subject of Root's T20 place came up. Root also made a rather useful 90 not out from 49 balls on Twenty20 international debut against Australia in 2013, from no. 5, even if he was already in an impossible situation, as England found themselves struggling in the face of Aaron Finch's then world-record score of 156.

It is said that the best players are simply the best players in any format, and Root is living proof of that. As the former England captain Michael Vaughan said to any young players listening to BBC *Test Match Special* during this match: 'I'd advise them to copy Joe Root. That's the kind of cricketer you want to be.'

It is sound advice. A DVD copy of Root's century here would enhance any young player's learning. Root played that well.

NINE
MORGAN SENSES HIS DESTINY

GAME FIVE –
ENGLAND V. AFGHANISTAN

OLD TRAFFORD, MANCHESTER

18 June 2019

How long would Jason Roy be out for? Indeed, would he play again in the World Cup? Those were the questions being asked during the preamble to England's next match, against Afghanistan at Old Trafford. All England would say officially was that he was out of this match and the one three days later, against Sri Lanka at Headingley. 'I certainly believe Jason will play again in this tournament. If not Australia [on 25 June], maybe the following game [against India on 30 June],' said Eoin Morgan.

But it was telling that England did not reveal the severity of the hamstring tear that Roy had suffered against West Indies at Southampton. There are three grades for this type of injury. A grade-one tear is just a mild pull that might mean as little as one week out of action. Grade two is a partial tear, where the recovery time might be somewhere between two and six weeks. A grade three is a complete tear, which is a much more serious injury and could even require an operation.

England very deliberately did not reveal which grade this was, and Morgan faced a tricky situation when pushed on this issue at the press conference. He said that he had seen the report on Roy's injury, but he had not noticed the number associated with it. 'I've looked at it, but it doesn't register a lot with me,' he said. 'It's how long is he going to be out for and how optimistic can we be? Jason is going to be assessed continuously over the course of the next week. It's a matter of giving him enough time to allow him to get himself back into the tournament. He's obviously a huge part of what we've been doing. He's in the best form of his life.'

It transpired that Roy had suffered a grade-two hamstring tear, and that the England medical staff were seriously concerned that he might be out for four weeks and would not be able to play any further part in the group stages. Had that been the case, England might never have won the World Cup.

Roy, whilst obviously worried, was adamant that he would be fine. And he did indeed make that India match on 30 June. But England were already discussing potential replacements. They were, of course, willing to give Roy as long as possible – replacements could only be summoned once a player was ruled out of the rest of the tournament – but plans needed to be in place.

This was where the name of Alex Hales was raised again. He was the ideal batsman, but he had of course been axed from the squad for failing a second drugs test. He had also not played any cricket recently. The match against Afghanistan was on 18 June. His last match had been on 12 May.

Morgan said that potential replacement players had been considered at the time of the original squad selection, but that none had been considered at this point. He told the BBC that if national selector Ed Smith came to him and Trevor Bayliss suggesting Hales was the best option, then they would have to weigh up the 'stigma' of such a selection.

The use of the word 'stigma' was pretty damning, but in general England were being careful what they said. When asked whether Hales was eligible for selection, they replied that he was. The truth was that Hales was never going to be considered. The two players in the frame were Kent's Joe Denly, who had been in the 15-man provisional World Cup squad before being replaced by Hampshire's Liam Dawson, and Middlesex's Dawid Malan.

The good news, though, for England was that captain Morgan was fit after his back spasm. 'I'm drastically improved,' he said. 'I've had extensive treatment and medication the last two days, which has helped me no end.' The ECB had arranged for a driver to take him back from Southampton to his house in Primrose Hill, London, and he lay flat all the way home. Rest and a lot of anti-inflammatory drugs had worked their magic.

England had only played one official ODI against Afghanistan before, in the 2015 World Cup in Sydney, winning by nine wickets, but that was a miserable day, the denouement of their torrid tournament. They had also met in the second of England's warm-up matches before this competition, with England again winning by nine wickets as Jason Roy smashed 89 not out from 46 balls.

'It's good luck for us Jason Roy is not playing,' Gulbadin Naib, Afghanistan's captain, said before this match. Maybe it was, but instead they were gunned down by Morgan, who played one of the most remarkable innings the ODI game has ever seen. He made 148 with a world-record 17 sixes.

As Mike Atherton wrote in *The Times*: 'There comes a point in a player's career when he recognises the moment and senses his destiny. For Eoin Morgan, that time has come.'

Indeed it had. From an early age Morgan had wanted to play for England. That was obviously not the case with too many of the other Irish boys growing up on the humble housing estate in the small town of Rush, 20 miles up the Fingal coast from Dublin, but Morgan was different.

'Any comments you would get would be around, "Why are you playing a British sport?" It didn't bother me at the time, but it is wrong when you look back at it, completely wrong,' Morgan told the ECB website in a revealing documentary when he returned home to Rush in 2018.

Morgan also recalled how the Dublin number plate on his father's car would make him uncomfortable when they drove north for junior cricket tournaments. 'A lot of our age-group inter-provincial cricket was played up north in the first 12 days of the marching season,' he said. 'This was around the time of the Troubles, with a hard border. It was actually very similar to touring the sub-continent at the moment, with a lot of army and police around, but being in situations you couldn't control as a kid is quite scary.

'If you find yourself going into the wrong area, people turn your car upside down and just burn it. So, experiences of that and people associating cricket with being a British sport always makes me think about travelling up to the north in the middle of the summer.'

Ireland were not a Test nation then, as they now are, and Morgan knew England represented his route to the top in the game he loved. Of course, he played for Ireland, 63 times in all between the ages of 16 and 22, including a World Cup in 2007. And things could have of course been very different. 'People who don't know anything about cricket have a go at him, but at the time England was the only career path open to him,' Matt Sheridan, the former president of Rush CC, told *The Times*. 'If he'd been born ten years later, he might still be playing for Ireland, now we're a Test nation, but that just wasn't to be.'

Morgan just did not want to be another sad Irish story. 'In a community there is always a story within the town or village where people haven't quite made it, there is always an excuse,' he said. 'If I was going to be good or make the most of my potential, I wasn't going to be able to do that in Ireland.

'My first year at secondary school, my dad and I met with the new Cricket Ireland coach at the time, Adi Birrell. We said that I wanted to play Test-match cricket. I was meeting with the head coach, and I wasn't even close to playing for the senior team. My dad spoke for both of us and said we were keeping them in the loop so that it wasn't a surprise further down the line. The national coach was shocked. He couldn't believe it.'

Morgan knew where he was going.

'I first heard of him when he was ten or 11. He was already making waves at that stage,' said Kenny Carroll, who played alongside Morgan at that 2007 World Cup. 'He never hid the fact that he wanted to play for England from an early age. He was over there playing in the school holidays from age 14. Everyone is free to make their own choices.'

Morgan's decision when he won the toss against Afghanistan was to bat first. But it was not an especially easy pitch on which to bat. Afghanistan opened with the mystery spin of Mujeeb ur Rahman, and his initial six overs went for only 18.

168

Rock bottom: Eoin Morgan trudges off as England lose their opening match of the 2015 World Cup to Australia and soon feared he could be sacked after his side crashed out in the first round.

Wise choice: Director of cricket Andrew Strauss (left) appointed Trevor Bayliss as England coach based on his record of one-day success around the world.

Cleared: Ben Stokes leaves Bristol Crown Court after he was found not guilty of affray but the incident led to a review of the team's culture.

You cannot do that: Stokes celebrates his wonder catch on the boundary in the opening game of the World Cup as England beat South Africa.

Banished: Alex Hales is a fine opening batsman but was axed by Morgan for letting down his teammates when he was suspended by the ECB for failing a second drugs test.

In vain: Jos Buttler celebrates his hundred against Pakistan at Trent Bridge but England lost a bad tempered match.

Bounce back: Mark Wood shows what a key player he would become as he bowls England to victory in the win over Bangladesh in Cardiff.

Carnage: Eoin Morgan smashed a world record 17 sixes as England demolished Afghanistan at Old Trafford.

On the brink: Lasith Malinga rolled back the years with some devastating yorkers as England lost to Sri Lanka at Headingley to put their World Cup hopes on the line.

Proving a point: Jonny Bairstow hits back at his critics with a brilliant hundred against India to put England back on track.

Take that: Jofra Archer cuts Alex Carey's face with a bouncer as England demolish Australia to reach the World Cup Final.

Sorry: Stokes apologises to New Zealand after his bat deflection goes to the boundary to give England a lucky six to keep their run chase hopes alive.

Sweet spot: Jimmy Neesham hits Jofra Archer for six in the Super Over to put New Zealand in control.

Heroes: Stokes gives Archer advice before he bowls the Super Over that won the World Cup.

All over: Buttler runs out Martin Guptill to win the World Cup off the final ball of the Super Over in front of a jubilant Lord's.

Champions: Eoin Morgan lifts the 2019 Cricket World Cup trophy on a gloriously sunny evening at Lord's.

Jonny Bairstow played cleverly during this period. In the opening powerplay, England had reached only 46 for one, their lowest score at that stage in this tournament, and their lowest score since they had been 34 for four after ten overs against Australia on the same ground a year earlier.

James Vince had been the man to go. In Roy's absence, this match had represented a huge opportunity for him. But he made just 26 from 31 balls, top-edging via his helmet to short fine leg. It was a classic Vince middling score, the type that is so annoying because he rarely looks uncomfortable at the crease.

He was out here attempting to pull off the front foot, which some great players have done well – Sir Vivian Richards and Ricky Ponting, to name a couple. But doing so has become a very modern trend, with batsmen using the power-hitting position to launch their versions of the front-foot pull, oblivious to the benefits of going back in the crease and giving themselves more time and a greater chance of coping with the bounce of a short ball.

Bairstow was not going to throw it away like that. He was waiting for his moment. When he passed fifty, it was the slowest (61 balls) of his ODI half-centuries as an opener. But he accelerated excellently from that point on, hitting the spinners extremely powerfully, eventually making 90 from 99 balls before being caught and bowled by Gulbadin Naib. When he was dismissed, England were 164 for two in the 30th over and now looking to increase the tempo.

There had been some consideration given to promoting Jos Buttler up the order – with time starting to run out and a lot of wickets in hand, it seemed an ideal scenario for him, especially given the fitness clouds over Morgan leading into the game – but out walked the captain to join Joe Root, who was just cruising along with 45 from 49 balls.

England's ambitions at this stage were not that lofty. 'When I came in, I thought we were on target for about 280, 290, maybe 300 – it was quite cagey,' Morgan said afterwards. 'The wicket was a little bit tacky, and we were always talking about getting a late 200s score.'

Then an incident in the 32nd over of the innings changed everything. It seemed innocuous at the time, but it would have huge repercussions for Afghanistan. It was a no ball from their captain Gulbadin Naib.

Morgan had faced six balls and scored just one run at this stage. He did not score from the no ball either, but now he had a free hit. It was a horrible slower-ball long-hop that simply demanded to be hit. And hit it Morgan did, smashing it for six over deep square leg. He was up and running. The next ball he hit for six too, this time over long-on.

Batsmen often talk about one shot changing an innings, even one stroke reversing a slump in form. This was certainly an example of where an innings was altered quite dramatically by one moment. Quite often free hits do not yield a boundary – the bowler knows what to expect, and the batsman swings too hard – but this was very different.

It was the start of a quite extraordinary innings from Morgan. By the time he had finished with the thoroughly dispirited Afghan bowlers, he had made his 148 from just 71 balls, his career-best ODI score (his previous best had been 124 not out, ironically for England against Ireland in Dublin in 2013).

Leg spinner Rashid Khan suffered the most, returning the worst figures in a World Cup match, conceding 110 from his nine overs, but Morgan did play him exceptionally well, always appearing to pick his variations and being savagely severe on anything short. Morgan faced 20 balls from Rashid and scored 58 runs, hitting seven sixes. In Rashid's seventh over, the captain hit three sixes, with the last of them, his 11th of the innings, taking him past 100 off 57 balls. It was his 13th ODI century, and it goes without saying that it became England's fastest World Cup century, beating Jos Buttler's effort earlier in the tournament.

By the end of the tournament, it was still the fourth-fastest century in a World Cup. Another Irishman, Kevin O'Brien, stands at the top of that list, having passed the milestone off just 50 balls against England in 2011.

It would be easy to say that Root was a mere bystander here, but he actually made 88 from 82 balls, even hitting a six too when lofting Rashid over long-on, as well as switch-sweeping Nabi for four. Root had put on 120 with Bairstow, and now with Morgan he put on 189, which was their 12th hundred partnership since the 2015 World Cup – the most of any pairing.

Root had passed his fifty – off 54 balls with just two fours, his fourth such score in five games in the tournament – when on 28 Morgan had a slice of fortune, dropped at deep square leg by Dawlat Zadran off Rashid. The fielder completely misjudged the flight of the ball and it flew over his head. It went for four, and Morgan responded by hitting two sixes in an over that went for 18.

Talk about another costly mistake. During the drinks break at the end of that over, Dawlat offered an apology to Rashid. Little did he realise the magnitude of regret he should have been expressing.

Morgan brought up his fifty with a pulled six off Nabi – already his fifth six, off just 36 balls – and then he just destroyed the Afghanistan bowling. He hit Mujeeb ur Rahman for six in the next over, then Nabi for two sixes in the over after that. It was carnage.

Somewhere along the line, Afghanistan bowled 28 dot balls

at Morgan. It certainly did not seem that they had managed that many. Morgan hit 60 off his last 16 balls alone, and nine sixes in his last 19 balls, and Root made just 33 in their stand of 189. Root was out, caught at long-on, in the same over, the 47th of the innings, in which Morgan went too. The captain was caught at long-off the ball after he had passed the record number of sixes, held jointly by West Indies' Chris Gayle, India's Rohit Sharma and South Africa's A.B. de Villiers.

Gulbadin, who had taken the wicket, immediately shook Morgan's hand. He knew, as did everyone in the ground, with a standing ovation ensuing, that something truly special had just occurred.

You can point to the quality of the bowling, which might not always have been top-class, although it was an attack that included leg spinner Rashid Khan, who was then third in the ICC's ODI bowling rankings and was still ninth even after a modest World Cup, but it was an incredible display of sustained hitting.

As he departed, Morgan was a picture of satisfaction, smiling broadly as his poker face cracked for once, and the next man in, Ben Stokes, respectfully waited at the boundary edge for him. They punched gloves, and then Stokes joined Buttler, two of England's most devastating hitters of a cricket ball. They both smiled and shook their heads in disbelief at what they had just seen. Even they felt that they could not follow Morgan's incredible performance.

As Jonny Bairstow said on television when interviewed in between innings: 'It was a ridiculous knock. The striking was of the highest order. We were seriously entertained.'

Indeed, everyone in the ground was. Not bad for a player who had not even been totally certain of playing until the morning of the game. Yes, Morgan had said that he was playing the day before, but he still required a late fitness test, during which he did not exactly look like he was the most flexible man in the world.

Once he began batting, it was a very different story. This truly was an innings to remember, an innings that even surprised Morgan a little in its brutality and brevity. There had been a time when Morgan, with his sweeps, reverse sweeps and power hitting, had been the odd one out in England's batting line-up. Now everyone was at it, but this was a reminder of what Morgan could do too, that he could keep up with the new kids. 'I would never have thought I could play a knock like that. I'm delighted,' he said. 'It's something that I never thought I would do. It's a nice place to be, but the hundred I scored today [off 57 balls] is considered a slow one in our changing room. Guys talk about doing that all the time. It's a tough school.

'For the last four years, I've probably played the best in my career, but that hasn't involved a 50- or 60-ball hundred. I've scored one at Middlesex, so I thought I would have it in the locker. All the work over the last four years, over my career, it comes to the front now.'

The 17 sixes he hit was just one short of the number the whole England team managed in the tournament in 2015, when Morgan himself hit only three. 'It is weird, but that record will become a target for guys in the changing room to take down,' Morgan said.

It was yet another perfect illustration of the difference between England's World Cup campaigns in 2015 and 2019. Morgan had made just 90 runs in five innings in that tournament, averaging only 18 and making a duck in the match in which England were knocked out of the tournament by Bangladesh. At the end of the 2015 campaign, Morgan had said: 'I've absolutely no regrets.' He was in denial. Now he was in heaven.

In 2019, he scored more runs than in his other World Cup campaigns put together. He had averaged only 29 with a strike rate of 72 before this tournament. 'This is where it matters,' he said.

Morgan's hitting in this match was just so clean and crisp. It was classic power hitting of the modern era. He stands still in his stance at the crease, with his bat already raised, and then he does not make any great movements towards the ball. But his back-lift from his original position is high, as indeed is his grip on the bat, with his bat almost flipping over ahead of his hands before coming down. His hand speed is quick, and he uses his hips and body shape to generate great pace through the ball. Morgan's head position is also excellent, and his weight distribution into the ball is so sharp that he is able to strike the ball incredibly sweetly.

Some of his strikes down the ground can appear more like golf shots – with his bat coming down slightly across the line rather than straight – and while Jonny Bairstow mentioned this in his mid-match television interview – 'he has been striking them well on the golf course, and he has taken it out to the middle' – it was interesting that Morgan himself referenced golf afterwards. 'It's like hitting a golf ball off the tee,' he said. 'If you think it's going straight, you're the only person who knows at the time. It's a very special feeling.'

Morgan played Test cricket once upon a time, of course, between 2010 and 2012, and made two centuries in his 16 matches at a perfectly respectable average of 30.43, but he has always admitted that he was not quite good enough. 'I had my chance to play Test cricket,' he once told ESPNcricinfo. 'I played in a very good team, in a very good environment, under an exceptional captain in Andrew Strauss.

'I think a lot of people that come and go in Test-match

cricket and don't make the most of their opportunity some-times look back and wish that they could have been part of a better team or a more expansive or disciplined team. I think people find it hard to say they just weren't good enough, and I don't think I was.'

There were two good reasons for Morgan not cracking Test cricket: his defence was not quite adequate, and he always found the short ball from the quicker bowlers, as evidenced in this World Cup, a problem. But he had always worked on those areas of his game, and even when he had given up hope of more Test cricket he would try to fit in some first-class cricket for Middlesex around his IPL commitments, where possible, to work on his defensive technique for the early stages of his one-day innings.

He did not play a first-class game at all in 2016 or 2017, but in 2018 he managed six for Middlesex, and then in 2019 before the World Cup he played in three matches, two in the County Championship and a first-class match against Oxford MCCU. 'Red-ball cricket helps my technique,' he said. 'The most vulnerable part of your batting is the first 30 balls.'

He does cock his wrists in his pick-up, and that can often mean that it is difficult for him to slow his hands down when trying to defend. But as a ball striker, especially of spin bowl-ing, Morgan stands amongst the most destructive the game has seen.

Against Afghanistan, it was not the batting for which he initially made his name – all those sweeps and reverse sweeps, which might have come courtesy of a hurling back-ground, although he himself plays this down – but instead it was simply a display of violent hitting, mainly in an arc between long-off and mid-wicket. The sixes he hit were not ones that just cleared boundaries that had been brought in to increase the entertainment value, which does happen from time to time. Most of his sixes in this match sailed high over the ropes and into the stands.

Once Morgan was out, the game was already done. But there was more to come from England. Moeen Ali smote 31 in just nine balls, including four sixes, in England's total of 397 for six, their highest World Cup score. It remained the highest score in the 2019 World Cup and the sixth highest in the tournament's history.

England's previous record of 386 for six, made against Bangladesh in Cardiff, had lasted just ten days. The 25 sixes they hit in their innings was also a record for a one-day international, beating their own record of 24 from earlier in the year against West Indies in Grenada.

In reply, Afghanistan made their highest World Cup total of 247 for eight. It was not easy for England to be at their sharpest, given that the game was already won, and Jonny Bairstow uncharacteristically dropped two catches, one at slip and another at fine leg. The pace of Jofra Archer and Mark Wood, allied to the spin of Adil Rashid, was too much for the Afghans, as those three bowlers shared eight wickets and England won by 150 runs.

There was a nasty moment when Hashmatullah Shahidi was hit on the helmet by Wood. It was a sickening blow, but Shahidi was up quickly and went on to top-score for his side with 76. 'I got up early because of my mum,' he said afterwards. 'I lost my father last year, so I didn't want her to hurt. My whole family was watching, even my big brother was here in the ground watching. I didn't want them to be worried for me.'

It was certainly a day for the family, as Morgan was accompanied to the post-match press conference by his young nephew, Callum Walsh. Afterwards, Morgan sat him in the chair in which he had conducted his press duties and took a photo of him holding his uncle's man-of-the-match award. 'Share that with your brothers,' Morgan told him.

It had been Morgan's day.

TEN

CRASHING BACK DOWN TO EARTH

GAME SIX – ENGLAND V. SRI LANKA

HEADINGLEY, LEEDS

21 June 2019

As England prepared to play Sri Lanka in Leeds, the team's mood was buoyant. Their six-hitting exploits in Manchester had reaffirmed England's position as tournament favourites, and victory at Headingley would put them top of the table above Australia and in touching distance of a semi-final place. This would grant them the luxury of resting and rotating players in their final three matches against the best opposition in the tournament: Australia, India and New Zealand. If they beat Sri Lanka, they could approach those final three group games without the pressure of having to win them to reach the last four – a big prize given they had not beaten any of those teams in World Cup cricket since 1992.

Apart from Afghanistan, Sri Lanka were the poorest team in the tournament so far, with four points from five games, including two washouts. In fact, their ODI cricket had been a mess for four years. Dimuth Karunaratne had been appointed captain on the eve of the tournament having not played a one-day international since 2015, and the team was reliant on ageing superstars such as Lasith Malinga and Angelo Mathews. There was no mystery spin to fear, and the legends Kumar Sangakkara and Mahela Jayawardene were now in the commentary box. Sri Lanka's hapless preparation was the polar opposite of England's carefully plotted campaign.

A two-year match-fixing investigation had dragged Sri Lankan cricket through the mire, and they arrived in Leeds unhappy with the world. The team manager, Ashantha de Mel, had lodged an official complaint to the ICC about the way they had been treated in England, moaning about green pitches and poor facilities. 'Instead of three nets, they gave us only two, and the hotel we were put up in at Bristol did not have a swimming pool, which is essential for every team – for the fast bowlers, especially, to relax their muscles after practice,' he said. 'The hotels that Pakistan and Bangladesh were put up in at Bristol had swimming pools.'

The complaint was dismissed by the ICC. 'At the heart of our planning is the philosophy that all ten teams are treated equally to enable them to have the best possible preparation for the event,' read an official statement. Get on with the game was the unsaid message.

Sri Lanka had good memories of Headingley. They beat England there in a Test match in 2014 that almost precipitated the resignation of Alastair Cook as captain. James Anderson was reduced to tears when he was the last man out after a valiant rear-guard action led by Moeen Ali, who scored his maiden Test hundred in only his fifth game. It was not enough as Sri Lanka gained a famous 1–0 series win. Mathews was captain that day and starred with bat and ball.

The game in Leeds would be Moeen's 100th ODI, a significant landmark in any player's career. With the team on a run of three successive wins, they felt confident enough for him to handle all of the pre-match interviews rather than the usual protocol of the captain speaking the day before the game. Some said it smacked of complacency; England just wanted Moeen to be centre of attention on his big day.

But Moeen was coming to terms with his own poor form after some mixed performances in the World Cup. He had bowled well, but his batting was non-existent, a continuation of his troubles in the winter in Test cricket, when he never settled on a place in the order and seemed to suffer from an identity crisis. Once again, he was trying to work out whether he was a bowler first and a batsman second, or the other way around, and for the first time it had affected his ODI cricket.

Headingley was a good ground for Moeen. In seven ODIs, he averaged 56 with the bat. Leeds provides a batsman full value for his shots, because of its fast outfield, and gone are the days of the groundsmen there preparing green seamers. But on the ICC's watch in the World Cup the surfaces were different, sucking the life out of pitches for strokemakers like Moeen.

No matter. England went into the game having won huge respect from their opponents. Karunaratne praised their batting revolution. 'I think England is the best batting line-up against the spinners around the world,' he said. 'If you take the Asian countries, England play it better than them.' It sounded genuine too.

Moeen never dreamt of playing 100 ODIs, and has happily talked already of having achieved cricketing fulfilment.

His faith keeps his sport in perspective, and his position as a role model is guaranteed as a result of his hard work and likeable public persona. He is popular among team-mates for his wit and loves to take the mickey out of his close friend Adil Rashid, cracking up when he did a video for the ECB's website quizzing Rashid on general knowledge, the latter answering 'Hillary Clinton' when asked who was the president of the United States. They live in each other's pockets on tour, and Moeen has been a tremendous pillar of support for Rashid, who lacks his friend's self-belief.

With a new daughter having arrived at the start of the World Cup, Moeen was in a happy place in his life, even if his cricket was faltering, so it was a good time to reflect on the 100-ODI landmark. 'I'm 32 now, and I feel it,' he said. 'Since that debut, I feel it more now. I'm getting old. Obviously, it is an amazing achievement for myself, and in a blink of an eye it has gone so quickly. When I think of all the fun I've had, it is a great thing. I won't even look back at the number of caps when I'm done. I think the most important thing will be remembering all the fun I've had with the guys in the dressing room and the friends I've made.

'I'm made to feel like a senior player, which is great. I was thinking about it this morning, and how I never thought I'd be a senior player in a county side let alone the England side. When you break into a county side, that is your aim, so it is an incredible feeling to have achieved that with England.'

Moeen loved playing under Eoin Morgan, happily describing him as the best captain he had played for, and he clearly missed his presence when appearing in Test cricket. Morgan is obviously a fine player of spin himself, but, unusually for an England captain, he is also good at handling his own slow bowlers. Before this match, he arranged for Steven Gerrard, legendary midfielder for Moeen's favourite team, Liverpool, to send him a good-luck message. Morgan presented him with his 100th cap in the dressing room, saying 'your contribution to the team is worth its weight in gold' before showing him the video of Gerrard. 'I'm a big fan of yours,' Gerrard said. Handling players is not just about telling them which end to bowl from; it is going that extra mile to make them feel wanted and special.

Moeen felt that keeping things light would help the team win the World Cup. So much easier said than done, as they would discover over the next ten days. 'We know there are big pressure games to come, but we've spoken about this, and in the World T20 in India we literally had a laugh all the way through. We had such a good time,' he said. 'At the Champions Trophy [in 2017], we didn't do that towards the end, and we probably took it a bit too seriously. We have spoken about it, and this time we want to stay true to ourselves even more as the pressure grows, both in the way we play and in the way we are as a team. We actually need to have more of a laugh and try to enjoy it as much as we can. We are only going to do this once, and it is a great opportunity to win the World Cup at home.'

Moeen bowled another ten very tidy overs at Headingley, but it was not an occasion for smiles and jokes. Sri Lanka batted from a bygone ODI age, scoring 232, but it was a day of frustration and disappointment for England, one that left Moeen facing some serious questions about his mindset and his team's big-match temperament.

England started well. Jofra Archer and Chris Woakes were again quick and accurate with the new ball, leaving Sri Lanka three for two and reeling after Karunaratne was caught behind for one in the second over and Kusal Perera slashed a catch to third man in the third over. But a new star was about to emerge. Avishka Fernando, a 21-year-old right-hander, was brought in for his first World Cup match and showed the intent that had been missing from Sri Lanka's batting so far.

Avishka dismantled England in the 2016 Under-19 World Cup and scored two hundreds against them in an age-group bilateral series as well. A bruising, hard-hitting batsman, built like a rugby hooker, there was little by the way of deft touch about his batting. He clobbered Archer for a huge six over mid-wicket and smacked him for 24 off 15 balls, forcing Morgan to take him out of the attack. Mark Wood, however, persisted with the short ball, and Avishka, one short of his first ODI half-century, guided a catch to deep third man in the 13th over.

Mathews and Kusal Mendis were Sri Lanka's experienced middle-order core. They had to battle it out for their side on a pitch that was starting to slow down. Mathews had been in woeful form, and past glories were keeping him in the team after scores of nine, zero, zero and one in his previous four innings as he struggled with English conditions. He took 13 balls to get off the mark here, and the Sri Lanka innings was stuck in neutral. England had a grip on proceedings, with Jonny Bairstow fielding brilliantly in the deep, cutting off boundaries by flinging himself everywhere on his home turf, and the two spinners combined well to give Sri Lanka nothing to hit.

Mathews continued to grind out the runs, though, doggedly protecting his wicket, because he knew his team's hopes rested on him seeing them to a workable target. Mathews and Mendis put on 71, the highest stand of the match, in 17 overs of obdurate resistance. It was crabby, gritty stuff that felt as if it were losing Sri Lanka the match given England's awesome power with the bat.

Mendis made 46 crucial runs before Rashid took two wickets in two balls. Mendis was brilliantly caught by Morgan at mid-wicket, diving low to his left. Next ball, Jeevan Mendis tamely popped a return catch to Rashid, and Sri Lanka were 133 for five and threatening not to bat through their 50 overs.

Mathews began to time a few more out of the middle, and he was supported by Dhananjaya de Silva's 29, but Morgan summoned Archer and Wood to see off the innings, both taking two wickets, as Mathews was left unbeaten on 85 from 115 balls.

Still, their total of 232 felt 30 or 40 runs below par, despite Mathews' sunnier outlook on their efforts. 'It was not the easiest wicket to bat on, topping and turning a bit,' he said. 'But I think it was a par total. At halfway I thought 260 to 270 would have been a good score, but their bowlers came out all guns blazing. Us experienced guys had to come into the game. I'm glad that I was able to scrap through to 230.'

But surely it would be a stroll for England given the way they'd battered Afghanistan's spinners a few days before. Maybe not.

Jason Roy had jogged on the outfield and faced a few throw-downs the day before the match until he was told by the medical staff to go and sit down and not make his hamstring injury worse. It meant James Vince had another chance to open the batting with Bairstow and establish an ODI career.

Bairstow had played brilliantly at Old Trafford, batting responsibly for the team and putting away the big shots. This was his home ground, and he was desperate to put on a show in a World Cup match. England win when they get off to a good start, and Bairstow looked back on an even keel after his first-baller against South Africa.

But there would be no fairy-tale Yorkshire homecoming. There was an ominous sign when he absent-mindedly went out to bat with two left-handed gloves before noticing his mistake. He was out first ball again, this time adjudged leg-before to Malinga to a ball that was just trimming leg stump. It was umpire's call on review. A close decision, but Bairstow had to depart and did not look happy.

Vince can be a sublime player – his cover drive is one of the best in the game. But this was another classic Vince innings – plenty of lovely shots, but ultimately no substance – and he failed to take the opportunity to establish his place in the side and silence some of his critics in the process.

One of those critics was watching from Headingley's new Emerald Stand, built for the World Cup. Geoffrey Boycott was not working for radio or television during the tournament, but he was there at Headingley as guest of honour to watch Vince strike a couple of beautiful drives before edging Malinga to slip for 14.

'I'm sat here in the Emerald Suite, stunning view right behind the bowler's arm,' he wrote on Twitter, although probably typed by someone else given his inability to work modern technology. 'Just waiting to see how Vince gets himself out.'

A few moments later, another post followed. 'Didn't have to wait long. No sooner had I sent that tweet and he was out driving on the up caught at slip.'

It was as if Vince had played the shot just to wind up Geoffrey. Vince knew he was keeping a place warm for Roy, but with Alex Hales having burnt his bridges, there was a longer-term future to play for, especially as the four-yearly cycle of regeneration after a World Cup offers opportunities to new or fringe players. Making runs in the pressurised environment of a World Cup was also the best possible way to seal an Ashes place for later in the summer, but his lack of mettle in a big match was highlighted once again.

Ominously for Vince, Roy was talking a good game about his fitness. He told *Test Match Special* his hamstring was healing well and he hoped to be fit for the match against Australia. That was wishful thinking but it was positive news for England because it showed Roy was making progress.

But even with Vince gone and England 26 for two in the seventh over, it still felt a comfortable total to chase. Then it all started to slowly unravel as the senior players looked tentative, poking at Sri Lanka's spinners without any real conviction. It was a strange performance given their usual dominance over slow bowling. England just could not find a partnership that would bind them together.

Morgan could not find his timing on the slow pitch, smacking a low full toss straight back at left-arm seamer Isuru Udana in the 19th over. And Root was not his usual self as he laboured to 57 off 89 balls before he fell in the 31st over, strangled down the leg side by Malinga, a fittingly lame dismissal. England were 144 for five and in trouble after a Malinga special hit Buttler low down on the front foot, and he was leg-before for ten. Malinga now had 51 wickets in World Cup cricket and four in this game alone. He had joined Glenn McGrath, Muttiah Muralitharan and Wasim Akram with 50 World Cup wickets to his name. He had left England still needing 89 off 18 overs and relying on their untested lower order, which had barely been required all summer.

Ben Stokes was watchful, resisting the temptation to smash his way out of trouble. Once again he was playing the percentages, trying to be a responsible senior player for his side in a crucial game. When Moeen slotted Dhananjaya straight down the ground for six, it felt as though England, at 170 for five, would coast home.

But the very next ball Moeen tried to repeat the shot. This time the execution failed to match the ambition, and he holed out for 16. He knew it was a bad shot as he walked off, head bowed. Chris Woakes was then caught behind trying to cut the off spinner Dhananjaya, and four balls later Rashid fell for one.

Stokes sensed the emergency and tried to calm Archer, talking him through two tense overs. But Archer tried to smash a slower ball from Udana out of the ground only to be caught in the deep and England were 186 for nine, with only Wood left with 6.2 overs remaining.

Malinga had one more over, and Stokes knew they would be six crucial balls. He did not take a risk, turning down singles to protect Wood at the other end. He tried to smash the fifth delivery of the over for a boundary but could not keep the ball down and was lucky a catch just dropped short of the fielder on the rope. Stokes took a single off Malinga's final ball to steal the strike.

When he slammed Udana for two consecutive sixes at the start of the next over, a famous escape was on, and the biggest cheer of the day came when Wood managed to successfully block out the final ball of the over.

With 30 required from four overs, Stokes was sensing victory. He pulled Pradeep for consecutive fours and took a single off the fifth ball to leave Wood just one ball to keep out. He failed. Pradeep found the perfect delivery for a no. 11, the ball moving late and taking the outside edge. Stokes was distraught and left stranded on 82. Somehow England had lost by 20 runs. The tournament had the upset it needed, but England had paid the price for some tentative batting early on and for panicking when they sensed danger.

The coaches and captain closed ranks behind Moeen, refusing to blame him for their defeat. Michael Vaughan was less sympathetic. 'England did not play with any smartness,' he said. 'At 170 for five, the game was won. Moeen Ali hits a six then tries to hit another. I hope we are not in an era where you can't sit in the dressing room and point a finger and say: "Sorry, Moeen, that is not good enough." Jofra Archer was out there with Ben Stokes and tries to club one into the stands and gets caught. It was just not smart cricket.'

Once again England had failed to adapt to the situation on a tricky pitch. But behind the scenes there was more anger at batsmen higher up the order for failing to take on Sri Lanka's spinners rather than with Moeen. There was also disappointment that two all-rounders, Woakes and Archer, fell playing cross-batted shots to the off spinner when they should have been more positive hitting down the ground. It had been a mess of a run chase.

'In the chase, we did not do the basics of getting substantial partnerships going,' admitted Morgan. 'There were a couple of good individual performances, but Sri Lanka deserved to win. We did not do enough to win. Even if we had nicked it at the end, I think we would have robbed the game with one great individual performance. We resort to aggressive, smart, positive cricket when we lose. Let's hope that's the case against Australia on Tuesday.'

England now had to win at least one, and probably two, of their final three matches to go through, and Australia were next on the agenda at Lord's.

Moeen knew he would be scapegoated. Writing in his column for the *Guardian* newspaper, he revealed his frustration. 'My belief is that we got too obsessed with the trickiness of the pitch, and we lacked some of the intensity that has been our approach over the past four years of one-day cricket. When I got out attempting a second six in a row, I walked off knowing people were going to get stuck into me. I targeted Dhananjaya de Silva, and if I had cleared the fielder – a metre in difference – our chase would have got that bit of extra momentum. And to be honest, I'd still rather get out playing that shot than . . . trying to guide a single only to edge behind when the ball seamed.

'The difference is, you get out playing a defensive stroke or a guided shot like that, the criticism isn't nearly the same. More credit goes to the bowler too. But break it down and the two reactions don't make sense. Both shots are played on merit, and both are failures in execution, rather than selection. Yet attacking shots attract more heat.'

The problem was Moeen did not clear the fielder. He played a poor shot for an experienced campaigner in his 100th ODI and should have been there at the end for Stokes. The group game against Australia a few days later would be his final appearance of the World Cup, the shot at Headingley having put enough doubt in the minds of the management about his form at a crucial juncture. A World Cup campaign that had been going so well was suddenly in choppy waters.

Farbrace had seen Morgan react to defeats before. Speaking after the match, he said Morgan would not be shouting and screaming. But there would be quiet, pointed, conversations with individuals about the shots they played. He said the key message though would be positive. 'We will still win this World Cup but we will have to learn quickly.'

Very quickly. England had three games left to put it right, but they were up against difficult opponents, including two former winners – Australia and India – and New Zealand. A place in the last four of a home World Cup, the absolute minimum expectation, was on the line. That four-year project suddenly looked like it could be another let-down.

'I don't tend to ever read the riot act,' said Morgan. They would need his calmness over the next ten days.

ELEVEN
SQUEAKY BUM TIME

GAME SEVEN –
ENGLAND V. AUSTRALIA

LORD'S, LONDON

25 June 2019

The story had taken an unexpected twist. A World Cup match, even if just in the group stages, between England and Australia at Lord's, especially in a summer when the Ashes was to come later, was always going to be special, but nobody had envisaged that it would carry quite as much significance in the grand scheme of the tournament. But England's shock defeat by Sri Lanka four days earlier at Headingley had altered things considerably. Qualification for the semi-finals was anything but certain now.

England were in a bit of a pickle. Of course, this was not a side that had suddenly become poor because of one defeat (two in the tournament). And there were some relevant statistics in their favour ahead of this match. They had not lost back-to-back one-day internationals since January 2017, when in India, and they had not done so in England since September 2015 – against Australia, as it happened. They had also beaten Australia in the previous six ODIs between the teams, indeed in 11 of the last 13.

But there was also one more worrying statistic: Australia had won the last three World Cup matches between the two teams. In fact, the last time England had defeated Australia in a World Cup match was in 1992 when Ian Botham, with four wickets and a half-century, was cutting those celebratory shapes that Chris Woakes and Joe Root had been so keen to ape. This match was going to be tense.

'The games we've played against them in the last two years, probably the scoreline hasn't been as fair as both sides have played,' said captain Eoin Morgan, who wasn't showing any signs of panicking. 'It's not must-win yet. We don't need to win every game to get to the semi-final. It's another game where we try and produce a performance that's worthy of winning.

'We're not a side that goes up and down like a yo-yo. There is no question mark about producing under pressure. Primarily it's trying to keep things as simple as possible, being truthful and honest about our previous performance, and trying to learn and rectify the performance almost immediately.

'And I think because we have quite a strong identity in the way that we play – I wouldn't say that we can flip back to it immediately – it almost becomes a little bit easier and less confusing to the guys, the direction in which they need to go.

'Honestly, we're in control of our performances from here on in, so we don't need to look elsewhere yet. Every game's a one-off. It's a chance to prove ourselves. It's a chance to play the way we've been playing, if allowed to.'

Given that James Vince had made only 14 against Sri Lanka, it was no surprise that there was again talk about Jason Roy playing. He did bat in the nets at Lord's, but he was ultimately ruled out of the game, and Morgan still could not say with any certainty when he might return. 'We'll monitor his progress during the week and assess him,' he said. 'To put one game on it, I don't think it's sensible. Let's just see how it goes. Hamstrings can be funny things.'

The pressure was on Vince again, even if he had made 64 in the unofficial warm-up match against Australia before the tournament. 'James Vince is an extremely talented, gifted player,' Morgan said. 'You can see that from just watching him. We have every faith in him to go on and get a score at some stage, to continue playing in his own way. It's important that he does that.'

There was no such pressure on Australia. They had won five of their six matches at this stage – losing only to India at the Oval – and were second in the table behind New Zealand. Head coach Justin Langer was therefore more than happy to big up England. 'Just look at their team. Nothing has changed in a week,' he said. 'We have seen how they have played for four years. They are the best team in the world.'

The build-up to this game would not have been complete, of course, without reference to Steve Smith and David Warner, this being their first official match against England since returning from their year-long bans for their roles in the ball-tampering scandal during the third Test against South Africa in March 2018. There had been a lot of booing for them around the grounds already, and Morgan was asked about his views on it, especially in light of the actions of Indian captain Virat Kohli in their match against Australia, who had gestured for fans to stop booing and apologised for the behaviour of the India supporters afterwards. Footage of Kohli trying to shush the crowd was the most watched video on the ICC's Twitter feed of the entire tournament.

But Morgan told the BBC that there was no way that he would use his position as England captain to influence how fans should behave. He pointed out that, while Smith and Warner had served their bans, it did not necessarily mean that they would be welcomed back with open arms. Restoring trust takes time, he said.

Morgan revealed that he had given considerable thought to what Kohli had done but said that he did not feel that it was something he would emulate. 'I didn't see it, but when I heard about it, I thought about it for quite a while,' he said. 'I thought: "Would it help in the right way? Is it right?" But it didn't sit right with me.'

For their part, Australia seemed unperturbed. 'It hasn't affected our boys one bit. If anything, it's given them more motivation,' said captain Aaron Finch. 'Whatever the public do, you're not going to change it. Whether someone says do or don't, it's going to happen regardless.

'I'm sure that's the last thing on Steve or Davey's mind when they are walking out to bat. If a handful of people or a whole stadium are booing them, it doesn't make any difference to how hard they watch the ball.'

Before the game, England had a selection dilemma: whether to keep an unchanged side from the defeat by Sri Lanka, meaning retaining two spinners in Moeen Ali and Adil Rashid – they had done that in three of their previous five ODIs at Lord's – or to recall Liam Plunkett, who had missed both England's defeats in the tournament, and who could boast a good ODI record at Lord's, having taken four for 46 in the victory over India in 2018. But they decided to go with the same team, after Jofra Archer had faced a late fitness test on the side injury that would dog him for the rest of the tournament and force him out of the first Ashes Test in July.

Eoin Morgan won the toss and decided to bowl first. 'The wicket's a bit soft on top,' said Morgan. 'We haven't seen much sun down south, so it might do a bit this morning.'

It did more than a bit. With dark clouds hovering above and the pitch retaining a greenish tinge, the ball darted around all over the place in the opening overs, and yet England could not claim a wicket. Somehow Australia's openers had taken the score to 123 before the first wicket fell in the 23rd over. The game was won and lost right there. The Australian openers Aaron Finch and David Warner had some luck, but any batsman would have needed the hand of good fortune in these circumstances.

Finch's first scoring shot in Chris Woakes's opening over, from his second ball, was off the edge and went flying over second slip, where Joe Root may have just got a fingertip to it. Archer began with a floaty half-volley that Finch duly drove to the cover boundary, but he might have snared the Australian captain on 15 when James Vince got a hand to a very difficult chance at backward point. On 18, Finch then survived a perilously close leg-before decision against Woakes. It was given not out initially, but England reviewed with some conviction. The ball was just clipping the bails, meaning it was umpire's call.

These were Test-match batting conditions, and Finch, amongst his good fortune, was batting rather well, which was ironic given that he had failed in his quest to convert to a Test-match opener in 2018, being dropped after five Tests. In ODIs, on the other hand, Finch remained outstanding, especially in replacing Tim Paine as captain and reinvigorating a side that, in losing an ODI series 5–0 in England in 2018, he admitted had tried too hard to copy England rather than playing their own style.

Here he made his 15th ODI century and, remarkably, his seventh against England. He was out the ball after passing his century, mis-hooking to fine leg, where Woakes, having misfielded to give him two for his hundred, took the catch.

Warner played superbly too, scoring 53 and becoming the first batsman to make 500 runs in the tournament. He was dismissed when a short ball from Moeen Ali stuck in the pitch and he cut to backward point.

Woakes was undoubtedly the most probing of England's seamers, bowling a fuller length in general than either Archer or Mark Wood, whose first three overs from the Pavilion End cost 24, though he did rally later from the Nursery End. Adil Rashid bowled decently, with his ten overs going for 49, but he was again unlucky, as Jos Buttler missed a straightforward stumping of the left-handed Usman Khawaja from a googly in the 28th over.

England's out-cricket was often shoddy, but the bowling definitely improved in the second half of the innings. Wood got rid of the dangerous Glenn Maxwell, who had just hit Archer into the Mound Stand. And while Steve Smith, noticeably booed more than Warner had been, did make 38 from 34 balls, he was out – hitting Woakes to long-on – when he might have taken his side to something grander than their eventual score of 285 for seven. That total was achieved mainly because of Alex Carey's perky 38 not out from just 27 balls.

England desperately needed the sort of start Australia had had, but James Vince lasted just two balls, bowled for a duck driving hard at Jason Behrendorff's left-arm inswing. Ah, the frustration Vince brings. The brutal truth was that England were hoping against hope that Vince would come good, a batsman with one fifty and an average of 24.09 in 11 ODI innings, and they simply should not have been doing that in a World Cup. It also emphasised how stupid Alex Hales had been. He could, and should, have been playing here.

It caused some observers to wonder how a player like Sam Billings might have done in the tournament. The Kent batsman was at Lord's doing some radio work, and it was hard not to feel some sympathy for him. Had he not dislocated a shoulder in April, he could have been opening here.

Billings might be better known as a middle-order batsman, but he has opened in four ODIs and scored two fifties (one more than Vince) in that time. His most recent innings for England had been a stunning 87 from 47 balls in a Twenty20 international in the Caribbean three months before the World Cup.

Australia, meanwhile, had seen England bowl too short early on and had made a decision to go much fuller. 'They didn't hit the stumps,' said Behrendorff, who would end up taking five for 44. 'Or the balls were going over the stumps too often. It's something we were assessing when they were bowling. We made a conscious effort to try to pitch up. We executed that quite well, and we were able to get off to an excellent start.'

There was left-arm inswing from the other end, propelled much more swiftly by Mitchell Starc. He soon dismissed Joe Root lbw with an absolute beauty. Eoin Morgan arrived at the crease next and immediately seemed in discomfort as Starc bowled fast and short. Kevin Pietersen thought it looked like more than discomfort. With typical gaucheness, he took to Twitter to say he thought Morgan 'looked scared'. 'That is a horror sign,' Pietersen tweeted. 'The England captain stepping to square leg when Starc bowled his first delivery made me think England could have a little problem. I hope not, but I've not seen a captain show such a weakness for a while.'

Asked about this afterwards, Morgan replied sarcastically: 'Really? Excellent,' before saying: 'No, no. It didn't feel that way at all.'

Morgan had been concussed by a Starc bouncer at Old Trafford in 2015, and his spell here revived memories of that. Morgan has a habit of staying leg side of the ball, but he has not been alone in doing that in the history of the game. Indeed, Australia's David Warner often does as much.

Morgan was soon out trying to hook the same bowler here, caught at fine leg. England were 26 for three before six overs had been bowled. It was a long way back from there, especially when Jonny Bairstow went for 27, pulling a ball from Behrendorff that was too wide for the stroke.

Australia's fielding was also much sharper than England's. Usman Khawaja took a brilliant running catch on the square-leg boundary to dismiss Jos Buttler for 25, and in the 42nd over Glenn Maxwell and Aaron Finch combined superbly to get rid of Chris Woakes, with Maxwell lobbing the ball back inside to Finch before stepping over the boundary at deep mid-wicket.

As it had been in the previous game against Sri Lanka, it was all down to Ben Stokes again. And what a fist he made of it. This was another very special effort from him. The sixth over is very early for your no. 5 to be appearing, but it did mean that Stokes had plenty of time in which to play himself in. He duly took 12 balls in getting off the mark, but he did so in emphatic manner by skipping down the pitch to Behrendorff and slapping the left-armer through the covers for four.

This was typical Stokes; this is his method. Manoeuvring

the ball around early on is not necessarily his forte. There are not many deft touches in his armoury, but there is a very solid technique to underpin his game. When you can catch up with the pace later on, it is not a problem if you use up a few dot balls at the start of an innings.

The way that Stokes was setting about his innings in this tournament was clear confirmation that it was not just as a person that he had matured since standing trial in 2018 for his actions outside that Bristol nightclub the year before. His batting was now so much more discerning too. He had always looked like a proper batsman rather than just a hitter, but it was now obvious that he had attached to that solid technique and fierce determination a calmer, smarter mind.

With every innings he had played in the World Cup, it was becoming ever more evident that he was attempting to make up for the time he had missed – an Ashes tour, no less – and all the negative publicity and upheaval that had naturally come with that. Clearly chastened, he was obviously determined not to waste his opportunity in the tournament or indeed in the rest of his career.

If Joe Root was the glue at the top of England's order, England knew that Stokes could perform a similar role later on in an innings, as well as being able to hit the ball out of the park, if need be, when the finish line was in sight. His bowling wasn't too bad either. He finished the tournament with England's second-best economy rate (4.83), behind only Jofra Archer (4.57). Of those who bowled 50 overs in the tournament, he was eighth on the list.

'The thing I have been most happy with has been my bowling,' he said. 'I had a chat with Morgs and a few others to get my head around my role. Being the fourth or fifth seamer, I sometimes put too much pressure on myself to influence the game. So, I spoke to them about not trying to take wickets every ball. It was a clear plan to go at five or six an over, and I might get a wicket doing that, that's helped offer the team more. In the last couple of years, it's probably where I have let the team down.'

Stokes had been building up to all this. After a poor IPL season with Rajasthan Royals, his English summer did not begin especially well, but it was towards the end of the ODI series against Pakistan – with England cleverly pushing him up the order to no. 4 to play some longer innings – that he had started to show his real form with the bat.

And he was showing it again now at Lord's. When on nine, he could so easily have done exactly the same as David Warner had to Moeen Ali earlier and cut to point as the ball held in the pitch. Fortunately for Stokes, the ball fell into untenanted territory.

Bairstow soon went in the 14th over, but Buttler arrived, and it was a measure of Australia's concerns about the danger he posed that they wasted a review on him when he was obviously well down the pitch and outside the line to Marcus Stoinis.

Stokes went to his fifty off 75 balls, but it was already obvious that he was struggling physically – possibly with cramp – in the heat and humidity. With the attention being paid to his calves at every opportunity, you did wonder if there was something more serious wrong.

'It was cramp,' Morgan said afterwards. 'It's a hot day, and Ben plays a role in every facet of our game. He runs around, he bowls fast, then makes a major contribution with the bat. It's nothing to worry about.'

Stokes disagreed on the diagnosis. 'It wasn't cramp; it was just tight calves,' he said. 'I suffer with it every now and then, especially on muggy days like this. Nothing to worry about.'

Buttler departed in the 28th over, and England still needed 162 from 22.4 overs, but Stokes responded by hitting Maxwell's off spin for two glorious sixes in an over. And when the 36th over of the innings, bowled by Pat Cummins, went for 12, with two fours from Stokes, both when charging down the pitch, and one from Chris Woakes, hopes were raised.

Aaron Finch decided to return to Mitchell Starc. This was a huge moment in the game, with England needing 113 from 14 overs. Starc duly delivered for his captain. Stokes had added only one more run when he was castled by a wicked in-dipping yorker that hit off stump. There was little he could do about it. It was undoubtedly the ball of the day. It was probably the ball of the tournament.

'He's a fantastic player, and he's one of their key batters,' said Starc. 'We knew while he was batting that we couldn't just rest up, we couldn't cruise. We had to try and take that wicket. Fortunately, I got one through the gate, but he was batting fantastically well.'

When asked if it was the best ball he had ever faced, Stokes replied dryly, 'What, a 90mph, inswinging yorker? It was a good ball, yep.'

On the pitch, Stokes could not believe it. He dropped his bat and then kicked it away (it wouldn't be the last time he kicked his bat at Lord's in the tournament). He was still shaking his head in disbelief when he made it inside the Lord's pavilion. He was gone for 89 from 115 balls, and with him went England's chance of winning the game. They ended up 64 runs short, with five overs and two balls remaining of their innings. It was a thrashing.

But Stokes could have done no more. With every game his presence was growing. He had just played two remarkable knocks in consecutive defeats. It was clear even then that he would soon play one in victory.

'Ben contributes in all three facets of our game plan,' said Morgan. 'Today was quite a big day for him. He's obviously in very, very good form, and it's partly disappointing that an innings like that almost goes to one side because we lost the game.'

England had two games left in the group stage, first against India at Edgbaston and then against New Zealand at Durham. Their destiny was still in their own hands, but things were getting serious. This was probably not the worst of their three defeats in the competition, but it predictably provoked a searching inquest. It was the old enemy after all. At Lord's, too.

How had it come to this? Had we been deceived all along? Was that pre-tournament no. 1 ranking, garnered in more gentle bilateral series, hiding problems that had then become clear faults under the spotlight of the World Cup itself? Had the Alex Hales situation had more of an effect on the squad than we imagined? There were a lot of questions being asked.

There seemed little doubt that we were seeing the vital differences from those bilateral series, where often teams were not at full strength – especially among their fast bowlers – and there was another day to prosper. One-off games naturally bring with them different pressures, especially when not played on the flat pitches on which most of England's home one-day internationals had taken place over the previous four years. England had now chased unsuccessfully in all three of their defeats. They had simply been unable to deal with surfaces that had not allowed them to play their usual aggressive game. They had gone into their shells.

'Australia outplayed us, showed us how strong their basics were, and ours need to be better,' said Morgan. 'This game and the last [defeat by Sri Lanka], we struggled with the basics of what we call our batting mantra – strong intent, building partnerships and doing it in our own way, and we haven't done those for long enough periods of the game to either chase down 230 or chase down 280, and that's disappointing.

'The wickets are going to be slow, low, they will wear. That's the way – the nature of ICC events. Our basics get challenged a lot more when we don't play on batter-friendly wickets – when you have to rotate the strike, as opposed to find the boundary more often than not.'

Stokes cut a defiant figure afterwards. 'We have to dig deep and go back to what we do well,' he said. 'This is our World Cup. We are not going away from our method of playing. We are not going to take a backward step now in the next two games.

'We have to take each game as it comes. We have a good record against India at home. We have had great support over the past four years. We know how much this means to the fans. And to the players. We are at home in a World Cup. There is no better time to be an England cricketer. In terms of progression, we make better decisions now than we did starting out on this run, and we are a confident team.'

As for Australia, they were through to the semi-finals.

'The competition's still very open. England are probably still firm favourites being the home country,' said Behrendorff. 'We'll just keep aspiring to play good cricket, but we're not favourites that's for sure.'

Was England's confidence affected? 'It will take a bit of a hit, but I don't think it's knocked anybody,' said Morgan. 'Normally when we lose we go back to what we do well. We'll still strive to do that for Sunday's game [against India].

'I like to lead from the front. Captains tend to have success that way. I will be trying to ensure my contributions have an impact in the next two games. Hopefully I can do that.'

Indeed, but as Mike Atherton said in *The Times*: 'It is squeaky bum time now.'

TWELVE
BULLETPROOF BAIRSTOW

GAME EIGHT –
ENGLAND V. INDIA

EDGBASTON, BIRMINGHAM

30 June 2019

In the large nondescript anteroom next to the home dressing room at Edgbaston, a very important meeting took place that turned the fortunes of England's World Cup campaign.

Two days before the game against India, the squad were in crisis. Two consecutive defeats had put their semi-final place in doubt. They had needed to win a minimum of two of their last three group games, and now Jonny Bairstow had become embroiled in a media spat that had brought unwanted attention to the team at the worst possible time.

The players had looked tentative and nervous during their defeat to Australia, as if the pressure of a home World Cup was becoming too much to bear. David Young, the team's psychologist, and the management knew something had to change. They called a meeting, that would last an hour, to clear the air and plot a way forward.

It started with the showing of a video lasting two minutes 35 seconds, edited by Greg Stobart, the ECB's digital editor, the details of which can be revealed here for the first time. It featured clips of the players talking about each other, complimenting their skills, all set to footage of individuals in action. It used feelgood background music, the kind you hear at a party conference before a politician takes the stage. The video started with a shot of the players lifting a one-day series trophy before Morgan spoke about Stokes, talking over film of him smashing the ball in all directions. 'Ben is brilliant to captain because you have a player who can change the game,' Morgan said.

Jason Roy spoke about several of his team-mates, each set to clips of them doing well. 'Yes, he is class,' he said about Chris Woakes. 'He is so pure. He probably has the best cover drive you have ever seen.'

Mark Wood talked about Roy: 'He is unbelievable. He doesn't let you settle. He is so good against the short ball.' Roy naturally spoke about his opening partner Bairstow. 'When he gets on a roll, he just keeps going.' As if to remind Bairstow to concentrate on his cricket, Morgan added: 'The last year and a half, Jonny has been phenomenal.'

About Jofra Archer, Morgan said: 'Jofra coming into the team has obviously added a lot. His death bowling is up there with the best in the world.'

Every player was mentioned, even those who were just squad members, such as Liam Dawson and Tom Curran. The idea was to foster team spirit and remind each other they were good at what they do.

Clips of good moments from the 2019 World Cup were also included, such as Stokes's blinding catch at the Oval. And Morgan said about Root: 'He is one of the world's best cricketers. He is going to be one of the best players of our generation in all formats of the game.'

It was Wood who spoke about Morgan, overplayed to footage of him celebrating a hundred. 'I have played under five world-class captains, and I would put Morgan on top of them all,' he said.

It was clear that Morgan was not going to allow an environment to develop in which players started blaming each other in difficult times. 'Honestly, it is such a pleasure to be around the group. Everyone is just good mates, enjoying their cricket. It is a great privilege to play with these lads,' said Curran. The film ended with commentary from a previous England win by Nasser Hussain. 'Brilliant at the start, brilliant at the end. Normal service resumed.' It was stirring stuff, and the room was silent after the video was played, but could normal service be resumed?

The meeting was only attended by players, coaches and Young. No physios, analysts or media officers. This was about the players and the team environment. The players were told it was OK to admit they were unhappy and to tell the group, but they also had to recommit to their principles.

Young invited everyone to talk, regardless of seniority. Each was asked what the World Cup meant to him. The message was to be courageous, get on the front foot and start to enjoy this once-in-a-lifetime experience. Be true to themselves. Trust each other again.

Young later told the *Daily Telegraph*: 'Perhaps some of them didn't feel as bulletproof as a month earlier. Several players said they felt they perhaps couldn't talk openly about this, and they were the only ones who felt like this.'

To outsiders these meetings can feel a bit corny, particularly for uptight Englishmen. Much of what is said comes across as stating the obvious. The video might be viewed by old-timers as a bit embarrassing, an example of the touchy-feely twenty-first-century world, when a good old-fashioned rollicking was called for instead. But for a group of modern players, young men feeling the pressure of expectation, it changed the mood, and they opened up for the clear-the-air discussion they needed.

It was important, because it looked as though a siege mentality was taking hold. Morgan had been snappy in his post-match press conference after the defeat to Australia, letting himself become easily wound up by an Australian journalist looking for a reaction from an under-pressure England captain. He had also been caught off guard by Kevin Pietersen's questioning of his courage when facing Mitchell Starc. The other players were incensed by Pietersen's suggestion that Morgan was backing away from Starc for fear of being hurt.

In fact, it apparently put on hold plans by the ECB to try to reintroduce Pietersen to the England set-up. Consideration had been given to inviting him to spend a couple of days with the Ashes squad before a Test match later in the summer, as fellow 2005 Ashes legend Marcus Trescothick had been. Not now. The players simply would not have countenanced it. Questioning the captain's bottle had crossed a line.

In addition to all of this, Bairstow's comments in an interview to publicise Yorkshire Tea's sponsorship of National Cricket Week, an initiative run by Chance to Shine, a charity that promotes cricket in state schools, had made the back pages of most newspapers, showing the extra scrutiny on a group of players used to living in the shadow of football.

Bairstow had sat down with a group of journalists he knew well for a 35-minute chat two days before the players were due to meet up at Edgbaston. He was in a good mood and joked about a London taxi driver sledging him after the Australia defeat.

Bairstow is an experienced media performer, but he is an emotional character too, who can rise easily to criticism. In the moments after the defeat to Australia, Michael Vaughan told BBC radio that England's campaign was in danger of unravelling. 'This is looking like turmoil for England. I've been involved in a couple of atrocious World Cups. If they're not careful, this could turn out to be top of the tree,' he said.

Vaughan and Bairstow had clashed before. In 2018, Vaughan wrote in his column for the *Daily Telegraph* that Bairstow had to 'stop sulking' and accept he had to bat at three for England after briefly losing his place in the Test side as wicketkeeper to Jos Buttler. So, when Bairstow was asked to react to Vaughan's comments about England's faltering World Cup campaign, he could not resist having a go back. 'I was on the radio this morning. I was surprised with a clip of Vaughan's comments at 8.30. Bloody hell. That's pretty rich,' he said. 'It's part and parcel of modern life, I'm afraid. That's the world at the moment. You can't be seen doing anything without someone having an opinion on it. You walk down the street wearing the wrong pair of trainers, and your sponsors fire you. It's as dumb as that. It's the world we live in. That is where we're at.

'People now are paid to have an opinion. Because we've done so well, any opportunity for someone to see we've lost two games, they were always going to jump on it. People were waiting for us to fail. They are not willing us on to win. In many ways, they are waiting for you to get that loss so they can jump on your throat. It's a typical English thing to do, in every sport.'

It was the 'people are waiting for us to fail' line that was picked up and turned into headlines. The following day, the back pages were full of it. The *Sun*'s headline read: 'You Lot Want Us to Fail'. The *Daily Mail*'s read: 'Moaning Bairstow: The Whole World Is Against Us'. *The Times*': 'Bairstow Takes Aim at Pundits'.

Vaughan hit back on social media. 'How wrong can Jonny Bairstow be? Never has an England team had so much support, but it's you and your team that has disappointed, Jonny. Win two games and you are in the semis. With this negative, pathetic mindset I am concerned, though. It's not the media's fault you have lost three games!!!'

Bairstow was stunned by the furore. He had appeared at the Yorkshire Tea press day without an ECB media minder, which had obviously backfired, but as a senior player he had to take responsibility for his comments.

England handled the situation calmly. Ashley Giles, the team's director, called Bairstow to offer him some advice gained from personal experience of the time when he had reacted badly to criticism as he attempted to cope with the pressure after Australia won the opening Test of the 2005 Ashes series. Giles struggled in that match and Dave Houghton, then coach of Derbyshire, said picking him was like taking to the field with ten men. Giles's skin has thickened with age, but at that time he was sensitive and reacted badly. 'It's always been an easier game from the sidelines, but it's disappointing that former players should lead the criticism of the England side,' he said. 'It's very easy for them to criticise, but they should know the pressure we're under. They should know better. I don't know if they just want a couple of minutes of fame, or what it is, but lots of them would struggle against this Australia team, and they have been a bit quick to criticise.' Sound familiar?

When he called Bairstow, Giles simply told him hitting back is not worth the aggravation. Concentrate on the cricket, because fighting battles on the field is hard enough without courting them off it. He also told Bairstow to let his talent do the talking for him, knowing it can bring the best out of him, for he is one of the mentally toughest players in the side.

Giles was at England nets the following day to lend personal support. Most of the players simply reacted with a roll of the eyes and put it down to 'Jonny being Jonny'. Jason Roy made sure the press knew that Bairstow's view was not shared by the rest of the dressing room.

Bairstow had no problem arguing with Vaughan. But he was upset by the perception his comments were critical of the public and that he was referring to England fans when he said people were 'waiting for us to fail' when he was in fact talking about media pundits. But it came across as a privileged, wealthy sportsman having a go at punters who had paid a lot of money to ensure every England World Cup game was a sell-out. It was not a good look when the team was losing.

It dominated the build-up to the India match, but this was perhaps a good thing, because it allowed Morgan to concentrate on bringing the side back together behind the scenes.

Vice-captain Jos Buttler gave the press conference two days before the game and said all the right things. 'It's just typical Yorkies,' he joked about Bairstow and Vaughan. '[But] talking about goodwill and people wanting you to do well, I think it's been great from the country. Everyone has been really behind the team.

'Naturally, being a good side, when we don't perform to

that level, it is frustrating. People give their opinion in the media or whatever and are frustrated. As are we as a team, and as individuals as well. But there's been lots of goodwill.'

He was asked if Bairstow was just revving himself up for another big score? 'I can assure you that's not what he's trying to do,' he said. 'But, as a player, when Jonny seems to have a point to prove, he performs outstandingly well.'

Those were prescient words. No England player likes to prove his critics wrong more than Bairstow. He was bristling with a sense of injustice, but the biggest boost for England's cause was the fitness of his opening partner. There is no way Roy would have played against India had England beaten Australia a few days earlier. But they were in deep trouble and needed him back in the side. They took an almighty gamble, because if he had aggravated the injury, he would have faced a lengthy spell on the sidelines, missing the rest of the World Cup and probably the start of the Ashes series when he was pencilled in for a Test debut.

Morgan likes to gamble on horses. Now he was willing to take a punt on his thoroughbred opener. Roy came in for James Vince. There was one other crucial change too. Moeen Ali was replaced by Liam Plunkett, because England had realised the tacky pitches suited his bowling. He would not let them down.

India attract huge support whenever they play overseas. However, it is in England where they have the strongest backing. When buying tickets for the World Cup, supporters were asked to tick which team they supported. The figures showed India would enjoy 55 per cent of the support at Edgbaston. In reality it was more like 80 per cent. This was a home game for Virat Kohli's side. It was a day out for the Bharat Army not the Barmy Army.

Be courageous, be positive. Those were the words ringing

in the England players' ears as the national anthems were sung. The clear-the-air meeting two days previously had given them direction. Roy and Bairstow were charged with making it happen after England won the toss and batted first.

The way Roy and Bairstow attacked India's spinners, the dangermen on a dry surface, proved the players had been listening to Young and each other. Roy and Bairstow put on 160 for the first wicket, sending a clear message about the mindset of the team in a match that was billed as the most important for England since the 2005 Ashes.

Two weeks after tearing his hamstring, Roy belted 66 off 57 balls and Bairstow scored his first World Cup hundred, making 111 from 109 balls, hitting ten fours and six sixes. But they got off to a slow start, struggling against the seamers, with Bairstow lucky to survive as 11 of his first 17 runs came off the edge. Roy would have been out on 21 had India reviewed a thin edge down the leg side off Hardik Pandya, but once the spinners came on, the openers took control and established England's authority that was to last for the rest of the game.

Roy reverse-swept leg spinner Yuzvendra Chahal for four in his second over, and two balls later Bairstow hit him over cow corner for six. Left-armer Kuldeep Yadav, India's other wrist spinner, went for 13 in his first over. Bairstow then clouted Chahal for two more sixes as he went past fifty. In all, India's two spinners conceded 160 runs from 20 overs of carnage as England lived up to Sri Lanka captain Dimuth Karunaratne's warning that they were the best players of the turning ball in the world. There was nothing subtle about their approach. It was just brutal.

Roy received a painful blow on the arm while batting that needed lengthy treatment, but more importantly it offered England a convenient excuse for him not to field later in the day and risk his hamstring. After the game, he wore casing on his hand. Not many were fooled.

Roy was out trying to smack Kuldeep for another six but was brilliantly caught by Ravindra Jadeja in his role as India's super-sub fielder. Bairstow carried on, reaching his hundred three overs later off 90 balls before India's seamers came back to give Kohli an element of control.

England managed just 25 runs in a ten-over spell in which they lost Bairstow, caught at point off Mohammed Shami, and Morgan, who was bounced out again, this time by Shami, as the innings threatened to fizzle out. But Ben Stokes ensured there would be another charge. England scored 121 from the last 13 overs. Stokes made his third successive score of more than 50, going after Chahal in particular, hitting him for 14 in his penultimate over.

Root lent support with a useful 44 off 54 balls as Stokes thrashed away at the other end, hammering Shami for four, six and four in consecutive balls in the 49th over of the innings. Jasprit Bumrah typically bowled a brilliant final over, conceding only three runs, befuddling Stokes with his slower balls before getting him out. But England set India 338 to win, which would be a record World Cup run chase if they were to pull it off.

'Having Jason back was great, but Jonny played unbelievably well – free flowing,' said Morgan. 'The two big threats were the two spinners, but they were put under pressure, and that is not easy to do, trust me. I thought that set things up nicely. Even if we went at a run a ball after the opening partnership, I thought we would still do well here.'

But Morgan knew the danger India's batting posed. In Rohit Sharma they had the World Cup's in-form opener, and Kohli is the greatest batsman one-day cricket has ever seen. They had been weakened by the loss of Shikhar Dhawan through injury, but Rishabh Pant's selection bolstered the lower order, and Hardik Pandya is a superstar hitter of the IPL. This was a team capable of setting a new run-chase record, especially when cheered on by such vociferous support in Birmingham.

However, it was a strange start to what would be an odd run chase. India were just 28 for one at the end of the powerplay, the lowest of the World Cup so far, as Chris Woakes started with three maidens and dismissed K.L. Rahul in the process. It would have been even better for England if Root had not dropped Sharma on four at slip off Archer. Kohli and Sharma settled in after seeing off Archer and Woakes, and started to take the attack to England, but Morgan had a plan. They hung the ball wide of off stump to Kohli, playing on his ego and challenging him to take the bait. He had no choice given the weight of India's target and fell to Plunkett, driving one of his cutters to backward point.

Batting was becoming harder as the day wore on and the surface slowed. Plunkett is a master in such conditions. He mixed up slower balls, cutters and back-of-a-length deliveries to make it very hard for the batsmen to score fluently. At 34 and with more than a decade of international cricket behind him, this tournament represented Plunkett's last chance to land a big prize. Injury, losses of form and the emergence of others had prevented him playing the number of games for England that his talent deserved, but he had thrived under Morgan's leadership.

Plunkett was Morgan's go-to bowler in the middle overs, and by the time he finished his spell India's required run rate had risen to more than ten an over. He returned later in the innings, and with his first ball dismissed Pant, caught brilliantly by a diving Woakes on the boundary. In his last over, he removed Pandya, caught at long-on, desperately trying to get enough power and elevation on another of the bowler's slower balls.

Plunkett had been left out of three games in the World Cup, and England had lost them all. There were doubts about his place in the squad leading into the tournament, after a winter in which it looked as though he had lost his zip and age, as well as a long list of injuries, was catching up with him. But Plunkett's three for 55 against India underlined his importance to Morgan. The captain needed someone he could trust in such a big game, with the team's World Cup place on the line. Plunkett would not be left out again, and he would continue to take the prized scalps. Kohli was not the last big name that would join his hit list.

Sharma continued to threaten for India, hitting four fours in seven balls as he reached his hundred from 106 balls, but the run chase went into reverse when he edged behind an off-cutter from Woakes. M.S. Dhoni was then booed by the crowd as he dawdled and played a bizarre innings that lacked urgency, as if he was oblivious to the mounting run rate as the overs ticked by. With 71 needed off the last five overs, the game was up for India, particularly as Dhoni and Kedar Jadhav played out seven dot balls and hit 21 singles from the 31 balls they faced together. India finished on 306 for five, their challenge petering out as their fans started to leave the ground well before the end.

India had lost their unbeaten record in the tournament. England were back in it. A last-four place beckoned. They still had to win their final group game against New Zealand in Durham to be certain of reaching the semi-finals, given their rivals would still have matches in hand after that, but the buzz was back.

Bairstow was man of the match. 'He played great. He set the tone with Jason Roy. You could see from the steel in his eyes he had to put in a performance, and his team had to put in a performance,' said Vaughan on *Test Match Special*. 'He let his bat do the talking. He is better at that.'

Bairstow credited his time in the IPL playing for Sunrisers and working with V.V.S. Laxman for the way he attacked India's spinners rather than any perceived criticism. It did not wash. 'I'm not saying I want everyone to come out and abuse me!' he said. 'But along the way people have questioned technique and conditions, and it's important to recognise different scenarios you can try and play your best in.

'It was a difficult week. To read how my comments were taken was very disappointing. But I was pleased to get over the line with a century in a World Cup. Was it my most important innings? I'd like to think it was definitely up there. With the speculation, and the position we found ourselves in, it was really pleasing to relax and play and contribute to what was a brilliant win.'

For the next few days, Trevor Bayliss jokingly offered ten-pound notes to anyone willing to slag Bairstow off. It became a running gag around the England team. 'Jonny winds himself up like that for most innings, because that is what makes him tick,' said Morgan. 'He is a magnificent player, as we have seen here. To score a hundred like that is match-winning for us.'

Stokes pinpointed the major reason why England had rediscovered their form. 'Having a forceful personality like Jason back in the team is a massive boost,' he said. 'He and Jonny feed off each other.'

England were back, and it had all started in that little ante-room overlooking the Edgbaston outfield. Mark Wood later said the chat set the team straight because they opened up to each other and were able to talk about their fears and concerns. The junior members of the side felt more confident after hearing that senior players harboured the same worries. Mentally, the side were back in a good place.

England were riding a wave of optimism and confidence. A semi-final place was now within their grasp again.

THIRTEEN
FATE PLAYS ITS HAND

GAME NINE –
ENGLAND V. NEW ZEALAND

RIVERSIDE GROUND, DURHAM

3 July 2019

'I don't think I need to prove anything. My record speaks for itself. I just go out there and express myself.' That is what Jonny Bairstow wrote in his column for the *Daily Telegraph* before England's final group game against New Zealand.

Just 24 hours later he was releasing a guttural roar, punching the air and bizarrely rubbing his head in celebration of a second successive century. The head rub was a dig at Michael Vaughan and his hair transplants, with Bairstow taking the moment to send another message to his critic.

Vaughan had just been doing his job after England's defeat to Australia, and by his standards of forthright punditry, his comments about England had been pretty gentle. But the team benefited from Bairstow's sense of injustice. His 106 against New Zealand, and another century stand with Jason Roy, guaranteed England their first World Cup semi-final place since 1992. Panic over.

Not many people behind the scenes believed Bairstow's insistence that he does not need a prod every now and then to provoke a reaction on the field. It happened when he had lost the wicketkeeping gloves in Sri Lanka in November 2018, after an ankle injury playing football gave Ben Foakes the chance to keep wicket in the first Test in Galle. Foakes scored a century, and Bairstow was not picked for the next match despite being fit. He scored a hundred in Colombo a week later, batting at no. 3, and celebrated it as if he had scored the winning goal in the FA Cup final, raising his bat towards the media centre in the process.

'There are different things you go through when you get castigated about being injured doing X, Y and Z when people don't actually see what's gone on,' he said afterwards to general bemusement, because criticism for getting injured in a kickabout had been fairly low.

But Bairstow is a different character to most sportsmen. His childhood experience of losing his father David has to be taken into account when assessing his character because such a traumatic experience has partly shaped his life. He has said in the past how it made him grow up quickly. He is generally liked, and most team-mates accept him for the character he is. He knows he can be moody and will warn others to keep their distance if he is having a bad day. But he also wants to be liked and can be friendly and warm towards those outside the team bubble.

On tour, England teams are often invited to functions with the British High Commissioner. One such event was at the

High Commissioner's residence in Johannesburg in January 2016. The England one-day men's and women's teams were there. Most players sit around, joking among themselves, and they rarely interact with the guests at these events. It is not rudeness, just the awkwardness of young men and women who don't really know how to relate to people outside the team environment. But while his team-mates were sitting on sofas looking at their mobile phones, Bairstow was working the room, shaking hands with embassy staff and talking to as many people as possible, making contacts in the process.

Throughout his career Bairstow has had an ability to take his chances. It is a ruthlessness that feeds into a self-confidence that others lack. Bairstow was a fringe player in the ODI side for the first two years of Eoin Morgan's regeneration. When he got a chance, he took it. We have mentioned that when Jos Buttler broke a finger and missed an ODI against New Zealand at Chester-le-Street in the summer of 2015, Bairstow stood in, smashed 83 from 60 balls and was man of the match in a series-winning game. But even more impressive was the fact that his maternal grandfather, who had played a large part in filling the void left behind by his father, had passed away a few days previously. It was a sure sign of his mental strength.

He still could not find a regular place in the side until Jason Roy's loss of form in the 2017 Champions Trophy. Bairstow was asked to open the batting in the semi-final when patience with Roy finally ran out and he was dropped. Bairstow made 43 in a doomed cause, but it was enough to ensure he would continue in the role for the one-day series against West Indies later that summer. He played three games, opening with Alex Hales, who then got involved in the Ben Stokes altercation in Bristol and was suspended. Roy was back in. He and Bairstow put on 126 in their first game and 156 in their second, with Bairstow making 141 across the two matches.

They complement each other. Bairstow is strong pulling and cutting, and can punch down the ground too. Roy hits hard straight, so bowlers have continually to change their length. Both play orthodox cricket shots, rather than fancy flicks and ramps. Bairstow puts his one-day power down to his childhood playing hockey, using the same snap of the wrists to generate power, with little follow through, as he would on the hockey field.

'We know we are able to get through tough periods from the bowlers because we have done it before. It means the pressure does not build on you internally. You draw on those previous successes,' said Bairstow. 'Communication is honest. We help each other by talking clearly and simply at the crease. It is a case of just geeing each other up with the odd word, bat taps and glove punches.

'On Sunday [against India] the atmosphere was brilliant, and it was such a big game that actually we did not have to say much to each other to keep going. It was such a great spectacle and crowd to be playing in front of that it was a case of feeding off that energy.

'We communicate about the bowlers, sharing views on if it is seaming, what a particular bowler is trying to achieve and traps they are trying to set for us, and how we go about scoring runs. We will discuss what shots are working, those that are not, and build a shared view on the pitch, communicating this back to the dressing room. The way he [Roy] is striking the ball at the moment and enjoying his cricket brings a calmness to proceedings too. His confidence is infectious.'

A brilliant all-round sportsman, Bairstow could have arguably made it professionally at both football and rugby league. He puts his athleticism in the outfield in ODI cricket down to his years playing rugby, a sport in which it is important to be able to hit the ground and get up again quickly – a bit like diving, picking up and throwing in cricket.

His partnership with Roy just clicked. Roy knows how to handle Bairstow's personality, and they have developed a natural understanding between the wickets, running as well as any other pairing in the England side (Bairstow and Joe Root also run well). Bairstow feeds off Roy's confidence. He feels comfortable to play his own shots when he knows Roy is in control at the other end. It allows Bairstow to concentrate on his own game.

By the time of the group game against New Zealand, they were already the best combination in England's ODI history for any wicket and deserve to be ranked alongside the best of all time. Before this match, they had opened together 30 times, made nine century stands and averaged 65.86 for the first wicket – the best of any opening partnership in history (minimum qualification of 1,000 runs together).

New Zealand knew a good England start could win the game. Everyone also knew Bairstow was still ticking from finding himself the centre of a media storm the week before, even if he denied it in public. 'I was able to divorce myself from the controversy, because I knew it did not matter,' he said. 'I did not pay attention to it. I heard whispers of what had been said, but when you know that the comments were misinterpreted, then you can put it to one side. I guess it is a reminder that during a World Cup everything is magnified.

'I would much rather go out there and just perform and score hundreds or keep wicket without any focus on me. I have scored eight ODI hundreds, and for seven of them I have flown completely under the radar before the game, so to suggest I need criticism to produce a performance is misguided.'

It did not matter as far as Morgan was concerned. He had his own demons to exorcise after that disastrous World Cup game against New Zealand in 2015. Morgan rebuilt his team in the style of that New Zealand side and used Brendon McCullum as his model, but there was no time for sentiment now. England had a semi-final place to grab, and New Zealand stood in their way. Lose, and England thought they would probably go out. All that hard work, all those years of planning would have been for nothing, just another glorious failure to add to a long list of disappointments down the years.

But the tide was turning for England. New Zealand were faltering in the tournament. They had lost to Australia at Lord's and Pakistan in Birmingham. Martin Guptill, their opener, was badly out of form, and the team were relying heavily on Kane Williamson and Ross Taylor.

When it emerged that Lockie Ferguson would not be fit for the match, it gave England a huge boost. His pace was a weapon that could really unsettle the big hitters in the team. The weather too was improving. It was sunny and warm in the north-east, and Durham were generous hosts, producing a flat, dry batting pitch that suited England's batsmen. Trevor Bayliss was delighted when he peeled back the covers the day before the game and saw the surface.

Morgan had now settled on his best XI too, with Liam Plunkett the extra seamer in place of Moeen Ali and Roy fit enough to play, if not fully recovered from his hamstring injury.

The meeting with the team psychologist before the India game in Birmingham had brought back the calm environment Morgan had spent four years building. 'Part of the meeting the other day was to emphasise the process we've been through,' he said. 'The hard work we've put in and also the hard work you have to put in in order to earn the right to win a game of cricket. It will be a matter of staying in the moment and trying to stick to that process. And not being lured into worrying about consequences.'

So, England no longer feared failure. They believed in themselves again. It was perfect timing with so much at stake.

The toss would be huge. Morgan called correctly and opted to bat first, as putting runs on the board had become the way to go in this World Cup. In total, 12 of the last 15 games of the tournament before the match in Durham had been won by the side batting first. Chasing was hard on pitches that slowed under the afternoon sun, a reversal of what you would normally expect. Going into the World Cup, England had won 19 of 50 games batting first. They were a chasing side, but not any more.

Ferguson's injury and winning the toss immediately produced an air of confidence around the team. It felt as though events were conspiring to make this the day they qualified for their first World Cup semi-final since 1992.

A big crowd at Durham was partisan and had local boys Mark Wood, Ben Stokes and Liam Plunkett, now at Surrey but from Middlesbrough, to get behind. The north-east loves its own, and Wood had written a song about Plunkett for the occasion. The Barmy Army sang it all day.

Ooh aah Liam Plunkett,
Ooh aah six or four
Ooh aah Liam Plunkett he just keeps on getting poles
Ooh aah Liam Plunkett
Ooh aah six or four
Ooh aah Liam Plunkett he just keeps on getting poles

It was sung to the tune of Gina G's 'Ooh Aah Just a Little Bit'. Naff and cheesy, but at least England were laughing and smiling again.

Wood is the funniest man in the team. His team-mates fear what he would be like if he had a drink. Wood and Stokes had been inundated with requests for tickets from friends and former club cricket team-mates. Wood joked half of his home town of Ashington would be at the game.

Wood would have a hand, quite literally, in a special day for England.

It started with business as usual from Roy and Bairstow. Williamson brought back the old tactic of opening with spin to England, and Mitchell Santner nearly speared an arm ball into Roy's stumps in the first over, but that was the only early alarm. Bairstow and Roy maximised the pace in the pitch and lack of movement in the air. They took the attack to New Zealand, not quite as viciously as McCullum had in Welling-ton four years previously, but just as decisively. This was the match-winning stand.

They put on 123 in 18.4 overs, brutally taking down Tim Southee, playing his only match of the tournament as a late call-up for Ferguson. Southee had taken the third best-ever World Cup figures in Wellington four years ago, and now was the time for revenge from England. He showed that net bowling is no substitute for match practice as he got his line and length wrong and was hammered. His first two overs cost 23, and he would concede 70 from nine in total. Roy hit eight fours in making 60 off 61 balls before falling to Jimmy Neesham, having just walloped him for fours off his previous two balls.

Bairstow carried on the attack, moving into the 90s with a straight six off Southee. At the other end, Joe Root became the first England batsman to make 500 runs in a World Cup tournament as England rattled along at 6.7 an over.

Bairstow has a habit of getting out in the 90s, but not this time. He hammered two fours in three balls off Southee to bring up a second consecutive hundred.

After 30 overs, England were 194 for one and totally dominant. Williamson was forced to turn to his main wicket-taking threat, Trent Boult. He removed Root with his first ball, and in the following over after a drinks break Bairstow played on. England lost momentum as the pitch became tackier and New Zealand took pace off the ball and restricted them to four an over. A succession of batsmen holed out trying to force the pace, but Adil Rashid and Plunkett put on 29 in three overs to take England beyond the 300 barrier. It looked to be plenty of runs unless Williamson played a great innings.

'It was about quickly identifying the wicket was changing and becoming more difficult to bat on and reacting accordingly,' said Morgan about England's batting. 'There were probably a couple of soft dismissals, but that is being extremely hard because of the nature of the wicket. It is not easy to come in and adapt when trying to push on from the great start we had.'

Chris Woakes struck with his fifth ball, hitting Henry Nicholls on the pads in front. The batsmen conferred, but Nicholls, a junior player in the side, did not want to waste their only review and was out for a golden duck. It was a mistake. Hawkeye tracked the ball missing the stumps.

Archer bowled quickly at the other end, nipping out Guptill, caught behind down the leg side in the sixth over for eight. It was Archer's 17th wicket of the World Cup and took him past Ian Botham's 16 in 1992 as the record for most at a World Cup by an England bowler.

The dismissal brought together Williamson and Taylor at 14 for two for what felt like the crucial stand of the innings. They brought a sense of calm, guiding their side to 61 for two without taking any risks. England looked to be out of ideas on how to dismiss Williamson, arguably the most accomplished batsman in the world. It would take something special or a mistake to get rid of him.

In the end it was a downright bizarre dismissal that proved it was England's day. Taylor drove a good-length ball from Wood back at the bowler. He instinctively stuck his hand out. The ball brushed his fingertips on the way to hitting the stumps at the non-striker's end. Williamson was short of his ground. A review checked if Wood had made contact, with the stump microphone picking up a slight deflection. Williamson was out for 27.

'I have tiny hands. He doesn't know how unlucky he is for me to get a hand on it,' said Wood. 'He is like Joe Root for us, the guy who often sees them home. He is one of the best players I have ever bowled at, so to get him out without actually having to bowl the ball at him was especially pleasing.'

Taylor was run out in the next over taking a second run after playing a shot to fine leg. It was a poor decision to go for the run but evidence of the improvement in England's fielding. The fielder on the rope was Rashid, a player many teams would have taken on down the years. But he proved again how hard he has worked on his fielding with the coaches, and this time picked and threw with accuracy and pace to Buttler, with Taylor a long way short of his ground.

Jimmy Neesham, Colin de Grandhomme and Mitchell Santner are a strong lower-middle order but fell to the northeast double act of Wood and Stokes. Neesham played on to Wood, who trapped Santner in front leg-before, while Stokes strangled de Grandhomme with a loosener that he slapped straight to deep square leg.

Tom Latham proved there were still runs in the pitch with a fluent 57 from 65 balls, but New Zealand could not muster any support at the other end. Wood's homecoming was completed when he bowled Matt Henry, a reward for consistently bowling at 90mph and pushing the batsmen back, finishing with three for 34.

New Zealand were beaten by 119 runs when Rashid turned one past Boult, who was stumped smartly by Buttler. England had made it to the semi-finals. They had won two games in a row to save themselves. They had been positive and fallen back on the values that had made them so strong in the first place.

'I'm buzzing,' said Wood. 'It was a must-win game, almost more like a quarter-final than a group game. I'm just delighted we have managed to qualify after a couple of ropey games. It is nice to come back strong and really show what we are made of, show some mettle.

'We are very high in confidence now. Not just confidence, but the fact we are getting back to the methods we used to play with. In the last couple of games, we have showed that by sticking to the values and methods we have used previously, it stands us in good stead. In some ways it shows a lot of courage to do that, especially when your backs are up against the wall. To then say "Look, this is how we are going to play, this is what we are going to do" then to carry that forward and win the game is really pleasing.'

In the Indoor School at the Riverside, the ICC set up its mixed zone, a roped-off area where media interviews are conducted. Players or coaches move from one group to another – from broadcasters to local media, foreign media and the UK national press. Bayliss was first to speak. The coach had seen it all before. He had of course taken Sri Lanka to the World Cup final in 2011, but this was different. Winning the World Cup this time was why he had been appointed England's head coach. Now his team were two games away from achieving it.

'The semi-finals are the business end of this competition,' he said. 'Our first aim was to get to the semi-finals, and we have got there now on the back of two very good games.'

Morgan was jubilant. He knew his side had ticked off the minimum requirement of reaching the last four, where they expected to play India in Birmingham. But the players now had eight days until the semi-final at Edgbaston, enough time for old doubts to creep in again. 'For us it is about staying true to the work we have done and the way we play,' said Morgan. 'My plan is to spend as much time as possible away from the cricket field now. The last few weeks have been very intense, and we have gone through the highs and lows of winning, and we are delighted to be through to semi-finals. Everybody is going to be encouraged to get away.'

Morgan went to Wimbledon, to sit in the Royal Box on Centre Court, where he, Root and Bairstow were introduced to the crowd, standing up to take the applause. It was on the middle Saturday of the championship, and Morgan spent a long time checking his phone. South Africa were playing Australia at Old Trafford in a match many people thought would go one way. Australia were on a roll, and South Africa had been poor throughout the tournament. But while watching Roger Federer and Rafael Nadal win on Centre Court, Morgan had a surprise.

South Africa, as they often do, raised their game against Australia. They pulled off a stunning win that meant England would now play Australia in the semi-final, not India. It would be at Edgbaston too, a ground suited to the Indians, and one where they would have received vociferous support, but a place Australians fear to tread. They had not won an ODI there for more than 20 years.

Fate had been kind to Morgan.

FOURTEEN
YOU ENGLISH HAVE WON NOTHING YET

SEMI-FINAL – ENGLAND V. AUSTRALIA

EDGBASTON, BIRMINGHAM

11 July 2019

You think you have seen most things as a journalist, and then you turn up at Edgbaston and discover that the Australian squad have been walking barefoot around the ground, apparently in order to capture 'positive energy coming out of the earth'.

It was certainly a very different way to prepare for a World Cup semi-final against England. It was, inevitably, the brain-child of head coach Justin Langer, who, as someone keen on philosophy and psychology, has always possessed a spiritual side and has written a book called *Seeing the Sunrise*, described as a 'handbook for overcoming self-doubt'.

'I'm also a bit of a hippy,' Langer said when he was

appointed Australia head coach in 2018. 'One month every year I like to grow a beard and not wear shoes.'

The Australians walked a lap of the outfield barefoot before gathering in a circle, where Langer spoke at length and the players then exchanged stories. 'It's something the coach has done before at other venues for a bit of grounding,' said batsman Peter Handscomb, who had replaced the injured Shaun Marsh (broken arm) in the Australian squad, and had probably never imagined that he would be answering questions on such a subject. The process seemed to be called 'earthing', and its advocates claim that it can reduce stress and inflammation, and improve sleep and wellbeing.

'It was just a moment to get a feel for the ground, literally,' said Handscomb. 'You get a feel of the grass on your feet, a bit of grounding, the positive and negative energy flowing through and coming out of the earth.

'You do that lap and you can see all the different views and where you might be fielding. It gives you an opportunity to take it all in before it all starts. You walk round with the group, have a bit of a laugh while you're going and talking. It is just a nice moment.

'There were some really good stories. It was an honest conversation, and it was great that some of the guys poured their heart out about what it meant to get to the semi-final, and their first memories of cricket growing up. It was really nice. It was great to see what playing in the finals means to this group.

'I actually liked Mitch Marsh's story. He was talking about the 1999 World Cup [which Australia won] with his dad [Geoff] coaching and having a photo done with the World Cup trophy, so Mitch wants to be there, and he wants to have a photo on the balcony at Lord's, which is pretty awesome.'

231

But the earthing story naturally attracted some ridicule, and it was difficult to escape the conclusion that Australia were spooked by their record at Edgbaston. They had not won at the ground since the Ashes Test of 2001, a run that included ten matches in different formats. England had also won their past ten matches at Edgbaston, whether in Tests or white-ball cricket, stretching back to a one-day international against India in 2014 for their most recent defeat.

The crowd at the ground, especially those in the Hollies Stand who had become rather well-oiled by mid-afternoon, is renowned for being raucous and loud. As Graeme Swann once said: 'It's the closest you get as a cricketer to knowing what it's like to be a professional footballer.' Little wonder England consider it their fortress (or they did until losing the Ashes Test there later in the year, anyway).

Of course, Handscomb tried to play all this down. He had to. 'It really doesn't make a difference,' he said. 'Nah, I mean, they're past games. We know the crowd is amazing here. It's electric, they come out, they let you know about it.

'That's part of it. That's part of playing cricket around the world, that different venues offer different things. We know this crowd is going to be tough, but that gets us going just as much as it gets them going.'

The England team were apparently thoroughly bemused by the barefoot business. Asked if he had heard of a team doing such a thing before, Joe Root said: 'I haven't, no. Each to their own. It is something that is important to them. They can prepare how they want. We will make sure we are ready in our own way.'

Some people in the Australia camp are thought to have wished it had been done in a closed session, without the media present. When Langer was asked about it before the match, he inevitably denied that it was anything to do with the spiritual earthing movement, saying that he and his Test-match opening partner Matthew Hayden used to do it regularly as a way of relaxing before a big match.

'"Haydos" and I used to do it before every Test as a bit of a ritual,' he said. 'We just took our shoes and socks off and did a lap of the ground. It's a nice place to be.

'We know we're going to be up against it, because England are a great team, and the best way to be at our best is to be nice and relaxed. We could have kept our shoes on, and no one would have said anything, so I wouldn't read too much into that. It wasn't the first time we've done it. We've done it about 15 times.

'You can walk on the best grounds in the world with your shoes off. We had a tough game against South Africa [who had beaten Australia by ten runs in their last group match], and it's just about staying as relaxed as possible.'

Indeed, it had been a tough game for Australia, the five-times winners of the World Cup. Nobody had been expecting them to face England here. It had been assumed that they would be playing New Zealand in the first semi-final at Old Trafford, where they had played South Africa. So, the defeat in that match had meant a change in travel plans, and a quick decision to do the barefoot walkabout upon arrival. You suspect they might have done things differently given their time again.

It really was a huge occasion. A World Cup semi-final between the old foes, with England having the opportunity to reach a final for the first time in 27 years. Given that they had thrashed New Zealand by 119 runs in their group match eight days previously, it seemed likely that it would be an incentive that England would meet the Kiwis, who had stunned India by 18 runs in the first semi-final, in the final three days later at Lord's (a ridiculously short turnaround for one team in a tournament that had lasted so long) if they beat Australia.

And captain Eoin Morgan was by now confident that his team had overcome the travails that had pockmarked their three group-stage defeats. 'We are a different team from that which played four games ago,' he said. 'The loss against Sri Lanka hurt us. It was an overhang into the game against Australia, and then when we came here [against India], we managed to produce something similar to the cricket we have been playing over the last four years. We went to Durham [against New Zealand] and improved again. It feels like we are back to the team that we are.'

Ben Stokes certainly recognised the magnitude of the occasion. 'Yes, to date, definitely, it is my most important game,' he said. 'It's a massive occasion for us as players and as a nation. The support has been brilliant. Playing against Australia is a big occasion in any sport. The rivalry goes way back, and we have the Ashes this summer too.

'Beating them is that touch better than any other team. Losing to them at Lord's [in the group stage] was massively disappointing, so I think there will be a bit of redemption for that, knowing we have the chance to beat them and get to the final.'

Crucially, of course, England now had Jason Roy back opening the batting. And he rather likes playing ODIs against Australia. His England ODI record score of 180 was made against them in Melbourne in 2018. He averaged 47.43 against them in 16 matches before this one, as opposed to his overall ODI average of 42.58. His strike rate was 114.30 against them, compared with 107.05 overall. He had also made two centuries and an 82 in his past four ODIs against Australia.

So, his return was rather important, but it was even more significant considering how the group game at Lord's had gone. Australia's openers, Aaron Finch and David Warner, had won the match there for their team.

It was certainly going to be a contrast of styles at the top of the order: the more belligerent Roy and Bairstow against the more conservative Finch and Warner. 'We know how they are going to play; they know how we are going to play,' said Finch. 'So, it will be whoever holds their nerves, whoever takes the half-chances, whoever starts off the game really well in the first ten overs, whether it is with bat or ball, it will be so important for either side.'

The opening salvoes here were going to be critical, especially as regards to how England's batsmen coped with the twin left-arm threat of Jason Behrendorff and Mitchell Starc, who had taken nine wickets between them in the group-stage match.

There was plenty of practice against left-armers at Edgbaston, with two coaches – Ant Botha, a South African former left-arm spinner, now an assistant coach at Nottinghamshire, and Jamaican-born Donovan Miller, who had worked at Essex and came recommended by Sir Alastair Cook – brought in specifically to throw left-armers with their dog sticks. Left-arm seamers had also been asked along to practice sessions regularly throughout the tournament (Warwickshire provided three here), and at Lord's before the group match against Australia, Sachin Tendulkar's son Arjun was there bowling his lively left-armers.

Eoin Morgan pointed to a combination of problems, including that hangover from the Sri Lanka match, surrounding the wickets taken by the left-armers in that Australia group match. 'Losing wickets early hurt us,' he said. 'I don't think we were anywhere near playing our best cricket. On top of that, there was a hangover from the Sri Lanka game, and since then we have played against quality bowling line-ups and overcome them, one of them obviously being a left-armer, [New Zealand's] Trent Boult. All we can do is practise as much as we can against left-armers, but we need to deliver now.'

Morgan was also questioned about Kevin Pietersen's 'scared' tweet. He told the BBC that he likened it to criticism from Geoffrey Boycott, that it was 'not good for a team environment.' Morgan said that he thought he had addressed problems with the short ball that had begun when Starc hit him four years previously.

And no Anglo-Australian match build-up would have been complete without some provocative words of encouragement from one of the Australians. Step forward their garrulous off spinner Nathan Lyon. 'They're full of world-class players, and they've been the no. 1 team for a couple of years now,' said Lyon. 'They should be going into this World Cup as favourites. It's all on them. It's their World Cup to lose, if you ask me. We've got nothing to lose; we've only got stuff to gain. That's the exciting thing.'

England were not about to rise to the bait. 'Nathan has a lot to say a lot of the time, so for me you just take it with a pinch of salt,' said Joe Root. 'It might be a way of taking pressure off himself and his team. We know what we need to do to perform well. I try not to get too involved, to be honest. There have been times within games when it has got a bit spicy, and there have been a few exchanges on the field, but generally we will go about things in our own way.'

Despite losing that group match against Australia at Lord's, as well as the warm-up fixture in Southampton, England had still won ten of their previous 12 ODIs against the old enemy. 'There has been a lot made of the fear factor of playing against Australia,' said Root. 'But as regards this group of players over the last four years, their experiences against

Australia are very positive. They have got a lot of success in the bank. We will be drawing on the confidence that, over a long period of time now, we have been successful against Australia, and we should take that into this game.'

And Root felt that the pressure of the matches against India and New Zealand had benefited England. 'I feel the last two games have been like knockout games for us, and that will hold us in good stead going into this game,' he said. 'We've found a good way of playing on this surface at Edgbaston. It suits the way we play one-day cricket. And you get a real sense of belief from the crowd here. It does make a difference. I do believe that. Whether it's the noise bouncing off the stands, I don't know whether it's just this ground, but I do feel there's a great element of support here. It's always been somewhere I've enjoyed turning up to play.'

And so it would prove again. Aaron Finch won the toss and batted. And Australia won the first ball of the day when David Warner cracked Chris Woakes through the covers for four. It was the last thing they won all day.

One ball from Jofra Archer, the seventh of the match, was all that it took to get rid of Finch. Archer had dismissed Finch in the group match at Lord's, but the problem then was that the opener had already made a century. At Lord's, Archer's first ball to him had been a gentle half-volley that was dispatched to the cover boundary. This delivery was very different. This one was pitched on a good length, as was the plan. It was brilliantly executed. The ball hit the seam, nipped back at Finch and thudded into his front pad. It looked out, and it was given out. Finch reviewed in desperation, but he knew. A golden duck it was.

Australia soon lost a second wicket, as Warner, undone by the extra bounce, fenced at Chris Woakes and edged to Jonny Bairstow at first slip. Peter Handscomb arrived at no. 4, but he looked just like a man who had not played in this tournament. He could easily have been out first ball leg-before, but England's review was just denied. He looked horribly out of touch throughout his 12-ball stay for four, before he was bowled by Woakes off the inside edge. Australia were 14 for three in the seventh over.

The game was almost decided. It is such a long way back from that kind of start. Just as Australia had dominated the opening stages at Lord's, so here England took charge. At the end of the powerplay, Australia were 27 for three.

Woakes's opening spell of six overs yielded just 16 runs and those two wickets. Archer did not take another wicket in his opening five-over spell, but he was quick and hostile, and he hit Alex Carey on the jaw with his fifth ball. It was a devilish bouncer, which the Australian left-handed batsman–wicketkeeper simply could not avoid. One of Archer's many outstanding attributes is that he bowls so close to the stumps that when he does bowl a short ball, there is no angle with which the batsman can work. That wicket-to-wicket quality, of course, is a problem for opposing batsmen with all of Archer's deliveries, but the others do not carry this sort of physical threat. Swaying one way or the other is almost impossible. To duck or play are really the only alternatives, and ducking is not easy because there also does not appear to be any obvious clue as to when Archer's bouncer is coming. With most bowlers, there is some sort of sign, however small. With Archer, that does not appear to be the case.

Carey was hit so hard on the chin that his helmet flew off. His reactions and awareness were quite superb for him to be able to catch it before it landed on the stumps. But he required lengthy treatment, and his face began to swell. At first the medical staff stopped the bleeding from his jaw with a plaster, but, such was the swelling, they returned later to put strapping around his head, making him look much like Rick McCosker once had during the Centenary Test in Melbourne in 1977 when he bravely batted with a broken jaw after being hit by Bob Willis. Carey played Twenty20 cricket for Sussex after the tournament. When Archer saw him in Hove, he pointed to the scar on Carey's face and asked him if he had cut himself shaving. He blends menace and a sense of humour.

Carey and Steve Smith rescued their side, putting on 103, before Carey hit Adil Rashid out to deep mid-wicket. It was the first of three wickets for the England leg spinner, and his best performance, statistically anyway, of the tournament. His first four overs of the match had gone for 29, and it would have been easy for Eoin Morgan to look elsewhere, but Morgan had long backed Rashid. He had long recognised his importance as a wicket-taker in the middle overs of an ODI.

It had not always been like this. After playing five ODIs in 2009, Rashid had been totally discarded by England. It was a combination of his not being ready and trust not being easily placed in him. By the time the revolution began after the 2015 World Cup, Rashid was more ready with his alluring mixture of accuracy and penetration. 'Since 2015, I've got a lot more accurate, and my game plan is a lot more solid with what I want to achieve,' he said. 'When I first started, I maybe didn't know what I wanted to bowl or how I wanted to bowl, but as the years have gone on I've concentrated on my game plan, and I've stuck by it. It is about being attacking, but that can also help keep the runs down, and that is what has happened.'

The team environment that Rashid returned to was now very different too. 'Different faces, young faces,' he told

Cricbuzz. 'It was, "Right, lads, we are going to play a different brand of cricket. We are going to be exciting. We are going to take the positive option regardless of whether we might lose games." A new England.'

Rashid was 31 at the 2019 World Cup, and his tale was a reminder that you need to be patient with wrist spinners, for their art is surely the most difficult of all the disciplines in cricket. Their roads are bumpier than most. Rashid had made his first-class debut in 2006, aged 18, and had taken six second-innings wickets for Yorkshire against Warwickshire. But there were many lessons to learn on and off the field. 'They say leg spinners develop in their late 20s, early 30s,' he said. 'When I was playing from 18 to 22 or 23, when there was a big game, I felt I needed to do well.

'But my lifestyle then is different to my lifestyle now. Now I'm a bit more relaxed, because I'm a bit more into my religion, which teaches you to take a day at a time and stay calm and accept whatever happens. My mindset before wasn't really thinking about anything and that cricket was the be all and end all.'

Rashid was the leading ODI wicket-taker in between World Cups, and at the end of the 2019 tournament he was, with 143, England's sixth-highest wicket-taker ever in the format, behind the seamers James Anderson, Darren Gough, Stuart Broad, Andrew Flintoff and Ian Botham. Chris Woakes was one behind him on 142, and Liam Plunkett was next on the list with 135. This further demonstrated the quality of the 2019 team, but it also pointed, in a way, to what might have been with Rashid.

His relationship with Morgan was critical. This was not a tournament in which spinners excelled, and once England decided that they had to play Plunkett and therefore drop a spinner it would have been easy to have gone with the safer hands – and the better batting – of Moeen Ali rather than Rashid. But Morgan wanted Rashid's wicket-taking ability.

'A hundred per cent Morgs is the best captain I have played under,' said Rashid. 'He knows my game inside out. I've been with him for four years, through good times and not so good times. He knows my strengths, what I'm capable of, and vice-versa as well.

'We have that communication. We have that trust as well. If he senses a feel, we'll go by it. If I sense a feel, we'll go by it – what plans we want or how we should bowl. It's very easy like that. We're easy-going like that. I trust him 100 per cent in the decisions he makes.'

Rashid had not been blessed with a great deal of luck in the competition. 'There's been some games where I felt as though I've been a bit unlucky,' he said. 'There's been a few dropped catches and missed stumpings.'

More importantly, Rashid had not been fully fit through-out the tournament. He had struggled with a shoulder problem, and bowling his dangerous googly had therefore become problematic for him. He did not play again in the 2019 season after the final and was told his rotator cuff would not take any more painkilling cortisone injections.

'Just before the World Cup I had an injection,' he said. 'In terms of variations, googlies and stuff, it's been a bit differ-ent to what it was pre-shoulder problem. Before the shoulder [injury], I was confident bowling everything. Once you have a niggle, it becomes a bit harder with the rotation – the arm gets a bit lower and you don't find that snap.'

But the googly was back against Australia, as he trapped Marcus Stoinis, who clearly did not pick it, lbw second ball. 'It was nice to make a batsman go for a cut on the back foot and spinning it back in with one that he doesn't pick,' said Rashid. 'That's a nice feeling.'

Rashid dismissed Pat Cummins too, caught by Joe Root at slip, but the wicket of the dangerous Glenn Maxwell by Jofra Archer was particularly clever. Maxwell had struggled with the short ball in the tournament, so Eoin Morgan immediately called Archer back into the attack upon the batsman's arrival in the middle. But it was not actually the short ball that proved Maxwell's downfall, rather it was a well-disguised knuckle ball that the batsman chipped to cover. Maxwell looked angrily at the pitch, but he had been deceived by the bowler rather than by the surface, with Archer changing his grip in his action and the batsman thinking it was a normal seamer. Archer had been working on the ball in the nets for the whole summer, but this was the first time he had used it in a match, and it brought instant success.

All the while Smith was desperately trying to hold his side together. He played superbly for his 85, but when he was brilliantly run out by Jos Buttler, all hope of Australia posting a substantial total went. They ended up 223 all out, with one over remaining.

It never looked enough, and England set off in pursuit like men in a hurry. Jonny Bairstow hit his first ball – from Jason Behrendorff – for four through the covers, and Jason Roy was soon doing the same to Mitchell Starc, twice in one over even. By the end of the sixth over, Roy had already played the shot of the match – maybe one of the shots of the tournament – as he flicked Starc, with an exaggerated wrist motion, for six over fine leg.

England were 31 without loss after six, then 50 off ten. At this point Aaron Finch decided to introduce the off spin of Nathan Lyon into the attack. A long-on was in position, but Roy just launched Lyon's first ball over his head for six. It was utterly dismissive. Lyon's five overs disappeared for 49. Starc's nine overs went for 70, even if he did trap Bairstow, who had earlier received treatment for a groin injury, leg-before for 34.

In desperation, Finch had turned to the leg spin of Smith in the 16th over of the innings. In days gone by, especially with England already cruising at 95 without loss, English batsmen might have approached him cautiously, maybe even fearing getting out to the part-timer. Not Jason Roy. He destroyed him, hitting him for three successive sixes from the last three balls of the over, the last six hitting the top tier of the huge new stand. Seasoned Warwickshire observers ranked it the biggest six hit at the ground.

'I thought it was going over [the stand],' Roy said, and when asked whether he had ever hit a bigger six, he replied: 'Absolutely not.'

The crowd were in raptures. There was rain around – even a weather warning for the area – and 20 overs needed to be bowled to make a match of it on the day (a reserve day was available), but nothing was going to stop England from here.

Those sixes took Roy and Bairstow past their fourth century opening partnership in the tournament. How different England looked with Roy back. When Bairstow did depart, he took a review with him, which was a little silly because it was plumb, and it would soon have ramifications for Roy. First, though, Joe Root came to the crease and gloved his first ball from Starc just out of the reach of wicketkeeper Carey and away for four. There were two more boundaries in that over as Root joined in on the fun.

Roy had passed fifty from 50 balls and was on 85 (off just 65 balls, with nine fours and five sixes) when Pat Cummins bowled him a short ball that went down the leg side. There was an appeal from the Australians, but it looked more like an attempt to avoid a wide being called. Remarkably, umpire Kumar Dharmasena, blundering again, gave Roy out, even though he appeared to doubt himself as he was raising his finger, hesitating for the slightest millisecond.

Roy could not believe it and called for a review. He had clearly not hit the ball. When he realised that a review was not possible, because Bairstow had already burned the one England had, he refused to go. Eventually Roy had to be ushered on his way by both umpires, with Marais Erasmus helping Dharmasena.

Roy was seething. He could be seen mouthing that it was 'fucking embarrassing' as he departed from the field. He threw his gloves when he reached the pavilion. That much could be seen on television. But it turned out that he then smashed a cool box full of drinks with his bat, cracking the box. One insider said it sounded as if a gun had gone off. There may have been an expletive or two as well.

You could understand Roy's frustration. He had been unjustly denied a century in a World Cup semi-final, and against Australia too. But you cannot behave as he did on the field. A meeting with match referee Ranjan Madugalle was inevitable. There was a possibility that Roy could even miss the final.

Thankfully, he was instead fined 30 per cent of his match fee and given two demerit points, taking his tally for the tournament up to three after having been given one point for shouting an audible obscenity in the match against Pakistan at Trent Bridge. Four demerit points would have meant a ban. Roy was seriously worried that might be the case and he could miss the final. Once he was told in the meeting that he could play in the final, he just said thank you and walked out. He was such a relieved man. It was also good to see Roy hugging umpire Dharmasena by way of apology before the final at Lord's. And, so we are told, he was back in good spirits swiftly after this match.

Chris Woakes was given the man-of-the-match award for his three for 20 from his eight overs. For that he received a trophy and an expensive Hublot watch, worth around £15,000, with watches only being given to the man-of-the-match winners in the two semi-finals and the final. Roy made no secret about who he thought should have got the award. 'That's my watch you've got,' he playfully told Woakes.

For Woakes, though, it was a special day on his home patch, which afterwards he called 'the greatest ground in the world'. Woakes was an unsung hero in the side. His nickname is 'the wizard', a moniker first given to him on an England Under-19 tour when the squad were playing darts and needed to give each other names, but in the press box he is probably more regularly referred to as 'the nicest man in cricket'. He is a delightfully polite, cheery and self-effacing man. His temperament is ideally suited to international cricket, whether opening the bowling or then returning for the 'death' overs, with his off-cutters and his bouncers both fast and slow. He can bat rather well too, even if, aside from the 40 he made when promoted to no. 3 against West Indies, he did not have too much opportunity to show that in this tournament.

He was a huge loss for England in the 2017 Champions Trophy when he pulled a side muscle after bowling just two overs in the opener against Bangladesh at the Oval. And, in truth, injuries, especially chronic tendonitis in his right knee, hampered him a lot between then and the 2019 World Cup.

But England knew how important he could be when fully fit, as he duly showed. He just got better and better as the tournament went on. Here he was simply outstanding.

'Chris is a cool customer,' said Eoin Morgan. 'He goes about his business, day in and day out, exceptionally. Today was his day. He stood head and shoulders above everybody else, purely for his accuracy. He and Jofra Archer were outstanding.

245

It was one of our bowlers' stand-out performances in the last four years.'

As for Woakes, he was typically unassuming. 'I'm pretty speechless,' he said. 'It was an incredible performance from the whole team – started well with the bowling and then the batting was outstanding.

'I don't think it was a bad wicket. We just found the right length, and they had to rebuild, and we kept the pressure on. The first ball I'd like to have had back [that four for David Warner], but other than that I felt I hit my straps and bowled the right lengths on the wicket.'

When Roy was out, captain Morgan had come to the crease. England were cruising, but that was not going to stop Australia from peppering Morgan with the short ball. Of Morgan's first 11 balls from Pat Cummins and Mitchell Starc, eight were short. At one point, Aaron Finch positioned himself on the boundary directly behind his wicketkeeper. A backstop in an ODI.

Morgan responded by jumping in the air and uppercutting Starc over point for a four that nearly went all the way for six. When Cummins eventually pitched a ball up (the 13th ball Morgan received), Morgan lofted him over mid-off for four. Morgan was soon able to pull the slower-paced deliveries of Jason Behrendorff and then both reverse-sweep and cut the off spin of Nathan Lyon. He finished with 45 not out from 39 balls (Root was unbeaten on 49 from 46 balls), fittingly hitting the winning runs as he heaved Behrendorff over mid-on for four. There were 107 balls remaining.

The scenes at the end were remarkable, with the utterly joyous crowd singing 'It's Coming Home' and 'Sweet Caroline'. Morgan and Root embraced one another, and a firework display began at the ground.

'The semi-finals are usually nervy, aren't they?' said Woakes. 'They tend to be tight. So, to win the way we did, and by the margin and in that fashion, was special from the whole team.

'We've built momentum nicely, and we know that's how we can play. To do that in such a big game, in a semi-final against Australia, adds a little bit to it as well. It's incredible.

'A few games ago, when we were under pressure to qualify, we probably didn't even think this was possible. So, to do what we've done and to put in this performance, myself as well, we're delighted.'

England were in their first World Cup final since 1992. 'We've got a great opportunity,' said Woakes. 'We turn up on Sunday, it's a new day against a completely new team [New Zealand] who are full of confidence after beating a great India side, so we know we have to be on the money, but we have that opportunity, which is a great thing.'

The England dressing room was ecstatic. But the celebrations did not last long. Just after 6pm, head coach Trevor Bayliss took off his famous blue England floppy hat – he was rarely seen without it during his time with England (mainly because he had always been warned of the dangers of skin cancer as a youngster), although it was stolen from his car just before this match and he was forced to wear a straw hat at training – and called all his players together.

As we have seen, Bayliss rarely says much, and both he and Eoin Morgan do not like long meetings or grandstanding speeches, so, as they had in their meeting in the Shangri-La hotel in Colombo the year before, the players knew something serious was going to be said.

And there was. Bayliss had a very important message. He started by telling them he was going to talk to them as an Australian, not as the coach of the England team. He did

247

not want any complacency. He knew that England cricketers always want to celebrate the hardest when they have beaten Australia. That is what the rivalry is all about. But this was not the right time.

'You English are all the bloody same,' he apparently said. 'You win a semi-final, and you think you have cracked it. Well, you've won nothing yet.'

The players were stunned. They put down their drinks, and silence descended upon the room. Then Morgan spoke too, reiterating what Bayliss had said.

Morgan had harboured regrets for two years over the way the side had reacted at the same ground to beating Australia in the 2017 Champions Trophy to reach the last four of the competition. They had celebrated until the early hours of the morning. It was as if they had already played their final. They were then beaten by Pakistan in the semi-final in Cardiff three days later.

Bayliss and Morgan had agreed they would speak up this time and make sure the same thing did not happen again. There would be no wild partying. That could wait until after the final. Instead, a few quiet drinks in the dressing room were permitted, while those with families went out and played with their children on the Edgbaston outfield.

There was still much to do.

FIFTEEN
ECSTASY BY THE BAREST OF MARGINS

THE SUPER OVER – ENGLAND V. NEW ZEALAND

LORD'S, LONDON

14 July 2019 – 7pm

L ord's was a cacophony of noise. Music was blaring out of the public-address system, and the atmosphere was tense, electric, as the World Cup final came down to a Super Over. Twelve balls would settle a seven-week tournament and decide the legacy of this England team.

Finding a quiet spot as the frenzy of the Super Over approaches is hard in a ground packed out with 27,000 supporters, and television cameras following the players from the middle, through the Long Room and up the stairs to the dressing room. But Ben Stokes has played at Lord's many times. He knows every nook and cranny. As Eoin Morgan tries to bring calm to the England dressing room and sort out their tactics, Stokes nips off for a moment of peace.

He is covered in dirt and sweat. He has batted for two hours and 27 minutes of unbelievable tension. At various stages he thought he had blown it, and he feels guilty about the deflection off his bat that went for four. He is also angry with his last stroke, because he hit it too straight to mid-on, so he and Mark Wood were unable to complete the two runs to win the match.

He had actually shown incredible restraint by not trying to hit it, a full toss on his legs, for the six that would have won England the World Cup. He did not want to risk ignominy by being caught on the rope and instead tried to guide it into the gap and run hard. It did not work.

He booted his bat ten yards, drop-kicking it as if it was a rugby ball, when he saw Wood had been run out. He is still upset with himself now, as he tries to come to terms with what happened. He has to compose himself quickly and ignore the pain from his toe because Morgan wants him to go back out and bat again in the Super Over.

What does Stokes do? He goes to the back of the England dressing room, past the attendant's little office and into the showers. There he lights up a cigarette very briefly before having a quick shower to refresh.

If the DJ at the ground had known this, he would surely have played Bach's 'Air on a G String', for the music from the Hamlet cigars advert from the 1980s would have been the perfect backdrop as Stokes tried to make peace with the task ahead of him.

Stokes already knew he would have to go back out. Morgan had asked him if he was willing to bat again as he struggled up the stairs on his way back to the dressing room at the end of the 50th over. Stokes had expected Jason Roy and Jos Buttler to do the job, but Morgan wanted a left- and right-hand combination at the crease. It also made sense because Buttler and Stokes were tuned in to the pace of the pitch, which had changed in the three hours since Roy had batted.

The dressing room was in chaos. Aleem Dar was explaining the rules of the Super Over, Jason Roy had lost his box and had to borrow one from Mark Wood, and Jofra Archer was having an injection in his side.

Stokes was putting a cooling spray on his hands because of cramps, Buttler let out his frustration by punching the physio's bench as he prepared to go out to bat again. It all happened very quickly. Bayliss and Morgan called the team together for one last chat.

Why do we have Super Overs? Thank Allen Stanford, the disgraced financier now serving a 110-year jail sentence in the United States. When he bankrolled England's $20m winner-takes-all Twenty20 match against the Stanford Superstars in Antigua in 2008, he had to decide what would happen in the event of a tie. A shared prize pot was not the story he wanted, so his organising committee came up with the Super Over idea, which was quickly borrowed by other Twenty20 leagues and the ICC.

The rules of the Super Over are that the batting team goes first but that the bowling side has the choice of ends. Trent Boult surprisingly chose to bowl from the Nursery End rather than use the slope from the Pavilion End. It meant a rethink for Morgan. Originally Roy was padded up to go in next. But after two balls, Morgan decided they needed a left-hander, because they would be hitting to the shorter boundary on the leg side under the Mound Stand. Despite his poor form, Morgan volunteered himself. He would go in if England lost a wicket.

Buttler and Stokes met again on the stairs going out to start the Super Over. Friends for years, they had batted together many times before but never under this pressure. Stokes had never been involved in a Super Over before and afterwards said: 'It's not one of the things I ever want to be involved in again, just because of the stress.'

Buttler drew on his IPL experience: 'I was chosen, but I had my hand up as well. I was ready to go. Morgs said get your pads on. There were ten seconds of: "Oh my God, the game is still going on." It was surreal. Luckily, I have been involved in a few Super Overs before, so it was not a one-off. There was quite a bit of disbelief [in the changing room] at what had just happened. Most people were almost laughing about the way the game was going. Credit to everyone, they were suddenly very switched on and got on with it.'

For Stokes it was time to focus again. 'I had to sort myself out and get back out there,' he said. 'It was a very quick turn-around. A three-minute discussion and that was it. I was the bloke to go out with Jos. I was disappointed we could not get over the line, so I had to go out and clear my mind and get back to the frame of mind I was in before that last over.'

It was no surprise New Zealand turned to Boult. He was the most experienced bowler on either side. A brilliant yorker bowler, albeit lacking the pace of Archer, Wood or, say, Lockie Ferguson – but in this situation accuracy and reliability were required.

It is 7.07pm. The World Cup final started eight hours 37 minutes ago. It feels like a lifetime with all the twists and turns of a five-match Ashes series packed into one day. Nobody has left the ground. Usually there is a reserved, low-sounding hum at Lord's. Now it is as partisan as Edgbaston's Hollies Stand on Test match fancy-dress day. Members are on their feet screaming support; the Barmy Army are in the Mound Stand trying to rally the team.

Sky flash up bullet points on the Super Over for the

uninitiated. Teams are allowed three batsmen. If two wickets fall, it is the end of the over. The last entry seems superfluous: it says in the event of a tie, the team that has hit the most boundaries across the match wins. England are well ahead on 24 to 16. But a Super Over never ends in a tie, does it? It sounds like the kind of arcane rule dreamt up in an ICC meeting room with someone saying: 'This will never happen, so it doesn't matter.'

Someone in the media centre asks: 'What is a par score for a Super Over?' Who knows? Who cares?

England are batting first, just how they like it. They can set the target and pile the pressure on the New Zealand batsmen, who have not been at the crease for hours and will have to recalibrate to its pace in the evening sunshine. A score with double figures is the bare minimum for England. Stokes is on strike.

Ball one: Boult aims for off stump, full length but not quite a yorker. Stokes clears his front leg and tries to whack it through the off side to the Grandstand boundary. The connection is not clean. It loops off the outside edge and over the short third-man fielder, who is up in the ring. Two fielders chase the ball while Stokes and Buttler run. Those sprints on the treadmill in the West Indies are paying off. England's quickest two players are at the crease. Buttler, fresher than Stokes, almost laps his partner. They run for three. Ian Smith, commentating for Sky, is on his feet. His passion and energy bring alive the two overs. 'They can push for three because Buttler is very quick. Stokes is out on his feet, but he will make it,' he says. England: 3–0.

Ball two: Buttler is on strike. Boult goes for his stock ball, the leg-stump yorker. Buttler heaves it to the leg side, lots of bottom hand and bat speed, over the infield and one bounce straight to the fielder at deep mid-wicket. The timing was not quite there. England scramble one. England: 4–0.

Ball three: Boult again bowls full, aiming at Stokes's off stump. Stokes goes down on one knee, sweeps and hits it hard to the short boundary on the leg side. Two fielders on the rope try to cut it off, but it is placed perfectly, and all Guptill can do is deflect the ball into the boundary sponge. 'Has he found the gap? Yes he has. He has. The fielder dived despairingly at full length. He got a hand to it, but he simply ran the ball into the boundary,' says Jonathan Agnew on *Test Match Special*. Phil Tufnell can be heard in the background: 'Get in.' England: 8–0.

Ball four: Boult, despite years of experience and playing his 89th ODI, is flustered. He goes for a wide yorker, gets it horribly wrong and produces a full toss that is waist high. Stokes has to reach for it, but it is a gimme. However, despite the heroics, Stokes is tired and has actually struggled to time the ball all day. This is no different. He slaps it straight to the cover fielder. A metre either side and, with no boundary sweeper posted, it would have been four. It is a missed opportunity. Boult is reprieved. England run one. England: 9–0.

Ball five: Boult has gathered himself. This is better. Right in the blockhole on off stump. Buttler chips it away into the off side. The low evening sun makes fielding hard in a match that should have finished half an hour ago. Henry Nicholls at deep extra cover struggles to pick up the ball in the light. His momentary hesitation allows Buttler and Stokes to run two. England: 11–0.

Ball six: The last ball of the Super Over, and England have Buttler on strike, the 360-degree hitter. Kane Williamson knows the danger. He is worried about Buttler's ramp shot. He brings mid-wicket into the circle so he can move third man down onto the rope to cover the ramp. Boult goes for a leg-stump yorker, but it is off slightly. A full toss. Buttler hits it cleanly to mid-wicket. Two bounces and it is four, with the fielder nowhere to be seen. Stokes leaps in the air twice. Buttler barely breaks a smile. He has a thousand-yard stare. He is in the zone. This is a man who had spent half an hour after his dismissal thinking he had blown it for England, worrying about how he would ever play cricket again if they lost. Now he has clutched his lifeline. England: 15–0.

New Zealand need 16 to win. While England were batting, Jofra Archer had been bowling to Chris Silverwood, the England bowling coach, on the boundary edge in front of the pavilion. There was no mystery over who Morgan had chosen to defend their target.

New Zealand chose Jimmy Neesham to bat. Not a surprise given his hitting, and poignant too, since he was left out of the last World Cup squad in 2015 and watched the final from the stands with his mates. However, that last-ball boundary by Buttler meant that Williamson, New Zealand's best player, could not pick himself to do the job. It required hard hitting, not his level-headedness and deft touches. But who to bat with Neesham? Colin de Grandhomme was the natural choice, but he had struggled to pick Archer's slower-ball bouncers and laboured to 16 off 28 balls, failing to hit a boundary in the New Zealand innings. They instead gambled on Martin Guptill, a player bereft of confidence, for the biggest over in New Zealand's cricketing history. Why? Because he was the quickest runner in the team, and they figured they needed someone fast between the wickets for the twos and threes that would be so important, with Archer certain to take pace off the ball, making boundaries hard to hit. Guptill is a fine striker of the ball. Perhaps he would click.

Archer looked cool and composed. As he stood at his mark, Stokes walked over from mid-on with some advice that Archer will remember for ever. 'Stokesy told me, even before the over: "Win or lose, today does not define you."'

Stokes of course had been hit for four sixes in the last over of the 2016 World Twenty20 final, something that had fascinated Archer when they played together in the IPL. He had asked Stokes one night out of the blue how he'd recovered from that mauling in such a big game. Now he could be about to find out what it felt like. 'I knew that even if we did lose, it was not the end of the world,' said Archer.

Wood, due to his side injury, could not field and was replaced by James Vince. Wood could not take the tension in the dressing room. He sat down in the dugout for the Super Over by the boundary rope, talking Moeen Ali through each ball to come in a vain attempt to calm his nerves. Next to him the team doctor could not look. He stared at the crowd instead.

Despite the outward look of calm, Archer had actually started to mark out his run-up at the Pavilion End, until the umpires told him he had to bowl from the same end as Boult.

'It was an easy decision [to ask Jofra],' said Morgan. 'He's our best yorker bowler; he's one of the best yorker bowlers in the world. We just asked him to do what he's been doing since he became a professional cricketer.'

Simple. Just bowl six yorkers, Jofra, and you are the hero. This was a 24-year-old playing his 14th ODI. He had been in scrapes like this before in the IPL. But if you lose a close game in a Twenty20 league, there is always another match a few days later. There would never be another World Cup final at Lord's for this team. Everything was on the line.

Ball one: Archer goes for the wide off-side yorker, the hardest ball to hit. But it is a gamble. The umpires have two blue lines to help them judge if it is a wide. This one is so close to being perfect. But it's a centimetre or so the wrong side of the line. Neesham drives hard but misses. Kumar Dharmasena immediately shouts wide ball and holds his arms out. Archer spreads his arms too and screams in anger. 'It is a gimme,' says Agnew. New Zealand: 1–0.

Ball one (second attempt): Archer goes tighter to off stump. Another yorker. Neesham digs it out and times it perfectly, for it goes slowly along the ground to James Vince at long-off, and they have time to take two runs. New Zealand: 3–0.

Ball two: This is a poor ball. Archer's length is wrong. It is right in the slot for a big-hitting batsman. Neesham tucks in. He times it beautifully, and the ball makes a lovely cracking sound as it pings out of the middle of the bat. It flies high and fast 50 rows back into the Tavern Stand for six.

'It's huge. It's gone. It's out of the park,' says Smith. England are stunned. There are smiles and slaps on the back on the New Zealand balcony. Williamson remains stony-faced while Morgan is ice cool. 'The skipper really believed in me, even after the six,' said Archer afterwards. 'A lot of captains could have been hands in head, or head down and pacing all over the place. But he was really calm, really understanding.' New Zealand: 9–0.

Ball three: Seven runs are needed from four balls. New Zealand are so close. What does Archer do now? He stays around the wicket to the left-handed Neesham. It is another ball in the slot but slightly fuller. Neesham is on the back foot because he is expecting the short ball. He swings hard into the leg side but connects with a bottom edge. England should reduce them to a single and put Guptill on strike. But Jason Roy, such a solid fielder on the boundary, snatches at the ball as it bobbles. He fails to take it cleanly, allowing Neesham to get back for the second. England's nerves are stretched to breaking point. New Zealand: 11–0.

Ball four: Five needed from three. Archer goes full again. This time it is the right length. Neesham can only dig it out, hitting it hard but straight to Roy at deep mid-wicket. He picks up cleanly this time. New Zealand gamble on the second. Buttler has his arms high in the air calling to Roy to throw to the keeper. Roy makes a second error and throws to the bowler's end, where Guptill was always going to make his ground. New Zealand are within touching distance, and England are flapping under the pressure. New Zealand: 13–0.

Ball five: Three needed from two balls. In years to come, it will be the final ball of the Super Over that will be talked about by England supporters as they reminisce about an incredible day. But it was this penultimate delivery that was so important. Archer showed incredible skill and composure. He knew Neesham was picking the yorkers. He gambled by deciding in a split second to change his length. It was the difference between winning and losing the World Cup.

Archer bowls back of a length, wide of off stump. If Neesham finds a top edge, it will fly for four and the game will be over. But he swings hard, trying to pull it to the leg side.

It hits the bottom edge and trickles back to Archer. Neesham goes for the single. With ball in hand, Archer could run him out. Agnew speaks for a nation as he screams at Archer: 'Don't throw it. Don't throw it . . . He didn't throw it. Sorry. Archer had the ball and aimed for a moment, but nobody was at the non-striker's end.' Overthrows would have been the end. Now Guptill is on strike for the first time in the over for the biggest ball of his life. New Zealand: 14–0.

Ball six: Two needed from one. England know a tie is good enough. They have scored comfortably more boundaries. Over to Agnew: 'It has come to this. Here is the last ball of the World Cup final.' Archer goes full on leg stump. Guptill stays calm. He does not swing hard. He tries to place it and take the pace off, giving him and Neesham as much time as possible to run two. They make one. Roy advances off the mid-wicket boundary. No fumbles this time. No throw to the wrong end either.

Now remember Trent Bridge three years ago when Buttler demanded England start attacking in the field like they do with the bat. He urged his fielders to pick up and throw in one movement. Three years of honing that skill came down to this moment. 'It was like it was happening in slow motion,' Roy would later tell the *Daily Mail*. 'I could see the seam of the ball rolling down the turf as it came towards me. Everything seemed to stop. There was no noise. It gives me goosebumps now. But I knew if I collected it cleanly and got it in, there was no chance they could get two.'

Roy's throw is about two metres to Buttler's right. He has to move across the stumps to gather it in his right hand. He switches it to his left and dives at the stumps. They light up. Guptill dives, but he is short and knows it. 'I didn't really know where the ball was, I just put the head down and just

259

started running,' he said later. Ian Smith is breathless but captures the moment vividly with words that will always be remembered by England supporters. 'England have won the World Cup by the barest of margins. By the barest of all margins. Absolute ecstasy for England. Agony, agony for New Zealand.' Nine seconds of silence later, Smith says just one word: 'Wow.'

Buttler rips off his right glove, then his left, as he runs towards the pavilion chased by his team-mates. Bairstow sprints in from the boundary to punch the air two-fisted at his mum Janet and sister Becky who are sitting in the Tavern Stand. 'Dad and Grandad were there with me in spirit also,' he says later.

Archer is on the ground punching and kicking the turf like a toddler having a tantrum. Bairstow leaps into Root's arms. The two have played together since the age of 13. Root shouts: 'World Cup, World Cup!'

Liam Plunkett and Chris Woakes are in tears. Wood sprints ontp the field and is hoisted aloft by Woakes, who carries him across Lord's screaming: 'Woody, Woody, Woody!'

Somehow Morgan gathered himself to speak into a microphone. 'I still can't quite believe that we have got over the line,' he said. 'It has been an extraordinary day. It was the most incredible game of cricket. There was nothing between the sides. Sport sometimes is about very fine margins, and this was the finest of margins, and it could have gone either way. Thankfully it went our way. It has been phenomenal. People believed because we believed.

'To come through is extraordinary. It was almost super human from Stokes. He has really carried the team. The emotion going through the whole game he handled in an incredibly experienced way.'

The presentation podium was assembled under the Warner Stand facing out on to the rest of the ground. The game finished at 7.35pm. Five minutes later, the England players were back in the Long Room, while New Zealanders were still laid out on the turf, some in tears.

'I'm pretty lost for words. All the hard work over four years to get here, and to be champions of the world is an amazing feeling,' said Stokes.

Buttler mumbled: 'I thought I'd seen everything in cricket, and that game was just ridiculous.'

It takes another 20 minutes for the presentation to be organised. The Duke of York is the token royal brought in to hand over the trophy. Agnew fails to recognise him. The Duke is irrelevant. It is about Morgan. He is handed the trophy. The ground announcer calls it. 'ICC World Champions: England!' he says as Morgan lifts the trophy.

The four-year project had worked. England were world champions on a gloriously sunny evening at Lord's. It was the 193rd time Lord's had hosted an England match, but it had never seen anything like this before. Indeed cricket had never seen a game like this before.

SIXTEEN
THE CELEBRATIONS

Miss Pennys discount shop in Duckworth Lane, Bradford, is a pound shop, selling everything from saucepans to sticky tape, and made for an incongruous setting for the homecoming of a special local World Cup hero.

Javid Bashir, owner of the shop, is Adil Rashid's uncle. He asked him to pop down when he returned from London two days after the World Cup final because a few of his friends wanted to say hello to the city's famous son.

'Going from growing up in Heaton [in Bradford] to being on the world stage is a massive achievement for Adil. He is a local lad who played a pivotal role in England winning the World Cup, and I am sure the whole of Bradford is very proud of him. Hopefully youngsters want to follow in his footsteps and have been inspired by his hard work and dedication, and I am hoping we get a good turnout to welcome him home,' Mr Bashir told the local paper.

Rashid was mobbed and looked shocked to be at the centre of such a big scrum of people. Hundreds turned up at the small shop to greet the England player, who was wearing his World Cup winners' medal around his neck, and who 24 hours earlier had been at Downing Street for a very different reception with the Prime Minister.

Politicians love to stand next to successful sportsmen, or put the boot in when necessary – for example, if they are caught up in a sandpaper row and there is political mileage in taking a swipe. Theresa May, though, is a genuine cricket fan, and she congratulated the players, telling them their achievement 'will live forever in our sporting history'.

Eoin Morgan led the team on its walk down Downing Street, but he was more impressed by the homecoming for Rashid, as it emphasised that the words he'd said in the moments after the World Cup victory were true.

Morgan had constantly talked about the diversity of his England team. The man of the match in the final, Stokes, was born in New Zealand, Jason Roy in South Africa, Rashid and Moeen Ali are prominent British Asians and Jofra Archer an African-Caribbean, a community lost to English cricket in recent years.

Sitting at the post-match press conference with the World Cup trophy on the desk next to him to his left, Morgan was asked if England had enjoyed the luck of the Irish that day. 'We had Allah with us as well,' he replied. 'I spoke to Adil, and he said Allah was definitely with us. It actually epitomises our team. It is quite diverse backgrounds, cultures, and guys have grown up in different countries.'

England had drawn on all faiths, all personal beliefs, in their hour of need. They were lucky to beat New Zealand. They knew that. But as memories of the final fade, they will be remembered as winners who delivered on their talent rather than a team thankful for a bat deflection or a quirk of the Super Over rules.

It was close to 9pm by the time Morgan reached the press conference held in the real-tennis court at Lord's. The ground normally empties very quickly after a major match. Not this time. There were thousands of fans still milling around as the players celebrated on the field with their families.

Morgan looked as if he had just played any other cricket match. His cool, professional demeanour was unchanged in the hour of his sweetest victory. 'To me and to the team, and everybody who has been involved over the last four years, it means absolutely everything. The planning, the hard work, the dedication, the commitment and the little bit of luck really did get us over the line,' he said.

'It's been an absolutely incredible journey. To everybody around the country and around the world who has followed us and supported us, thank you so much. It's been phenomenal. Right from the very beginning of the tournament, all the way through, regardless of our performances, people believed because we believed.'

They won because they adapted. England spent four years planning for the World Cup. They built their team around two spinners, big-hitting batsmen and picking a group of players and sticking with them because they had identified experience and average number of caps as being vital markers of what was needed to win a World Cup.

When the crunch came, they dropped their second spinner, Moeen Ali, the pitches were slow and low, making batting a scrap in the dirt, and their Super Over was bowled by a player with 14 ODIs to his name. That was Morgan's triumph. Rigidity to playing one way cost them badly in 2015. In 2019, they realised they had to change. The captain had learned.

At one point in the press conference, Morgan was told that George Cohen, 1966 World Cup winner, once said to his nephew Ben, a member of the Rugby World Cup-winning team of 2003, that you play in very few games that change your life, but World Cup finals have the power to do that.

'I enjoy my life. I lead quite a quiet one, so I hope it hasn't changed too much. I would love it to change for everybody else who wants it to change, but I enjoy my life,' Morgan replied, smiling.

With the formalities done, it was time to rejoin his team. The players with children spent time with them on the out-field. The New Zealanders mingled in, taking their defeat with grace and class, reinforcing their status as the world's most popular cricket team.

Family and friends were invited into the inner sanctum of the England dressing room to continue the party before Morgan called all the players together for a few moments.

'Eoin addressed the group and told us this is our moment, enjoy it and soak it all in. He told us we had worked four years for this day. This was our time. We then all put our hands on the trophy together. The speech lasted just 15 seconds, but there was a photograph taken of us all together in that moment which we will treasure for ever,' said Jonny Bairstow.

They all sang the team song as each man placed a hand on the World Cup trophy before joining family and friends once again. It was a party atmosphere. Wood compared it to a wedding-night do. He told the families the players had to go up to the dressing room for a team-talk. It was a white lie. It was time for them to celebrate together, alone as a team. Hours flew by as players drank, sang songs and shared stories about the day.

Families returned to the team hotel, the Landmark in Marylebone, leaving the players at the ground, where they stayed until after midnight. Bairstow said: 'I don't know what time I got to bed. Time lost all meaning.'

Stokes had been presented with one of those expensive watches by sponsors Hublot for winning the man-of-the-match award. In the excitement, he left it behind in the dressing room, and someone had to take it back to the hotel on his behalf.

The ECB had made clear before the final there would be no open-top bus parade through London, citing the upcoming Ashes. They did not want to distract the players who would soon have to prepare to face Australia.

There had been constant criticism throughout the tournament about the fact the games were being shown behind a paywall on Sky. Some figures at the ECB feared it had not reached a wide enough audience and were worried the team could parade through London with nobody noticing. How embarrassing. But the lobbying from the ECB to persuade Sky to show the final on free-to-air television, partnering with Channel 4, brought it to a wide audience. Their fears would have been misplaced.

This World Cup win was about young people. Inspiring the next generation had been a theme throughout the tournament. This was the ECB's chance. They opted instead for a celebration party the day after the final at the Oval. The ground had been cleared of its ICC World Cup branding and only English media were invited. This was an ECB event, not ICC.

They took the opportunity to promote their own programmes, helped by Surrey, who arranged for 1,000 local school kids to come along. Volunteers from All Stars Cricket, an initiative aimed at children aged between five and eight, and Chance to Shine, the ECB-backed charity that promotes cricket in state schools, were invited to share the occasion, and children from both projects were allowed in. The ECB also sent out an invitation to England fans to attend on their Facebook page.

Some of the players had barely slept, but all were told they had to be on the team bus leaving the hotel for the Oval at 10am. One by one they were introduced to the crowd, walking down the steps from the dressing room at the ground, on to the field of play through a tunnel of flag wavers. Morgan carried the trophy, and children swarmed around him, trying to touch the World Cup. The players joined in cricket demonstrations with the kids, signing autographs and posing for pictures. Jofra Archer held a cup of coffee, looking like a man who needed a caffeine hit after a late night. James Vince never took his sunglasses off, and Ben Stokes had the bloodshot eyes of someone who had not slept for a week. It lasted about two hours. Liam Plunkett had been off the alcohol for months. Now he looked like a man who had tried to catch up and was paying the price.

Seven-year-old Jack Nagioff had his cap, bat and shirt signed by all the players. 'I got all of them. It was really exciting. I was about to burst at one point,' he told the *Daily Telegraph*.

Bairstow spotted a youngster who had been knocked over in the melee to touch the World Cup and was in tears, so he picked up the trophy and took it over to the young lad. Bairstow still could not quite comprehend what the team had achieved. 'Rooty and I sharing fish and chips with Rash when I was 15. Rooming together in Liverpool. Rash was playing England Under-19s, then all of a sudden me as a 15-year-old playing for Yorkshire Under-17s and told you're rooming with Adil Rashid. And now we've just won a World Cup,' he said.

Buttler was asked to relive the final moments of the Super

Over. 'It is pure elation. Feelings that you've never felt before. To do that in a game like that, at a home World Cup final at Lord's, is truly remarkable. I remember running off and throwing my gloves off and hat off, and then I saw Moeen Ali aeroplaning past me, and then I saw Jofra lying on the floor at some point, so I went and gave him a hug. It is fun today watching some of the videos back, all the TV angles, the people in the crowd who are filming it. It was a truly incredible ten seconds.'

Stokes was told he was now a national treasure and his life had changed. 'Whatever, I'm not bothered. I've got this medal around my neck, so it's all good,' he said. 'I don't know, it's not sunk in yet, but coming down here and seeing what a small portion of the support we've had feels about it – the kids, the adults – the energy they all had for what they saw yesterday is amazing.'

The players left the Oval at lunchtime to go back to the hotel to freshen up (and sober up) for the trip to Downing Street that evening.

England cricketers have history at Downing Street. In 2005, one of the players famously urinated in the Rose Garden, and they asked Euan Blair, son of the Prime Minister, to go out to buy some booze when they realised only soft drinks were on offer. It would be different on Morgan's watch. The players wore their number twos, smart-casual blue polo shirts and trousers rather than blazers, shirt and tie, and had their winners' medals hanging from their necks.

Morgan had been briefed to walk down Downing Street and the Prime Minister would emerge when they reached the front door. Theresa May had enjoyed few moments of cheer during her time as Prime Minister, and she was not going to miss this opportunity. She went off script, leaving Number Ten and greeting the team halfway along Downing Street.

She posed for photos, awkwardly holding aloft the trophy with Morgan.

The players behaved. A couple tried to sneak into the Cabinet Room for a drink, but it was only a half-hearted attempt, and they never pulled it off. One nearly accidentally knocked a clock over. But it was gentle stuff. When they started to get a bit lairy after a few drinks, Morgan sensed danger. The players started to sing the team song about their captain, with Jason Roy bashing a desk to keep the beat.

> Our captain is Morgan
> Taking the cap forward
> As World Champions
> Allez, Allez, Allez

Morgan cut them off before it got out of hand, telling them to shut it. They did.

Those watching on, including Sir John Major, could see that Morgan had a firm grip on his team. 'On the way out, we were making some noise, and we needed to quieten down, but that was just excitement. That's all,' said Morgan.

The players went back to the hotel to continue celebrating. On the Tuesday morning, they drove to Lord's and picked up their kit bags, which had been left in the dressing room after the final. Some were still wearing their medals as they thanked the Lord's stewards for looking after their gear. And that was that. Wood drove home to the north-east wearing his medal, wondering what had just happened to him, still coming to terms with the win.

Liam Plunkett told the *Daily Telegraph* he experienced a low as he came down from the greatest moment in his career. 'I went from winning the World Cup to all of a sudden I'm sat on my sofa watching Netflix a day and a half later. It was quite hard, and, honestly, I felt quite down. Everything was building up to that World Cup, and it was the highest point of my career. I'm not sure anything's going to happen like that again in cricket for me.'

Archer went back to Barbados to recover from his side injury, and there were soon photographs in the tabloid newspapers of him covered in paint and twerking with his girlfriend at a street party – a sign of his new-found fame and a warning that his private life is no longer his own. At least Archer was still wearing his England shorts.

When he returned home to Hove, he told the *Daily Mail* how he had been touched by the World Cup win. 'I knew how big the World Cup was straight afterwards,' he said. 'I was just walking back to my flat, and a guy who was gardening in one of the houses nearby stopped what he was doing, ran over and shook my hand. He said he was in the pub watching the final. And I've had that sort of thing the whole time since it was over.'

Six days after the final, the Test players were at an Ashes planning camp at the FA's St George's Park base. It was too soon. Root had to be there as Test captain, but the others should have been given more time to come to terms with what had just happened. At least Buttler and Stokes were excused from the match against Ireland at Lord's the following week, but for others it was back to the day job. Nine days after the World Cup final, Root, Bairstow, Roy and Woakes were playing against Ireland in a tense, tight Test match.

The players involved will never forget the experience. They devised a hand signal to be used for difficult moments on the pitch in the future. It is a finger drawing a small circle over the chest to indicate a World Cup winners' medal, a sign the players can achieve anything. During the Ashes series after the World Cup, the players could be seen giving the signal to Roy, to try and boost his morale as he struggled for runs.

The cricket cycle turns quickly, but some things will be stitched in time. Roy, Bairstow, Root, Morgan, Stokes, Buttler, Woakes, Plunkett, Archer, Rashid, Wood. Those 11 names will be remembered for ever as England's World Cup-winning team. It is the nature of sport that sides who achieve great things often never play together again. Some players pick up injuries, others retire. It is probably for the best. That way the memory of their achievement can never be spoiled by later failures. Plunkett was the first player to taste this reality when he was dropped by England after the World Cup. There was no room for sentiment. Plunkett took three wickets in the final. What a way to go out and he will always be remembered for that feat rather than for how his England career was ruthlessly ended aged 34 a few weeks later.

Over to Stokes, hero of the final: 'It's cool, but the best thing about it is that we won what we wanted to. We deserved to be in the final because of what we've done over the last four years. We would have been devastated if we hadn't managed to lift the trophy. Looking back over that game, I think it will go down in the history books as the best ever, with all the drama of a World Cup final. It's an amazing thing to have been a part of.'

England delivered on their promise. They were world champions for the first time at the end of an incredible four years capped off by the most remarkable day at Lord's. Courage, unity, respect. England had stuck to their principles and landed the biggest prize of all.

STATISTICS

BATTING

Most runs by an individual

Name	Team	Mat	Inns	NO	Runs	HS	Avge	SR	100	50
RG Sharma	Ind	9	9	1	648	140	81.00	98.33	5	1
DA Warner	Aus	10	10	1	647	166	71.88	89.36	3	3
Shakib Al Hasan	Ban	8	8	1	606	124*	86.57	96.03	2	5
KS Williamson	NZ	10	9	2	578	148	82.57	74.96	2	2
JE Root	Eng	11	11	2	556	107	61.77	89.53	2	3
JM Bairstow	Eng	11	11	0	532	111	48.36	92.84	2	2
AJ Finch	Aus	10	10	0	507	153	50.70	102.01	2	3
Babar Azam	Pak	8	8	1	474	101*	67.71	87.77	1	3
BA Stokes	Eng	11	10	3	465	89	66.42	93.18	0	5
JJ Roy	Eng	8	7	0	443	153	63.28	115.36	1	4

Highest batting averages (qualification – 5 innings)

Name	Team	Mat	Inns	NO	Runs	HS	Avge	SR	100	50
Shakib Al Hasan	Ban	8	8	1	606	124*	86.57	96.03	2	5
KS Williamson	NZ	10	9	2	578	148	82.57	74.96	2	2
RG Sharma	Ind	9	9	1	648	140	81.00	98.33	5	1
DA Warner	Aus	10	10	1	647	166	71.88	89.36	3	3
Babar Azam	Pak	8	8	1	474	101*	67.71	87.77	1	3
BA Stokes	Eng	11	10	3	465	89	66.42	93.18	0	5
F du Plessis	SA	9	8	2	387	100	64.50	89.58	1	3
JJ Roy	Eng	8	7	0	443	153	63.28	115.36	1	4
AT Carey	Aus	10	9	3	375	85	62.50	104.16	0	3
HE van der Dussen	SA	9	6	1	311	95	62.20	90.40	0	3

Most sixes hit

Name	Team	Mat	Runs	6s	Balls	Balls/6
EJG Morgan	Eng	11	371	22	334	15.2
AJ Finch	Aus	10	507	18	497	27.6
RG Sharma	Ind	9	648	14	659	47.1
JJ Roy	Eng	8	443	12	384	32.0
CH Gayle	WI	9	242	12	274	22.8
BA Stokes	Eng	11	465	11	499	45.4
JM Bairstow	Eng	11	532	11	573	52.1
HE van der Dussen	SA	9	311	10	344	34.4
N Pooran	WI	9	367	10	366	36.6

Most 50+ scores by an individual

Name	Team	Inns	50s	%Inns
Shakib Al Hasan	Ban	8	7	87.50
RG Sharma	Ind	9	6	66.66
DA Warner	Aus	10	6	60.00
JJ Roy	Eng	7	5	71.42
V Kohli	Ind	9	5	55.55
AJ Finch	Aus	10	5	50.00
BA Stokes	Eng	10	5	50.00
JE Root	Eng	11	5	45.45

List of centuries (31 scored in the tournament)

Score	BF	4s	6s	Name	Team	Against	Venue	StartDate
107	104	10	1	JE Root	England	Pakistan	Nottingham	03/06/2019
103	76	9	2	JC Buttler	England	Pakistan	Nottingham	03/06/2019
122*	144	13	2	RG Sharma	India	South Africa	Southampton	05/06/2019
153	121	14	5	JJ Roy	England	Bangladesh	Cardiff	08/06/2019
121	119	12	1	Shakib Al Hasan	Bangladesh	England	Cardiff	08/06/2019
117	109	16	0	S Dhawan	India	Australia	The Oval	09/06/2019
107	111	11	1	DA Warner	Australia	Pakistan	Taunton	12/06/2019
100*	94	11	0	JE Root	England	West Indies	Southampton	14/06/2019
153	132	15	5	AJ Finch	Australia	Sri Lanka	The Oval	15/06/2019
140	113	14	3	RG Sharma	India	Pakistan	Manchester	16/06/2019
124*	99	16	0	Shakib Al Hasan	Bangladesh	West Indies	Taunton	17/06/2019
148	71	4	17	EJG Morgan	England	Afghanistan	Manchester	18/06/2019

Score	BF	4s	6s	Name	Team	Against	Venue	StartDate
106*	138	9	1	KS Williamson	New Zealand	South Africa	Birmingham	19/06/2019
166	147	14	5	DA Warner	Australia	Bangladesh	Nottingham	20/06/2019
102*	97	9	1	Mushfiqur Rahim	Bangladesh	Australia	Nottingham	20/06/2019
148	154	14	1	KS Williamson	New Zealand	West Indies	Manchester	22/06/2019
101	82	9	5	CR Brathwaite	West Indies	New Zealand	Manchester	22/06/2019
100	116	11	2	AJ Finch	Australia	England	Lord's	25/06/2019
101*	127	11	0	Babar Azam	Pakistan	New Zealand	Birmingham	26/06/2019
111	109	10	6	JM Bairstow	England	India	Birmingham	30/06/2019
102	109	15	0	RG Sharma	India	England	Birmingham	30/06/2019
104	103	9	2	WIA Fernando	Sri Lanka	West Indies	Chester-le-Street	01/07/2019
118	103	11	4	N Pooran	West Indies	Sri Lanka	Chester-le-Street	01/07/2019
104	92	7	5	RG Sharma	India	Bangladesh	Birmingham	02/07/2019
106	99	15	1	JM Bairstow	England	New Zealand	Chester-le-Street	03/07/2019
100	100	8	0	Imam-ul-Haq	Pakistan	Bangladesh	Lord's	05/07/2019
113	128	10	2	AD Mathews	Sri Lanka	India	Leeds	06/07/2019
111	118	11	1	KL Rahul	India	Sri Lanka	Leeds	06/07/2019
103	94	14	2	RG Sharma	India	Sri Lanka	Leeds	06/07/2019
100	94	7	2	F du Plessis	South Africa	Australia	Manchester	06/07/2019
122	117	15	2	DA Warner	Australia	South Africa	Manchester	06/07/2019

Highest partnerships

Wkt	Part	Bat1	Bat2	Team	Against	Venue	StartDate
1	189	KL Rahul	RG Sharma	India	Sri Lanka	Leeds	06/07/2019
2	192	DA Warner	Usman Khawaja	Australia	Bangladesh	Nottingham	20/06/2019
3	189	JE Root	EJG Morgan	England	Afghanistan	Manchester	18/06/2019
4	189*	Shakib Al Hasan	Liton Das	Bangladesh	West Indies	Taunton	17/06/2019
5	130	JE Root	JC Buttler	England	Pakistan	Nottingham	03/06/2019
6	132	JDS Neesham	C de Grandhomme	New Zealand	Pakistan	Birmingham	26/06/2019
7	116	MS Dhoni	RA Jadeja	India	New Zealand	Manchester	09/07/2019
8	66	CH Morris	K Rabada	South Africa	India	Southampton	05/06/2019
9	39	Rashid Khan	Mujeeb ur Rahman	Afghanistan	Australia	Bristol	01/06/2019
10	41	CR Brathwaite	OR Thomas	West Indies	New Zealand	Manchester	22/06/2019

BOWLING

Most wickets taken

Name	Team	Mat	Balls	Mdns	Runs	Wkts	Avge	RPO	BB	4I
MA Starc	Aus	10	554	5	502	27	18.59	5.43	5-26	4
LH Ferguson	NZ	9	502	3	409	21	19.47	4.88	4-37	1
JC Archer	Eng	11	605	8	461	20	23.05	4.57	3-27	0
Mustafizur Rahman	Ban	8	433	2	484	20	24.20	6.70	5-59	2
JJ Bumrah	Ind	9	504	9	371	18	20.61	4.41	4-55	1
MA Wood	Eng	10	538	2	463	18	25.72	5.16	3-18	0
Mohammad Amir	Pak	8	438	5	358	17	21.05	4.90	5-30	1
TA Boult	NZ	10	594	4	479	17	28.17	4.83	4-30	2
Shaheen Shah Afridi	Pak	5	283	3	234	16	14.62	4.96	6-35	2
CR Woakes	Eng	11	510	6	446	16	27.87	5.24	3-20	0

Best bowling averages (qualification 5 wickets)

Name	Team	Mat	Balls	Mdns	Runs	Wkts	Avge	RPO	BB	4I
Mohammed Shami	Ind	4	211	2	193	14	13.78	5.48	5-69	3
Shaheen Shah Afridi	Pak	5	283	3	234	16	14.62	4.96	6-35	2
MA Starc	Aus	10	554	5	502	27	18.59	5.43	5-26	4
D Pretorius	SA	3	138	4	94	5	18.80	4.08	3-25	0
JDS Neesham	NZ	10	327	2	292	15	19.46	5.35	5-31	1
LH Ferguson	NZ	9	502	3	409	21	19.47	4.88	4-37	1

Name	Team	Mat	Balls	Mdns	Runs	Wkts	Avge	RPO	BB	4I
KAJ Roach	WI	4	198	4	121	6	20.16	3.66	3-36	0
AD Russell	WI	4	114	1	101	5	20.20	5.31	2-4	0
JJ Bumrah	Ind	9	504	9	371	18	20.61	4.41	4-55	1
Mohammad Amir	Pak	8	438	5	358	17	21.05	4.90	5-30	1

Best strike-rate by a bowler (qualification 5 wickets)

Name	Team	Mat	Balls	Mdns	Runs	Wkts	Avge	SR	BB	4I
Mohammed Shami	Ind	4	211	2	193	14	13.78	15.07	5-69	3
Shaheen Shah Afridi	Pak	5	283	3	234	16	14.62	17.68	6-35	2
MA Starc	Aus	10	554	5	502	27	18.59	20.51	5-26	4
Mustafizur Rahman	Ban	8	433	2	484	20	24.20	21.65	5-59	2
JDS Neesham	NZ	10	327	2	292	15	19.46	21.80	5-31	1
AD Russell	WI	4	114	1	101	5	20.20	22.80	2-4	0
LH Ferguson	NZ	9	502	3	409	21	19.47	23.90	4-37	1
Mohammad Amir	Pak	8	438	5	358	17	21.05	25.76	5-30	1
Mohammad Saifuddin	Ban	7	348	2	417	13	32.07	26.76	3-72	0
D Pretorius	SA	3	138	4	94	5	18.80	27.60	3-25	0

Best economy rates (qualification 150 balls bowled)

Name	Team	Mat	Balls	Mdns	Runs	Wkts	Avge	RPO	BB	4I
KAJ Roach	WI	4	198	4	121	6	20.16	3.66	3-36	0
C de Grandhomme	NZ	10	306	4	212	6	35.33	4.15	1-14	0
JJ Bumrah	Ind	9	504	9	371	18	20.61	4.41	4-55	1
Mujeeb ur Rahman	Afg	7	347	1	259	7	37.00	4.47	3-39	0
JC Archer	Eng	11	605	8	461	20	23.05	4.57	3-27	0
Mohammad Nabi	Afg	9	436	0	335	10	33.50	4.61	4-30	1
Hamid Hassan	Afg	5	156	3	122	1	122.00	4.69	1-53	0
MJ Santner	NZ	10	402	4	323	6	53.83	4.82	2-34	0
Imad Wasim	Pak	6	234	0	188	2	94.00	4.82	2-48	0
TA Boult	NZ	10	594	4	479	17	28.17	4.83	4-30	2

Five-wicket hauls (10 taken in the tournament)

O	M	R	W	Name	Team	Against	Venue	StartDate
10	1	46	5	MA Starc	Australia	West Indies	Nottingham	06/06/2019
10	1	31	5	JDS Neesham	New Zealand	Afghanistan	Taunton	08/06/2019
10	2	30	5	Mohammad Amir	Pakistan	Australia	Taunton	12/06/2019
10	1	29	5	Shakib Al Hasan	Bangladesh	Afghanistan	Southampton	24/06/2019
10	0	44	5	JP Behrendorff	Australia	England	Lord's	25/06/2019

O	M	R	W	Name	Team	Against	Venue	StartDate
9.4	1	26	5	MA Starc	Australia	New Zealand	Lord's	29/06/2019
10	1	69	5	Mohammed Shami	India	England	Birmingham	30/06/2019
10	1	59	5	Mustafizur Rahman	Bangladesh	India	Birmingham	02/07/2019
10	0	75	5	Mustafizur Rahman	Bangladesh	Pakistan	Lord's	05/07/2019
9.1	0	35	6	Shaheen Shah Afridi	Pakistan	Bangladesh	Lord's	05/07/2019

Most maiden overs bowled (in an innings)

O	M	R	W	Name	Team	Against	Venue	StartDate
10	3	36	1	CH Morris	South Africa	India	Southampton	05/06/2019
10	3	28	3	Shaheen Shah Afridi	Pakistan	New Zealand	Birmingham	26/06/2019
10	3	58	2	CR Woakes	England	India	Birmingham	30/06/2019
10	3	41	2	PJ Cummins	Australia	West Indies	Nottingham	06/06/2019
9.1	3	37	4	LH Ferguson	New Zealand	Afghanistan	Taunton	08/06/2019

Most maiden overs bowled (tournament)

Name	Team	M	Balls	Mdns	Runs	Wkts	Avg	RPO	BB	4I
JJ Bumrah	Ind	9	504	9	371	18	20.61	4.41	4-55	1
JC Archer	Eng	11	605	8	461	20	23.05	4.57	3-27	0
PJ Cummins	Aus	10	517	6	427	14	30.50	4.95	3-33	0
CR Woakes	Eng	11	510	6	446	16	27.87	5.24	3-20	0
Mohammad Amir	Pak	8	438	5	358	17	21.05	4.90	5-30	1
MJ Henry	NZ	9	482	5	392	14	28.00	4.87	4-47	1
MA Starc	Aus	10	554	5	502	27	18.59	5.43	5-26	4
CH Morris	SA	8	382	5	341	13	26.23	5.35	3-13	0

TEAM

Highest team totals

Score	Overs	Team	Against	Venue	StartDate
397-6	50	England	Afghanistan	Manchester	18/06/2019
386-6	50	England	Bangladesh	Cardiff	08/06/2019
381-5	50	Australia	Bangladesh	Nottingham	20/06/2019
352-5	50	India	Australia	The Oval	09/06/2019
348-8	50	Pakistan	England	Nottingham	03/06/2019
338-6	50	Sri Lanka	West Indies	Chester-le-Street	01/07/2019
337-7	50	England	India	Birmingham	30/06/2019
336-5	50	India	Pakistan	Manchester	16/06/2019
334-9	50	England	Pakistan	Nottingham	03/06/2019
334-7	50	Australia	Sri Lanka	The Oval	15/06/2019

Lowest team totals

Score	Overs	Team	Against	Venue	StartDate
105	21.4	Pakistan	West Indies	Nottingham	31/05/2019
125	34.1	Afghanistan	South Africa	Cardiff	15/06/2019
136	29.2	Sri Lanka	New Zealand	Cardiff	01/06/2019
143	34.2	West Indies	India	Manchester	27/06/2019
152	32.4	Afghanistan	Sri Lanka	Cardiff	04/06/2019

Highest match aggregate

Runs	Wkts	Overs	Home	Away	Venue	StartDate	Result
714	13	100	Australia	Bangladesh	Nottingham	20/06/2019	Australia won by 48 runs
682	17	100	England	Pakistan	Nottingham	03/06/2019	Pakistan won by 14 runs
668	15	100	Australia	India	The Oval	09/06/2019	India won by 36 runs
666	16	98.5	England	Bangladesh	Cardiff	08/06/2019	England won by 106 runs
653	15	100	Sri Lanka	West Indies	Chester-le-Street	01/07/2019	Sri Lanka won by 23 runs

Highest cumulative runs per over scored

Team	Matches	Runs	Wkts	HS	Avge	RPO	100	50
England	11	3183	78	153	40.80	6.27	7	17
Australia	10	2901	81	166	35.81	6.02	5	16
Bangladesh	9	2278	64	124*	35.59	5.96	3	11
West Indies	9	1969	65	118	30.29	5.76	2	13
India	10	2516	56	140	44.92	5.71	7	12
Pakistan	9	2025	61	101*	33.19	5.68	2	9
South Africa	9	1934	52	100	37.19	5.33	1	11
Sri Lanka	9	1621	62	113	26.14	5.20	2	7
New Zealand	11	2154	67	148	32.14	4.97	2	12
Afghanistan	9	1831	87	86	21.04	4.65	0	6

Best runs per over in each Powerplay – Batting

POWERPLAY 1			POWERPLAY 2			POWERPLAY 3		
Team	RPO	Avge	Team	RPO	Avge	Team	RPO	Avge
Sri Lanka	6.18	48.11	England	6.05	57.62	England	8.54	19.38
England	5.24	57.70	Australia	5.95	54.67	Australia	8.06	17.94
Bangladesh	5.20	52.00	Bangladesh	5.83	48.35	Pakistan	8.05	20.90
Pakistan	4.88	48.87	West Indies	5.82	32.33	India	7.83	25.24
Australia	4.68	42.54	India	5.52	62.65	South Africa	7.53	24.60
West Indies	4.57	28.15	Pakistan	5.43	38.76	Bangladesh	7.39	16.92
Afghanistan	4.55	37.27	South Africa	5.21	42.07	New Zealand	7.19	21.04
South Africa	4.53	39.70	New Zealand	4.75	40.93	West Indies	7.19	25.73
India	4.40	49.50	Sri Lanka	4.71	22.84	Sri Lanka	5.75	20.07
New Zealand	4.29	28.60	Afghanistan	4.59	22.15	Afghanistan	5.27	11.00

Best runs per over in each Powerplay – Bowling

POWERPLAY 1			POWERPLAY 2			POWERPLAY 3		
Team	RPO	Avge	Team	RPO	Avge	Team	RPO	Avge
India	3.91	35.20	New Zealand	4.64	31.27	England	6.18	16.39
England	4.24	33.35	South Africa	4.91	36.00	New Zealand	6.63	17.65
New Zealand	4.73	31.53	Afghanistan	5.15	41.66	Pakistan	6.91	17.48
West Indies	4.84	30.28	India	5.23	34.60	Australia	7.16	17.87
Afghanistan	4.93	63.42	England	5.33	36.64	India	7.38	18.55

POWERPLAY 1			POWERPLAY 2			POWERPLAY 3		
Team	RPO	Avge	Team	RPO	Avge	Team	RPO	Avge
Australia	5.16	51.60	Pakistan	5.49	47.00	South Africa	7.66	25.05
Bangladesh	5.16	82.60	Australia	5.72	36.13	Sri Lanka	7.70	16.78
South Africa	5.17	46.00	Sri Lanka	5.80	56.83	West Indies	8.43	23.66
Sri Lanka	5.18	45.37	Bangladesh	5.95	55.00	Bangladesh	8.50	19.71
Pakistan	5.21	37.90	West Indies	6.01	49.69	Afghanistan	8.93	31.71

Lowest cumulative runs per over conceded

Team	Matches	Overs	Mdns	TotVs	WktsVs	RPWVs	RPOVs	BB	4I	5I
New Zealand	11	466.3	22	2330	87	26.78	4.99	5-31	5	1
England	11	527.2	17	2767	95	29.12	5.24	3-18	0	0
India	10	422.1	15	2237	77	29.05	5.29	5-69	5	1
South Africa	9	379.3	17	2067	61	33.88	5.44	4-29	1	0
Afghanistan	9	382.1	10	2138	51	41.92	5.59	4-30	1	0
Pakistan	9	356.5	11	2029	61	33.26	5.68	6-35	3	2
Australia	10	450.2	18	2607	80	32.58	5.78	5-26	5	3
Sri Lanka	9	276.4	7	1621	40	40.52	5.85	4-31	2	0
West Indies	9	352.5	12	2142	58	36.93	6.07	4-27	3	0
Bangladesh	9	394.1	6	2474	63	39.26	6.27	5-29	3	3

Highest Powerplay 1 (overs 1 to 10)

Runs	Wkts	Team	Against	Venue	StartDate	Result
87	0	Sri Lanka	Australia	The Oval	15/06/2019	Lost
79	0	Sri Lanka	Afghanistan	Cardiff	04/06/2019	Won
77	0	New Zealand	Sri Lanka	Cardiff	01/06/2019	Won
73	0	South Africa	Australia	Manchester	06/07/2019	Won
71	2	West Indies	Pakistan	Nottingham	31/05/2019	Won

Highest Powerplay 2 (overs 11 to 40)

Runs	Wkts	Team	Against	Venue	StartDate	Res
235	2	Bangladesh	West Indies	Taunton	17/06/2019	Won
211	4	West Indies	Bangladesh	Taunton	17/06/2019	Lost
209	1	England	Afghanistan	Manchester	18/06/2019	Won
208	3	England	Bangladesh	Cardiff	08/06/2019	Won
207	4	West Indies	Sri Lanka	Chester-le-Street	01/07/2019	Lost

Highest Powerplay 3 (overs 41 to 50)

Runs	Wkts	Team	Against	Venue	StartDate	Res
142	4	England	Afghanistan	Manchester	18/06/2019	Won
131	4	Australia	Bangladesh	Nottingham	20/06/2019	Won
116	3	India	Australia	The Oval	09/06/2019	Won
111	3	England	Bangladesh	Cardiff	08/06/2019	Won
111	2	West Indies	Afghanistan	Leeds	04/07/2019	Won

287

LIST OF RESULTS AT ICC CRICKET WORLD CUP 2019

GROUP STAGE

Date	Venue	Bat first	Scpre	Bat second	Scpre	Result
30/05/2019	The Oval	England	311-8 (50)	South Africa	207 (39.5)	England won by 104 runs
31/05/2019	Nottingham	Pakistan	105 (21.4)	West Indies	108-3 (13.4)	West Indies won by 7 wickets
01/06/2019	Bristol	Afghanistan	207 (38.2)	Australia	209-3 (34.5)	Australia won by 7 wickets
01/06/2019	Cardiff	Sri Lanka	136 (29.2)	New Zealand	137-0 (16.1)	New Zealand won by 10 wickets
02/06/2019	The Oval	Bangladesh	330-6 (50)	South Africa	309-8 (50)	Bangladesh won by 21 runs
03/06/2019	Nottingham	Pakistan	348-8 (50)	England	334-9 (50)	Pakistan won by 14 runs
04/06/2019	Cardiff	Sri Lanka	201 (36.5)	Afghanistan	152 (32.4)	Sri Lanka won by 34 runs (DLS)
05/06/2019	The Oval	Bangladesh	244 (49.2)	New Zealand	248-8 (47.1)	New Zealand won by 2 wickets

Date	Venue	Bat first	Scpre	Bat second	Scpre	Result
05/06/2019	Southampton	South Africa	227-9 (50)	India	230-4 (47.3)	India won by 6 wickets
06/06/2019	Nottingham	Australia	288 (49)	West Indies	273-9 (50)	Australia won by 15 runs
07/06/2019	Bristol	Pakistan	--	Sri Lanka	--	Match abandoned
08/06/2019	Taunton	Afghanistan	172 (41.1)	New Zealand	173-3 (32.1)	New Zealand won by 7 wickets
08/06/2019	Cardiff	England	386-6 (50)	Bangladesh	280 (48.5)	England won by 106 runs
09/06/2019	The Oval	India	352-5 (50)	Australia	316 (50)	India won by 36 runs
10/06/2019	Southampton	South Africa	29-2 (7.3)	West Indies	--	No result
11/06/2019	Bristol	Bangladesh	--	Sri Lanka	--	Match abandoned
12/06/2019	Taunton	Australia	307 (49)	Pakistan	266 (45.4)	Australia won by 41 runs
13/06/2019	Nottingham	India	--	New Zealand	--	Match abandoned
14/06/2019	Southampton	West Indies	212 (44.4)	England	213-2 (33.1)	England won by 8 wickets

Date	Venue	Bat first	Scpre	Bat second	Scpre	Result
15/06/2019	Cardiff	Afghanistan	125 (34.1)	South Africa	131-1 (28.4)	South Africa won by 9 wickets (DLS)
15/06/2019	The Oval	Australia	334-7 (50)	Sri Lanka	247 (45.5)	Australia won by 87 runs
16/06/2019	Manchester	India	336-5 (50)	Pakistan	212-6 (40)	India won by 89 runs (DLS)
17/06/2019	Taunton	West Indies	321-8 (50)	Bangladesh	322-3 (41.3)	Bangladesh won by 7 wickets
18/06/2019	Manchester	England	397-6 (50)	Afghanistan	247-8 (50)	England won by 150 runs
19/06/2019	Birmingham	South Africa	241-6 (49)	New Zealand	245-6 (48.3)	New Zealand won by 4 wickets
20/06/2019	Nottingham	Australia	381-5 (50)	Bangladesh	333-8 (50)	Australia won by 48 runs
21/06/2019	Leeds	Sri Lanka	232-9 (50)	England	212 (47)	Sri Lanka won by 20 runs
22/06/2019	Southampton	India	224-8 (50)	Afghanistan	213 (49.5)	India won by 11 runs
22/06/2019	Manchester	New Zealand	291-8 (50)	West Indies	286 (49)	New Zealand won by 5 runs

Date	Venue	Bat first	Scpre	Bat second	Scpre	Result
23/06/2019	Lord's	Pakistan	308-7 (50)	South Africa	259-9 (50)	Pakistan won by 49 runs
24/06/2019	Southampton	Bangladesh	262-7 (50)	Afghanistan	200 (47)	Bangladesh won by 62 runs
25/06/2019	Lord's	Australia	285-7 (50)	England	221 (44.4)	Australia won by 64 runs
26/06/2019	Birmingham	New Zealand	237-6 (50)	Pakistan	241-4 (49.1)	Pakistan won by 6 wickets
27/06/2019	Manchester	India	268-7 (50)	West Indies	143 (34.2)	India won by 125 runs
28/06/2019	Chester-le-Street	Sri Lanka	203 (49.3)	South Africa	206-1 (37.2)	South Africa won by 9 wickets
29/06/2019	Leeds	Afghanistan	227-9 (50)	Pakistan	230-7 (49.4)	Pakistan won by 3 wickets
29/06/2019	Lord's	Australia	243-9 (50)	New Zealand	157 (43.4)	Australia won by 86 runs
30/06/2019	Birmingham	England	337-7 (50)	India	306-5 (50)	England won by 31 runs
01/07/2019	Chester-le-Street	Sri Lanka	338-6 (50)	West Indies	315-9 (50)	Sri Lanka won by 23 runs
02/07/2019	Birmingham	India	314-9 (50)	Bangladesh	286 (48)	India won by 28 runs

Date	Venue	Bat first	Scpre	Bat second	Scpre	Result
03/07/2019	Chester-le-Street	England	305-8 (50)	New Zealand	186 (45)	England won by 119 runs
04/07/2019	Leeds	West Indies	311-6 (50)	Afghanistan	288 (50)	West Indies won by 23 runs
05/07/2019	Lord's	Pakistan	315-9 (50)	Bangladesh	221 (44.1)	Pakistan won by 94 runs
06/07/2019	Manchester	South Africa	325-6 (50)	Australia	315 (49.5)	South Africa won by 10 runs
06/07/2019	Leeds	Sri Lanka	264-7 (50)	India	265-3 (43.3)	India won by 7 wickets

SEMI-FINALS

Date	Venue	Bat first	Scpre	Bat second	Scpre	Result
09/07/2019	Manchester	New Zealand	239-8 (50)	India	221 (49.3)	New Zealand won by 18 runs
11/07/2019	Birmingham	Australia	223 (49)	England	226-2 (32.1)	England won by 8 wickets

FINAL

Date	Venue	Bat first	Scpre	Bat second	Scpre	Result
14/07/2019	Lord's	New Zealand	241-8 (50)	England	241 (50)	Match tied and Super over – tied England won on higher boundary count

ENGLAND v SOUTH AFRICA

Venue:	The Oval, Kennington
Date:	30th May 2019
Toss:	South Africa
Result:	England won by 104 runs
Man of the Match:	BA Stokes (England)

ENGLAND innings

		R	B	4	6
JJ Roy	c Du Plessis b Phehlukwayo	54	53	8	-
JM Bairstow	c De Kock b Imran Tahir	0	1	-	-
JE Root	c Duminy b Rabada	51	59	5	-
*EJG Morgan	c Markram b Imran Tahir	57	60	4	3
BA Stokes	c Amla b Ngidi	89	79	9	-
+JC Buttler	b Ngidi	18	16	-	-
MM Ali	c Du Plessis b Ngidi	3	9	-	-
CR Woakes	c Du Plessis b Rabada	13	14	1	-
LE Plunkett	not out	9	6	1	-
JC Archer	not out	7	3	-	-
AU Rashid					
Extras	(lb 2, w 8)	10			
TOTAL	(for 8 wkts; 50 overs)	311			

SOUTH AFRICA innings

		R	B	4	6
+Q de Kock	c Root b Plunkett	68	74	6	2
HM Amla	c Buttler b Plunkett	13	23	1	-
AK Markram	c Root b Archer	11	12	2	-
*F du Plessis	c Ali b Archer	5	7	1	-
HE van der Dussen	c Ali b Archer	50	61	4	1
J-P Duminy	c Stokes b Ali	8	11	1	-
D Pretorius	run out (Stokes/Morgan)	1	1	-	-
AL Phehlukwayo	c Stokes b Rashid	24	25	4	-
K Rabada	c Plunkett b Stokes	11	23	2	-

LT Ngidi	not out	6	5	-	1
Imran Tahir	c Root b Stokes	0	1	-	-
Extras	(b 4, lb 5, w 1)	10			
TOTAL	(all out; 39.5 overs)	207			

SOUTH AFRICA bowling

	O	M	R	W	wb	nb
Imran Tahir	10	0	61	2	-	-
Ngidi	10	0	66	3	2	-
Rabada	10	0	66	2	2	-
Pretorius	7	0	42	0	-	-
Phehlukwayo	8	0	44	1	4	-
Duminy	2	0	14	0	-	-
Markram	3	0	16	0	-	-

ENGLAND bowling

	O	M	R	W	wb	nb
Woakes	5	0	24	0	-	-
Archer	7	1	27	3	1	-
Rashid	8	0	35	1	-	-
Ali	10	0	63	1	-	-
Plunkett	7	0	37	2	-	-
Stokes	2.5	0	12	2	-	-

Fall of wickets

	Eng	SA
1st	1 (2)	36 (3)
2nd	107 (1)	44 (4)
3rd	111 (3)	129 (1)
4th	217 (4)	142 (6)
5th	247 (6)	144 (7)
6th	260 (7)	167 (5)
7th	285 (8)	180 (8)
8th	300 (5)	193 (2)
9th	207 (9)	
10th	207 (11)	

HM Amla retired hurt on 5* (at 14-0) and returned at fall of 6th wicket (167-6)

Umpires:	HDPK Dharmasena & BNJ Oxenford
TV umpire:	PR Reiffel
Referee:	DC Boon

ENGLAND v PAKISTAN

Venue:	Trent Bridge, Nottingham
Date:	3rd June 2019
Toss:	England
Result:	Pakistan won by 14 runs
Man of the Match:	Mohammad Hafeez
Umpires:	M Erasmus & S Ravi
TV umpire:	RSA Palliyaguruge
Referee:	JJ Crowe

PAKISTAN innings

		R	B	4	6
Imam-ul-Haq	c Woakes b Ali	44	58	3	1
Fakhar Zaman	st Buttler b Ali	36	40	6	-
Babar Azam	c Woakes b Ali	63	66	4	1
Mohammad Hafeez	c Woakes b Wood	84	62	8	2
*+Sarfaraz Ahmed	c and b Woakes	55	44	5	-
Asif Ali	c Bairstow b Wood	14	11	-	1
Shoaib Malik	c Morgan b Woakes	8	8	-	-
Wahab Riaz	c Root b Woakes	4	2	1	-
Hasan Ali	not out	1	5	-	1
Shadab Khan	not out	10	4	2	-
Mohammad Amir					
Extras	(b 1, lb 8, w 11)	20			
TOTAL	(for 8 wkts; 50 overs)	348			

ENGLAND

		R	B	4	6
JJ Roy	lbw b Shadab Khan	8	7	2	0
JM Bairstow	c Sarfaraz Ahmed b Wahab Riaz	32	31	4	1
JE Root	c Mohammad Hafeez b Shadab Khan	107	104	10	1
*EJG Morgan	b Mohammad Hafeez	9	18	1	0
BA Stokes	c Sarfaraz Ahmed b Shoaib Malik	13	18	1	0
+JC Buttler	c Wahab Riaz b Mohammad Amir	103	76	9	2
MM Ali	c Fakhar Zaman b Wahab Riaz	19	20	1	0
CR Woakes	c Sarfaraz Ahmed b Wahab Riaz	21	14	1	1
JC Archer	c Wahab Riaz b Mohammad Amir	1	2	0	0
AU Rashid	not out	3	4	0	0
MA Wood	not out	10	6	2	0
Extras	(lb 3, w 5)	8			
TOTAL	(for 9 wkts; 50 overs)	334			

ENGLAND bowling

	O	M	R	W	wb	nb
Woakes	8	1	71	3	2	-
Archer	10	0	79	0	4	-
Ali	10	0	50	3	-	-
Wood	10	0	53	2	2	-
Stokes	7	0	43	0	-	-
Rashid	5	0	43	0	1	-

PAKISTAN bowling

PAKISTAN bowling	O	M	R	W	wb	nb
Shadab Khan	10	0	63	2	-	-
Mohammad Amir	10	0	67	2	3	-
Wahab Riaz	10	0	82	3	1	-
Hasan Ali	10	0	66	0	1	-
Mohammad Hafeez	7	0	43	1	-	-
Shoaib Malik	3	0	10	1	-	-

Fall of wickets

	Pak	Eng
1st	82 (2)	12 (1)
2nd	111 (1)	60 (2)
3rd	199 (3)	86 (4)
4th	279 (4)	118 (5)
5th	311 (6)	248 (3)
6th	319 (5)	288 (6)
7th	325 (8)	320 (7)
8th	337 (7)	320 (8)
9th	-	322 (9)
10th	-	-

ENGLAND v BANGLADESH

Venue:	Sophia Gardens, Cardiff
Date:	8th June 2019
Toss:	Bangladesh
Result:	England won by 106 runs
Man of the Match:	JJ Roy
Umpires:	HDPK Dharmasena & JS Wilson
TV umpire:	BNJ Oxenford
Referee:	DCBoon

ENGLAND innings

		R	B	4	6
JJ Roy	c Mashrafe Mortaza b Mehedi Hasan	153	121	14	5
+JM Bairstow	c Mehedi Hasan b Mashrafe Mortaza	51	50	6	0
JE Root	b Mohammad Saifuddin	21	29	1	0
JC Buttler	c Soumya Sarkar b Mohammad Saifuddin	64	44	2	4
*EJG Morgan	c Soumya Sarkar b Mehedi Hasan	35	33	1	2
BA Stokes	c Mashrafe Mortaza b Mustafizur Rahman	6	7	0	0
CR Woakes	not out	18	8	0	2
LE Plunkett	not out	27	9	4	1
AU Rashid					
JC Archer					
MA Wood					
Extras	(lb 3, w 7, nb 1)	11			
TOTAL	(for 6 wkts; 50 overs)	386			

BANGLADESH innings

		R	B	4	6
Tamim Iqbal	c Morgan b Wood	19	29	1	0
Soumya Sarkar	b Archer	2	8	0	0
Shakib Al Hasan	b Stokes	121	119	12	1
+Mushfiqur Rahim	c Roy b Plunkett	44	50	2	0
Mithun Ali	c Bairstow b Rashid	0	2	0	0
Mahmudullah	c Bairstow b Wood	28	41	1	1
Mosaddek Hossain	c Archer b Stokes	26	16	4	0
Mohammad Saifuddin	b Stokes	5	8	0	0
Mehedi Hasan	c Bairstow b Archer	12	8	2	0
*Mashrafe Mortaza	not out	4	9	0	0
Mustafizur Rahman	c Bairstow b Archer	0	3	0	0
Extras	(lb 9, w 10)	19			
TOTAL	(all out; 48.5 overs)	280			

ENGLAND bowling

	O	M	R	W	wb	nb
Shakib Al Hasan	10	0	71	0	2	-
Mashrafe Mortaza	10	0	68	1	-	-
Mohammad Saifuddin	9	0	78	2	2	-
Mustafizur Rahman	9	0	75	1	2	1
Mehedi Hasan	10	0	67	2	1	-
Mosaddek Hossain	2	0	24	0	-	-

ENGLAND

	O	M	R	W	wb	nb
Woakes	8	0	67	0	-	-
Archer	8.5	2	29	3	1	-
Plunkett	8	0	36	1	2	-
Wood	8	0	52	2	-	-
Rashid	10	0	64	1	2	-
Stokes	6	1	23	3	1	-

Fall of wickets

	Eng	Ban
1st	128 (2)	8 (2)
2nd	205 (3)	63 (1)
3rd	235 (1)	169 (4)
4th	330 (4)	170 (5)
5th	340 (5)	219 (3)
6th	341 (6)	254 (7)
7th	-	261 (6)
8th	-	264 (8)
9th	-	280 (9)
10th	-	280 (11)

ENGLAND v WEST INDIES

Venue:	The Hampshire Bowl, Southampton		
Date:	14th June 2019		
Toss:	England		
Result:	England won by 8 wickets		
Man of the Match:	JE Root		
Umpires:	HDPK Dharmasena & S Ravi		
TV umpire:	RJ Tucker		
Referee:	DC Boon		

WEST INDIES innings

		R	B	4	6
CH Gayle	c Bairstow b Plunkett	36	41	5	1
E Lewis	b Woakes	2	8	0	0
+SD Hope	lbw b Wood	11	30	1	0
N Pooran	c Buttler b Archer	63	78	3	1
SO Hetmyer	c and b Root	39	48	4	0
*JO Holder	c and b Root	9	10	0	1
AD Russell	c Woakes b Wood	21	16	1	2
CR Brathwaite	c Buttler b Archer	14	22	0	1
SS Cottrell	lbw b Archer	0	1	0	0
OR Thomas	not out	0	11	0	0
ST Gabriel	b Wood	0	3	0	0
Extras	(lb 5, w 12)	17			
TOTAL	(all out; 44.4 overs)	212			

ENGLAND innings

		R	B	4	6
JM Bairstow	c Brathwaite b Gabriel	45	46	7	0
JE Root	not out	100	94	11	0
CR Woakes	c sub (FA Allen) b Gabriel	40	54	4	0
BA Stokes	not out	10	6	2	0
JJ Roy					
*EJG Morgan					
+JC Buttler					
AU Rashid					
MA Wood					
JC Archer					
LE Plunkett					
Extras	(lb 2, w 15, nb 1)	18			
TOTAL	(for 2 wkts; 33.1 overs)	213			

ENGLAND bowling

	O	M	R	W	wb	nb
Woakes	5	2	16	1	1	-
Archer	9	1	30	3	1	-
Plunkett	5	0	30	1	3	-
Wood	6.4	0	18	3	1	-
Stokes	4	0	25	0	-	-
Rashid	10	0	61	0	1	-
Root	5	0	27	2	1	-

WEST INDIES bowling

	O	M	R	W	wb	nb
Cottrell	3	0	17	0	1	-
Thomas	6	0	43	0	2	-
Gabriel	7	0	49	2	7	-
Russell	2	0	14	0	1	-
Holder	5.1	0	31	0	1	1
Brathwaite	5	0	35	0	1	-
Gayle	5	0	22	0	2	-

Fall of Wickets:

	WI	Eng
1st	4 (2)	95 (1)
2nd	54 (1)	199 (3)
3rd	55 (3)	-
4th	144 (5)	-
5th	156 (6)	-
6th	188 (7)	-
7th	202 (4)	-
8th	202 (9)	-
9th	211 (8)	-
10th	212 (11)	-

ENGLAND v AFGHANISTAN

Venue:	Old Trafford, Manchester
Date:	18th June 2019
Toss:	England
Result:	England won by 150 runs
Man of the Match:	EJG Morgan
Umpires:	PR Reiffel & JS Wilson
TV umpire:	M Erasmus
Referee:	RS Madugalle

ENGLAND innings

		R	B	4	6
JM Vince	c Mujeeb ur Rahman b Dawlat Zadran	26	31	3	0
JM Bairstow	c and b Gulbadeen Naib	90	99	8	3
JE Root	c Rahmat Shah b Gulbadeen Naib	88	82	5	1
*EJG Morgan	c Rahmat Shah b Gulbadeen Naib	148	71	4	17
+JC Buttler	c Mohammad Nabi b Dawlat Zadran	2	2	0	0
BA Stokes	b Dawlat Zadran	2	6	0	0
MM Ali	not out	31	9	1	4
CR Woakes	not out	1	1	0	0
AU Rashid					
JC Archer					
MA Wood					
Extras	(lb 1, w 7, nb 1)	9			
TOTAL	(for 6 wkts; 50 overs)	397			

AFGHANISTAN innings

		R	B	4	6
Noor Ali Zadran	b Archer	0	7	0	0
*Gulbadeen Naib	c Buttler b Wood	37	28	4	1
Rahmat Shah	c Bairstow b Rashid	46	74	3	1
Hashmatullah Shahidi	b Archer	76	100	5	2
Asghar Afghan	c Root b Rashid	44	48	3	2
Mohammad Nabi	c Stokes b Rashid	9	7	0	1
Najibullah Zadran	b Wood	15	13	0	1
Rashid Khan	c Bairstow b Archer	8	13	1	0
+Ikram Ali Khil	not out	3	10	0	0
Dawlat Zadran	not out	0	0	0	0
Mujeeb ur Rahman					
Extras	(lb 1, w 8)	9			
TOTAL	(for 8 wkts; 50 overs)	247			

AFGHANISTAN bowling

AFGHANISTAN bowling	O	M	R	W	wb	nb
Mujeeb ur Rahman	10	0	44	0	2	-
Dawlat Zadran	10	0	85	3	4	-
Mohammad Nabi	9	0	70	0	-	-
Gulbadeen Naib	10	0	68	3	-	1
Rahmat Shah	2	0	19	0	-	-
Rashid Khan	9	0	110	0	-	-

ENGLAND bowling	O	M	R	W	wb	nb
Woakes	9	0	41	0	2	-
Archer	10	1	52	3	2	-
Ali	7	0	35	0	-	-
Wood	10	1	40	2	1	-
Stokes	4	0	12	0	-	-
Rashid	10	0	66	3	1	-

Fall of Wickets:

	Eng	Afg
1st	44 (1)	4 (1)
2nd	164 (2)	52 (2)
3rd	353 (3)	104 (3)
4th	359 (4)	198 (5)
5th	362 (5)	210 (6)
6th	378 (6)	234 (4)
7th	-	234 (7)
8th	-	247 (8)
9th	-	-
10th	-	-

ENGLAND v SRI LANKA

Venue:	Headingley, Leeds
Date:	21st June 2019
Toss:	Sri Lanka
Result:	Sri Lanka won by 20 runs
Man of the Match:	SL Malinga
Umpires:	M Erasmus & JS Wilson
TV umpire:	BNJ Oxenford
Referee:	RB Richardson

SRI LANKA innings

		R	B	4	6
*FDM Karunaratne	c Buttler b Archer	1	8	0	0
+MDKJ Perera	c Ali b Woakes	2	6	0	0
WIA Fernando	c Rashid b Wood	49	39	6	2
BKG Mendis	c Morgan b Rashid	46	68	2	0
AD Mathews	not out	85	115	5	1
BMAJ Mendis	c and b Rashid	0	1	0	0
DM de Silva	c Root b Archer	29	47	1	0
NLTC Perera	c Rashid b Archer	2	6	0	0
I Udana	c Root b Wood	6	4	1	0
SL Malinga	b Wood	1	5	0	0
ANPR Fernando	not out	1	1	0	0
Extras	(lb 4, w 6)	10			
TOTAL	(for 9 wkts; 50 overs)	232			

ENGLAND innings

		R	B	4	6
JM Vince	c BKG Mendis b Malinga	14	18	2	0
JM Bairstow	lbw				
	b Malinga	0	1	0	0
JE Root	c MDKJ Perera b Malinga	57	89	3	0
*EJG Morgan	c and b Udana	21	35	2	0
BA Stokes	not out	82	89	7	4

+JC Buttler	lbw b Malinga	10	9	1	0
MM Ali	c Udana b De Silva	16	20	0	1
CR Woakes	c MDKJ Perera b De Silva	2	4	0	0
AU Rashid	c MDKJ Perera b De Silva	1	2	0	0
JC Archer	c NLTC Perera b Udana	3	11	0	0
MA Wood	c MDKJ Perera b ANPR Fernando	0	4	0	0
Extras	(lb 1, w 5)	6			
TOTAL	(all out; 47 overs)	212			

ENGLAND bowling

	O	M	R	W	wb	nb
Woakes	5	0	22	1	-	-
Archer	10	2	52	3	2	-
Wood	8	0	40	3	1	-
Stokes	5	0	16	0	-	-
Ali	10	0	40	0	3	-
Rashid	10	0	45	2	-	-
Root	2	0	13	0	-	-

SRI LANKA bowling

	O	M	R	W	wb	nb
Malinga	10	1	43	4	2	-
ANPR Fernando	10	1	38	1	2	-
De Silva	8	0	32	3	-	-
NLTC Perera	8	0	34	0	-	-
Udana	8	0	41	2	1	-
BMAJ Mendis	3	0	23	0	-	-

Fall of Wickets:

	SL	Eng
1st	3 (1)	1 (2)
2nd	3 (2)	26 (1)
3rd	62 (3)	73 (4)
4th	133 (4)	127 (3)
5th	133 (6)	144 (6)
6th	190 (7)	170 (7)
7th	200 (8)	176 (8)
8th	209 (9)	178 (9)
9th	220 (10)	186 (10)
10th	-	212 (11)

ENGLAND v AUSTRALIA

Venue:	Lord's, London
Date:	25th June 2019
Toss:	England
Result:	Australia won by 64 runs
Man of the Match:	AJ Finch
Umpires:	CB Gaffaney & S Ravi
TV umpire:	HDPK Dharmasena
Referee:	RS Madugalle

AUSTRALIA innings

		R	B	4	6
*AJ Finch	c Woakes b Archer	100	116	11	2
DA Warner	c Root b Ali	53	61	6	0
UT Khawaja	b Stokes	23	29	1	0
SPD Smith	c Archer b Woakes	38	34	5	0
GJ Maxwell	c Buttler b Wood	12	8	1	1
MP Stoinis	run out				
	(Bairstow/Rashid/Buttler)	8	15	1	0

308

		R	B	4	6
+AT Carey	not out	38	27	5	0
PJ Cummins	c Buttler b Woakes	1	4	0	0
MA Starc	not out	4	6	0	0
NM Lyon					
JP Behrendorff					
Extras	(lb 4, w 4)	8			
TOTAL	(for 7 wkts; 50 overs)	285			

ENGLAND innings

		R	B	4	6
JM Vince	b Behrendorff	0	2	0	0
JM Bairstow	c Cummins b Behrendorff	27	39	5	0
JE Root	lbw b Starc	8	9	2	0
*EJG Morgan	c Cummins b Starc	4	7	1	0
BA Stokes	b Starc	89	115	8	2
+JC Buttler	c Khawaja b Stoinis	25	27	2	0
CR Woakes	c Finch b Behrendorff	26	34	2	0
MM Ali	c Carey b Behrendorff	6	9	1	0
AU Rashid	c Stoinis b Starc	25	20	3	1
JC Archer	c Warner b Behrendorff	1	4	0	0
MA Wood	not out	1	2	0	0
Extras	(b 1, lb 5, w 3)	9			
TOTAL	(all out; 44.4 overs)	221			

ENGLAND bowling

	O	M	R	W	wb	nb
Woakes	10	0	46	2	1	-
Archer	9	0	56	1	1	-
Wood	9	0	59	1	2	-
Stokes	6	0	29	1	-	-
Ali	6	0	42	1	-	-
Rashid	10	0	49	0	-	-

AUSTRALIA bowling

AUSTRALIA bowling	O	M	R	W	wb	nb
Behrendorff	10	0	44	5	1	-
Starc	8.4	1	43	4	-	-
Cummins	8	1	41	0	-	-
Lyon	9	0	43	0	-	-
Stoinis	7	0	29	1	1	-
Maxwell	2	0	15	0	-	-

Fall of Wickets

	Aus	Eng
1st	123 (2)	0 (1)
2nd	173 (3)	15 (3)
3rd	185 (1)	26 (4)
4th	213 (5)	53 (2)
5th	228 (6)	124 (6)
6th	250 (4)	177 (5)
7th	259 (8)	189 (8)
8th	-	202 (7)
9th	-	211 (10)
10th	-	221 (9)

ENGLAND v INDIA

Venue:	Edgbaston, Birmingham
Date:	30th June 2019
Toss:	England
Result:	England won by 31 runs
Man of the Match:	JM Bairstow
Umpires:	Aleem Dar and HDPK Dharmasena
TV umpire:	RSA Palliyaguruge
Referee:	RS Madugalle

ENGLAND innings

		R	B	4	6
JJ Roy	c sub (RA Jadeja) b Yadav	66	57	7	2
JM Bairstow	c Pant b Mohammed Shami	111	109	10	6
JE Root	c Pandya b Mohammed Shami	44	54	2	0
*EJG Morgan	c Jadhav b Mohammed Shami	1	9	0	0
BA Stokes	c sub (RA Jadeja) b Bumrah	79	54	6	3
+JC Buttler	c and b Mohammed Shami	20	8	1	2
CR Woakes	c Sharma b Mohammed Shami	7	5	1	0
LE Plunkett	not out	1	4	0	0
JC Archer	not out	0	0	0	0
AU Rashid					
MA Wood					
Extras	(b 2, lb 2, w 4)	8			
TOTAL	(for 7 wkts; 50 overs)	337			

INDIA innings

		R	B	4	6
KL Rahul	c and b Woakes	0	9	0	0
RG Sharma	c Buttler b Woakes	102	109	15	0
*V Kohli	c sub (JM Vince) b Plunkett	66	76	7	0
RR Pant	c Woakes b Plunkett	32	29	4	0
HH Pandya	c sub (JM Vince) b Plunkett	45	33	4	0
+MS Dhoni	not out	42	31	4	1
KM Jadhav	not out	12	13	1	0
K Yadav					
YS Chahal					
Mohammed Shami					
JJ Bumrah					
Extras	(lb 1, w 6)	7			
TOTAL	(for 5 wkts; 50 overs)	306			

311

INDIA

INDIA	O	M	R	W	wb	nb
Mohammed Shami	10	1	69	5	1	-
Bumrah	10	1	44	1	-	-
Chahal	10	0	88	0	2	-
Pandya	10	0	60	0	1	-
Yadav	10	0	72	1	-	-

ENGLAND

ENGLAND	O	M	R	W	wb	nb
Woakes	10	3	58	2	-	-
Archer	10	0	45	0	-	-
Plunkett	10	0	55	3	4	-
Wood	10	0	73	0	1	-
Rashid	6	0	40	0	1	-
Stokes	4	0	34	0	-	-

Fall of Wickets:

	Eng	Ind
1st	160 (1)	8 (1)
2nd	205 (2)	146 (3)
3rd	207 (4)	198 (2)
4th	277 (3)	226 (4)
5th	310 (6)	267 (5)
6th	319 (7)	-
7th	336 (5)	-
8th	-	-
9th	-	-
10th	-	-

ENGLAND v NEW ZEALAND

Venue: Riverside Ground, Chester-le-Street
Date: 3rd July 2019
Toss: England
Result: England won by 119 runs
Man of the Match: JM Bairstow
Umpires: S Ravi and RJ Tucker
TV umpire: PR Reiffel
Referee: DC Boon

ENGLAND innings

		R	B	4	6
JJ Roy	c Santner b Neesham	60	61	8	0
JM Bairstow	b Henry	106	99	15	1
JE Root	c Latham b Boult	24	25	1	0
+JC Buttler	c Williamson b Boult	11	12	1	0
*EJG Morgan	c Santner b Henry	42	40	5	0
BA Stokes	c Henry b Santner	11	27	0	0
CR Woakes	c Williamson b Neesham	4	11	0	0
LE Plunkett	not out	15	12	1	0
AU Rashid	b Southee	16	12	1	0
JC Archer	not out	1	1	0	0
MA Wood					
Extras	(b 4, lb 4, w 7)	15			
TOTAL	(for 8 wkts; 50 overs)	305			

NEW ZEALAND innings

		R	B	4	6
MJ Guptill	c Buttler b Archer	8	16	1	0
HM Nicholls	lbw b Woakes	0	1	0	0
*KS Williamson	run out (Wood)	27	40	3	0
LRPL Taylor	run out (Rashid/Buttler)	28	42	2	0
+TWM Latham	c Buttler b Plunkett	57	65	5	0
JDS Neesham	b Wood	19	27	1	0

C de Grandhomme	c Root b Stokes	3	13	0	0
MJ Santner	lbw b Wood	12	30	1	0
TG Southee	not out	7	16	0	0
MJ Henry	b Wood	7	13	0	0
TA Boult	st Buttler b Rashid	4	7	1	0
Extras	(b 2, lb 6, w 6)	14			
TOTAL	(all out; 45 overs)	186			

NEW ZEALAND bowling

	O	M	R	W	wb	nb
Santner	10	0	65	1	2	-
Boult	10	0	56	2	1	-
Southee	9	0	70	1	-	-
Henry	10	0	54	2	2	-
De Grandhomme	1	0	11	0	-	-
Neesham	10	1	41	2	2	-

ENGLAND bowling

	O	M	R	W	wb	nb
Woakes	8	0	44	1	1	-
Archer	7	1	17	1	1	-
Plunkett	8	0	28	1	1	-
Wood	9	0	34	3	2	-
Root	3	0	15	0	-	-
Rashid	5	0	30	1	-	-
Stokes	5	0	10	1	1	-

Fall of Wickets:

	Eng	NZ
1st	123 (1)	2 (2)
2nd	194 (3)	14 (1)
3rd	206 (2)	61 (3)
4th	214 (4)	69 (4)
5th	248 (6)	123 (6)
7th	272 (5)	164 (5)

6th	259 (7)	128 (7)
8th	301 (9)	166 (8)
9th	-	181 (10)
10th	-	186 (11)

ENGLAND v AUSTRALIA (Semi-Final)

Venue:	Edgbaston, Birmingham
Date:	11th July 2019
Toss:	Australia
Result:	England won by 8 wickets
Man of the Match:	CR Woakes
Umpires:	HDPK Dharmasena & M Erasmus
TV umpire:	CB Gaffaney
Referee:	RS Madugalle

AUSTRALIA innings

		R	B	4	6
DA Warner	c Bairstow b Woakes	9	11	2	0
*AJ Finch	lbw b Archer	0	1	0	0
SPD Smith	run out (Buttler)	85	119	6	0
PSP Handscomb	b Woakes	4	12	0	0
+AT Carey	c sub (JM Vince) b Rashid	46	70	4	0
MP Stoinis	lbw b Rashid	0	2	0	0
GJ Maxwell	c Morgan b Archer	22	23	2	1
PJ Cummins	c Root b Rashid	6	10	0	0
MA Starc	c Buttler b Woakes	29	36	1	1
JP Behrendorff	b Wood	1	4	0	0
NM Lyon	not out	5	6	0	0
Extras	(lb 6, w 10)	16			
TOTAL	(all out; 49 overs)	223			

ENGLAND innings

		R	B	4	6
JJ Roy	c Carey b Cummins	85	65	9	5
JM Bairstow	lbw b Starc	34	43	5	0
JE Root	not out	49	46	8	0
*EJG Morgan	not out	45	39	8	0
+JC Buttler					
BA Stokes					
CR Woakes					
LE Plunkett					
JC Archer					
AU Rashid					
MA Wood					
Extras	(lb 1, w 12)	13			
TOTAL	(for 2 wkts; 32.1 overs)	226			

ENGLAND bowling

	O	M	R	W	wb	nb
Woakes	8	0	20	3	-	-
Archer	10	0	32	2	2	-
Stokes	4	0	22	0	-	-
Wood	9	0	45	1	4	-
Plunkett	8	0	44	0	3	-
Rashid	10	0	54	3	1	-

AUSTRALIA

	O	M	R	W	wb	nb
Behrendorff	8.1	2	38	0	1	-
Starc	9	0	70	1	3	-
Cummins	7	0	34	1	2	-
Lyon	5	0	49	0	-	-
Smith	1	0	21	0	1	-
Stoinis	2	0	13	0	1	-

Fall of Wickets:

	Aus	Eng
1st	4 (2)	124 (2)
2nd	10 (1)	147 (1)
3rd	14 (4)	-
4th	117 (5)	-
5th	118 (6)	-
6th	157 (7)	-
7th	166 (8)	-
8th	217 (3)	-
9th	217 (9)	-
10th	223 (10)	-

ENGLAND v NEW ZEALAND (Final)

Venue:	Lord's, London
Date:	14th July 2019
Toss:	New Zealand
Result:	Match tied (England won on higher boundary count after tied Super Over)
Man of the Match:	BA Stokes
Umpires:	HDPK Dharmasena & M Erasmus
TV umpire:	RJ Tucker
Referee:	RS Madugalle

NEW ZEALAND innings

		R	B	4	6
MJ Guptill	lbw b Woakes	19	18	2	1
HM Nicholls	b Plunkett	55	77	4	0
*KS Williamson	c Buttler b Plunkett	30	53	2	0
LRPL Taylor	lbw b Wood	15	31	0	0
+TWM Latham	c sub (JM Vince) b Woakes	47	56	2	1

		R	B	4	6
JDS Neesham	c Root b Plunkett	19	25	3	0
C de Grandhomme	c sub (JM Vince) b Woakes	16	28	0	0
MJ Santner	not out	5	9	0	0
MJ Henry	b Archer	4	2	1	0
TA Boult	not out	1	2	0	0
LH Ferguson					
Extras	(lb 12, w 17, nb 1)	30			
TOTAL	(for 8 wkts; 50 overs)	241			

ENGLAND innings

		R	B	4	6
JJ Roy	c Latham b Henry	17	20	3	0
JM Bairstow	b Ferguson	36	55	7	0
JE Root	c Latham b De Grandhomme	7	30	0	0
*EJG Morgan	c Ferguson b Neesham	9	22	0	0
BA Stokes	not out	84	98	5	3
+JC Buttler	c sub (TG Southee) b Ferguson	59	60	6	0
CR Woakes	c Latham b Ferguson	2	4	0	0
LE Plunkett	c Boult b Neesham	10	10	1	0
JC Archer	b Neesham	0	1	0	0
AU Rashid	run out (Santner/Boult)	0	0	0	0
MA Wood	run out (Neesham/Boult)	0	0	0	0
Extras	(b 2, lb 3, w 12)	17			
TOTAL	(all out; 50 overs)	241			

ENGLAND bowling

	O	M	R	W	wb	nb
Woakes	9	0	37	3	4	1
Archer	10	0	42	1	5	-
Plunkett	10	0	42	3	-	-
Wood	10	1	49	1	2	-
Rashid	8	0	39	0	-	-
Stokes	3	0	20	0	2	-

NEW ZEALAND bowling

	O	M	R	W	wb	nb
Boult	10	0	67	0	2	-
Henry	10	2	40	1	-	-
De Grandhomme	10	2	25	1	1	-
Ferguson	10	0	50	3	3	-
Neesham	7	0	43	3	1	-
Santner	3	0	11	0	1	-

Fall of Wickets:

	NZ	Eng
1st	29 (1)	28 (1)
2nd	103 (3)	59 (3)
3rd	118 (2)	71 (2)
4th	141 (4)	86 (4)
5th	173 (6)	196 (6)
6th	219 (7)	203 (7)
7th	232 (5)	220 (8)
8th	240 (9)	227 (9)
9th	-	240 (10)
10th	-	241 (11)

ENGLAND

Super Over innings		R	B	4	6
BA Stokes	not out	8	3	1	-
+JC Buttler	not out	7	3	1	-
Extras		0			
TOTAL	(for 0 wkt; 1 over)	15			

NEW ZEALAND

Super Over innings		R	B	4	6
JDS Neesham	not out	13	5	-	1
MJ Guptill	run out (Roy-Buttler)	1	1	-	-
Extras	(w 1)	1			
TOTAL	(for 1 wkt; 1 over)	15			

NEW ZEALAND

bowling	O	M	R	W	wb	nb
Boult	1	0	15	0	-	-

ENGLAND

bowling	O	M	R	W	wb	nb
Archer	1	0	15	0	1	-

Fall of Wickets:

	Eng	NZ
1st	-	15 (2)

ACKNOWLEDGEMENTS

Reliving the 2019 World Cup and collating the stunning story behind England's victory would not have been possible without the help of colleagues and members of the England cricket team, both on and off the field.

Thank you to Scyld Berry, Daily Telegraph cricket correspondent, for reading through the manuscript, spotting errors and making wise suggestions to improve our storytelling.

David Luxton's support and vision for the book made it become a reality. Many thanks to Paul Farbrace for his time and insight into the England dressing room, and knowledge of the four-year plan to win the World Cup. From within the England camp, many thanks to Danny Reuben and Greg Stobart for facilitating interviews and helping to fill in the blanks. Nathan Leamon and Graham Thorpe provided insight from behind the scenes, and thank you to Andrew Strauss for giving up his time to both authors.

Eoin Morgan was inundated with interview requests but found time in his schedule to speak to the authors about his team's journey both before and after the World Cup.

Thank you to Les Snowden and Tim Hallissey at The Times for their help and understanding, and also to Adam Sills and Andrew Fifield from the Telegraph sports desk.

INDEX